Through the
the
Green

Through the Green

Green

The Mind and Art of a
Professional Golfer

Sal Maiorana
with the cooperation of
Davis Love III

ST. MARTIN'S PRESS

New York

Books are available in quantity for promotional or premium use. Write to
Director of Special Sales, St. Martin's Press, 175 Fifth Avenue, New York, NY
10010, for information on discounts and terms, or call toll-free (800) 221-7945. In
New York, call (212) 674-5151 (ext. 645).

Editor: George Witte
Production Editor: Eric C. Meyer
Design by Ann Gold

Library of Congress Cataloging-in-Publication Data

Maiorana, Salvatore.
    Through the green : the mind and art of a professional golfer /
Sal Maiorana with the cooperation of Davis Love, III.
        p.   cm.
    ISBN 0-312-09363-2
    1. Golf—Psychological aspects.   2. Love, Dennis.   3. Golf
tournaments—California—Los Angeles—Case studies.   I. Love,
Davis.   II. Title.
GV979.P75M35   1993
796.352—dc20   93-16467
                                                         CIP

First Edition: May 1993
10   9   8   7   6   5   4   3   2   1

To Christine: My caddie for life,
thank you for your patience,
your love and your support.

To Mom, Dad and Lisa:
Thanks for your love, guidance
and, most of all, your tolerance of me.
Together we're a pretty good foursome.

Acknowledgments

I would like to thank the following people for their cooperation and contributions to this project: Mark Love, Robin Love, Jeff Sluman, Joey Sindelar, Sandy Lyle, Tom Sieckmann, John Cook, John Daly, Fred Couples, Billy Ray Brown, Mike Carrick, Rich Jordan, Jolande Lyle, Joe LaCava, Chico Fernandez, Andy Martinez, Paul Hospenthal, Mike Ploski, George Willets, Steve Giovanisci, George Babikian, Jim Morrison, Jim Middleton, Bob Levey, Jan Fambro, Andrew Conway, Vinnie Giles and John Heller.

Special thanks to my wife, Christine, for her love and support; to Vic Carucci, whose advice, direction and friendship were instrumental in this book ever becoming a reality; to Basil Kane, for his belief in this book; and to George Witte of St. Martin's Press, for his skillful editing.

And finally, to Davis Love III, for allowing me to be his shadow for a number of weeks and for sharing his talent, knowledge, insight and honesty. Hit 'em long and straight, and may you always be under par on the golf course.

Prologue

Davis Love III takes his persimmon head driver back slowly, methodically, in a huge sweeping arc, his left shoulder turning and turning and turning. It is an upper body rotation that is the envy of many players on the PGA Tour. Because of that excessive shoulder turn and broad swing arc, Davis is able to hit golf balls prodigious distances. When the shaft of the driver reaches its apex and is parallel to the ground, he shifts his weight from the right side of his six-foot three, 175-pound frame to the left and starts the club moving forward with his powerful wrists, whipping it downward until it strikes the ball. The club continues moving after impact and his long arms end up coiled around his neck while the shaft presses against his back. Davis holds this position for a couple of seconds as he watches the flight path of the Titleist, a look of disinterest creasing his face as the ball cuts through the air like a missile, climbing into the blue sky. Davis relaxes his posture and pulls his driver back over his head, holding it loosely in front of him as the ball begins its descent and eventually comes to rest safely in the fairway.

It is the 18th hole of the South course at Torrey Pines Golf Club in La Jolla, California. The final round of the Buick Invitational of California is nearing its conclusion on a bright, sunsplashed Sunday afternoon. A little more than four hours ago, Davis had started play with a simple goal in mind: to shoot a good number and perhaps by the end of the day, be in position to win the tournament, or at the very least, finish in the top 10. Instead, as he strides down the fairway following his perfect drive, he is well out of contention. Moments later, after holing a putt for par, he signs a scorecard that reads 72, an even-par round that has been littered with stray shots, missed opportunities and breaks in concentration.

As he leaves the scorer's tent, Davis is frustrated because he never got it going, never gave himself a chance to make a run at the top of the leaderboard. He is also frustrated that the day is over, and only now that it is over does he think about what is happening to the Tour.

Throughout the 1980s and into the early '90s, the PGA Tour rode a wave of unbridled success as its assets, purses and popularity exploded through the atmosphere like one of Davis's drives. But the Tour now finds itself having to fight its way out of the rough.

Legal issues have cast a cloud over the once sunny future of professional golf. A $100 million lawsuit brought by Karsten Solheim, president and chief executive officer of Karsten Manufacturing Corp. over the legality of the company's Ping Eye2 U-grooved irons could deplete a huge chunk of the Tour's assets, which were estimated to be more than $175 million at the close of 1991. Because the suit deals with antitrust issues, damages would be trebled so a defeat could cost the Tour many, many millions, including payment of its own legal costs as well as Karsten's. Most alarming to the players is that their pension fund could be tapped as a source of payment.

Then, there is the recent ruling by the Internal Revenue Service which excluded two college football bowl games from the tax-exempt provisions governing nonprofit organizations, a status the Tour and its tournaments currently enjoy. In the past, a corporate sponsor could give money to an event and because the money went to charity, the sponsor did not have to pay taxes. Now, in the case of the two football games—the Mobil Cotton Bowl and the John Hancock Bowl—the IRS is calling these charitable contributions a form of paid advertising and plans on taxing at a rate of 34 percent. Should the IRS ruling be extended to include pro golf, Tour income from corporate sponsorship, already endangered by the ongoing economic recession, could decline as sponsors are forced to re-evaluate their advertising budgets and pull the plug on their involvement with the Tour.

An investigation of the Tour's business practices by the

Federal Trade Commission and a threatened strike by the recently unionized Tour field officials—led by Philadelphia attorney Richie Phillips, the man who directed the Major League Baseball umpires during three work stoppages and got their salaries and benefits boosted dramatically—also looms.

This morning, Davis arrived at Torrey Pines six shots off the pace being set by Tom Watson, Brad Faxon and Mike Springer. Six shots is not a lot to make up in thirty-six holes. But there weren't going to be thirty-six holes being played today, only eighteen, and overcoming a six-shot deficit in eighteen holes on the PGA Tour is like trying to win a one-on-one basketball game with Michael Jordan—and spotting him a few points at the start.

Saturday morning, dense fog had rolled in off the Pacific Ocean and refused to lift, leaving the entire seaside course shrouded in a gray mist. The players waited for hours to begin play, but it became apparent that there was no way the fog was going to allow it. Still, at about noon, officials decided to give it a go, using an unprecedented shotgun start to speed up play.

The players screamed. A shotgun start! A group on all 18 holes, teeing off at the same time and moving around the course like subway passengers maneuvering through turnstiles. "Did you pick up your tee prizes when you preregistered?" Mark O'Meara had jokingly shouted to John Cook. Others took a more indignant attitude toward the proposal. "Whatever happened to the integrity of the game, the integrity of the competition?" Tom Weiskopf asked. "This is not a tournament. It's an outing. It's corporate golf."

Davis, a twenty-seven-year-old in his seventh year on the PGA Tour, agreed. "That's not the way to play a golf tournament," he said.

As it turned out, the fog never lifted, the shotgun was avoided and the round was postponed. Or so the players thought. Having dodged the shotgun bullet, Davis and his fellow competitors figured they'd be playing thirty-six holes on Sunday to complete the tournament. But according to NBC, Buick and the Tour officials, that wasn't possible. NBC was scheduled to be on the air with final-round coverage from one to three o'clock pacific time

Sunday in order to get a six o'clock East Coast conclusion, so there wasn't time for thirty-six holes. Buick's only concern was that their officials were shown on national television presenting the first-place check to the winner on Sunday. The Tour's primary concern was making sure that NBC and Buick—the organizations paying the bills this week in La Jolla—were both happy. In the end the only person with a smile on his face was Steve Pate, who emerged as the winner, shooting a final-round 67 for a 54-hole total of 200, nine strokes fewer than Davis, who wound up tied for 38th place, his $4,000 check a fraction of Pate's $180,000.

"The emphasis isn't as much on golf championships as it is on taking care of the sponsors in the Pro-Am and making sure the sponsors are there the next year and getting a big high purse," Davis says. "It's more of a corporate game, corporate sponsorship and money, television, putting the whole package together so we can play for more money rather than doing what's best for just playing golf. We cut it to a fifty-four-hole event and it was like, that's the normal thing to do. We came here to play seventy-two holes, let's play seventy-two holes and get us a winner. But TV was on from one to three o'clock, so if we play thirty-six holes on Sunday to finish the tournament, we're finishing at five pacific time and TV doesn't get to show the trophy presentation. All they care about is the Buick president presenting the Buick check to Steve Pate. That's the important thing. It isn't that Steve Pate beat everyone else and won the golf tournament."

Of course, Davis is acutely aware that there is a catch-22. The players bristle about the corporate nature of their sport, but those companies provide the obscenely large bankrolls that the golfers play for every week.

"The valid argument was that if we tell Buick we're not going to play a shotgun to get the round in, we're telling them tough luck," Davis says. "But here they are, and they sponsor four of our events. Basically, we had to do whatever we could not to make them mad. Do you tell Buick to 'screw off, we're going to play seventy-two holes until we finish and crown us a champion whether it's Monday or Tuesday,' or do we say, 'we'll do whatever you guys want. You sponsor four events.' Buick gets pissed off, pulls out and there goes four events and five million dollars that they're spending. Now that's just a little bit of their whole advertising budget, but they can say, 'Screw it, we'll go somewhere else.' They can go away real fast, so we have to take care of them."

Davis's good friend, 1988 PGA champion Jeff Sluman, was a key figure in the foggy proceedings because he is a member of the Tour Policy Board, the ten-man group that establishes the goals and policies for the operation of the Tour. Just like Davis and the rest of the players, Sluman wants what is best for the golfers, and that means playing seventy-two holes. But Sluman explains that an unusual set of circumstances forced the cancellation of the third round, therefore shortening the tournament to fifty-four holes.

"It was Buick's first event in southern California," Sluman began. "The TV contracts say that if it rains or whatever, the network must show golf, so they usually show the tape of last year's tournament. Well, the problem with that was last year's tournament wasn't sponsored by Buick; it was sponsored by Shearson-Lehman. NBC was in a tough situation because the other Buick tournaments are held by CBS, so they didn't have any Buick tapes to run, so Buick wasn't crazy about that, which is understandable. But what was more important to Buick was to make sure that they had a Sunday finish on TV so they could award the prize to the winner. So with all these things going on that some of the other guys probably didn't think about, we decided to at least try a shotgun. Of course, the fog never lifted so it turned out to be a non-issue. But that's what we were up against.

"People are always going to question things without knowing one hundred percent of what's going on. That's why they selected the board members and we have to make the best decisions we possibly can. If you get one hundred fifty players together and people start making decisions, you're not going to have one hundred percent agreement. Davis wanted to play seventy-two holes, and the way we tried to play seventy-two holes he didn't like, so where do you go from there? I just hope everyone realized that we gave it our best effort. We always want to get seventy-two holes in because the best player of the week will generally win. If this had happened on the East Coast, we would have had all kinds of time to re-pair and wait for the fog to blow out, and even if we couldn't finish Saturday, we could have finished Sunday morning. But being on the West Coast, time was not our ally in this situation."

Sluman disagreed with Davis on the issue of the game caving in to the demands of the corporate world.

"I don't really think it's a corporate outing," he said. "I may have thought that prior to becoming a board member, but I think that the players aren't always totally informed about things, and that's just the way it is. I'm not in favor of playing a shotgun all the time, but this could only happen on the West Coast, under the freaky circumstances that occurred. TV and the sponsor really didn't have anything to do with it, Duke Butler [the Tour's executive director of tournament administration] made the decision."

Regardless of the decision-making process, Davis and many other players were not happy. Davis has always been one of the more opinionated, outspoken players on Tour. He has been around the world of professional golf since he was a child because his late father, Davis Love, Jr., used to play the Tour and later became one of the finest, most respected golf teachers in the world. Davis has seen the Tour grow from a mom and pop–type organization to the corporate, mega-bucks conglomerate that is facing monumental legal battles today.

He blames part of the Tour's current problems on its insistence on branching off into new business ventures behind the strong-armed leadership of Commissioner Deane Beman. Since Beman replaced Joseph C. Dey as the Tour's leading man on March 1, 1974, he has been instrumental in the organization's meteoric growth. The Tour's assets were around $730,000 at the time, and are now approximately $175 million. Total prize money on the PGA Tour was $8.2 million. This year, the PGA, Senior and Hogan tours will play for a combined $84 million in purses. Beman spearheaded the birth of the Senior Tour in 1980 and Hogan Tour in 1990. The Seniors began with two events, and in '92, they will play forty-three. In the previous six years, up to 1992, charitable contributions have topped $115 million. PGA Tour Investments, Inc. was created eleven years ago and includes 15 Tournament Players' Clubs around the country—as well as one in Japan—with more in the planning stages. Many Tour events are held on these courses and because they are owned by the PGA, the Tour does not have to pay the exorbitant rental fees that many private clubs charge. PGA Tour Productions, the Tour's first in-house TV/audio visual production entity, was born in 1985; it produces tournament highlight videos, commercials, golf films and the widely acclaimed television shows *Inside the PGA Tour* and *Inside the Senior Tour*, which are broadcast weekly on ESPN. Other Beman accomplishments include establishing a season-ending tournament for the top 30 money winners, which is like the Super Bowl of the Tour; the implementation of the PGA Tour Stats Program; electronic scoreboards at Tour sites; the Centinela Fitness Center; junior clinics at Tour sites; the Tuesday Long Drive contests and Shootouts; the players' pension fund; and the all-exempt Tour.

All of this has been done through brilliant planning, marketing and foresight, all the while being heavily reliant on corporate sponsorship. The boom was great, but it has gotten to the point, according to Davis, where the Tour is growing out of control.

"I think Deane has done a great job, but I think the Tour has grown beyond its purpose in the world," Davis says. "The Tour should be in the business of running golf tournaments for the players to play in. That's what the Tour should do. Organize the tournaments and do a really good job of it and not get into building golf courses and all this other stuff. They're working against the players too much when they should be working for the players. The Tour is getting too big and expanding too much, and they're not doing the things they should be doing like paying the Tour staff a reasonable amount of money. Who cares about building golf courses, we'll play where there's a golf course that the sponsors want us to play on. Let's not build courses for us to play on, let's not get into the real-estate business. We're a nonprofit organization. Why go out and have it be a for-profit deal? We're going to get burned."

One example Davis refers to is the Karsten lawsuit. It all stems from a Tour rule that took effect in 1990, banning the use of clubs made with U-shaped grooves in tournament competition. In 1987, Tour players were asked if they felt the U-grooves, which make the ball spin more off the clubface even on shots out of the rough, provided a competitive edge compared to the conventional V-shaped grooves. About 60 percent of the players responded to Beman's questionaire and the majority felt that the U-shaped grooves were taking away from the integrity of the game. The Tour had previously deferred all decisions about the legality of equipment to the governing bodies of golf, the U.S. Golf Association in America and the Royal and Ancient Golf Club in St. Andrews, Scotland. However, in this instance, Beman took matters into his own hands and banned the U-shaped grooves from Tour events, arguing that a professional sports organization has the power to make its own rules of competition. The Ping Eye2 irons were and still are the most widely used U-grooved clubs, both by Tour players and amateurs. Karsten complained that his company's sales and reputation would be damaged by the ban and later won an injunction against the ban in federal court. For now, Tour pros are still allowed to use the clubs.

"We've gotten into making our own rules, and that's gotten us into the major lawsuit," Davis says. "And this golf course design thing has the players unhappy. Some players get to design courses and some don't; the whole deal is bad. They argue that it's more money for the pension fund. Well, maybe, but it's a big pain. You see it in any business—if things grow too big, it brings the whole thing down—and I think the Tour is growing out of control."

Davis' feelings are not without precedent. Back in 1983, two golf legends, Arnold Palmer and Jack Nicklaus, led a group of players who complained to the Policy Board that the Tour was improperly moving into areas that were in direct competition with the players who made up the Tour's membership, such as golf-course design and construction, endorsements and television rights. The Policy Board sided with Beman and the issues had not resurfaced until now.

There isn't much Davis can do about these pressing issues except voice his opinion. For now, he's just glad to be finished at Torrey Pines. His attitude—which is the same as every other player in the field except Steve Pate—is let's get the hell out of here and get to Los Angeles, where the next tournament is scheduled. As he walks toward the locker room he tries to blend into the crowd, but his white Tommy Armour visor and the sound

8

of his golf shoe spikes scraping along the concrete distinguish him from the fans and once they recognize who he is, they cluster around him seeking his autograph. In robotic fashion, he mindlessly scribbles his name on the balls, hats, programs, pairings sheets and trading cards that are being thrust in front of him. They each thank him. He responds with a nod and a murmured "You're welcome." As he performs this ritual, he is asking himself, How am I going to get to Los Angeles?

Davis had the use of a courtesy car all week in La Jolla, but he never bothered to call for a rental car for the ride up the coast to Los Angeles. But because Los Angeles is only a couple of hours away, he is not worried about hitching a ride with someone. Sluman has a car, so does Fred Couples. Someone will have room for him and his brother-turned-caddie, Mark.

That someone turns out to be Bill Crist, an investment broker with Alex Brown, a brokerage house based in Richmond, Virginia. Crist had been in San Diego meeting with a few of his clients, one being Davis. He offers Davis a ride, Davis accepts, and within an hour, Crist, Davis and Mark are heading north on the Santa Ana Freeway.

As Mark stares out at the Southern California landscape speeding by, Crist asks Davis the typical questions that fans query of athletes and/or celebrities.

"Bill's not a regular out here, so he's like anyone else," Davis says. "People love to hear stories about the Tour. They like to hear about the inside stuff, they like to hear about what Ian Baker-Finch is like or whatever. Then they can go back and tell other guys what they heard. If you get a bunch of golfers together, there isn't much talk about golf, it's mostly fishing, boats, houses, stereos, things normal people talk about. If I go home, there's hardly any."

For most of the ride, Crist and Davis talk about money—how much Davis and his wife Robin have and where they should be investing it. Planning for the future has never been one of Davis's favorite tasks, but with his custom-built 6,500-square-foot house in Sea Island, Georgia, now completed and his daughter Alexia approaching her fourth birthday, he realizes that he has to put his earnings to work. Crist and Davis discuss a college fund, the current state of interest rates, what stocks are advancing and which are declining, all the things that, Davis admits, "I haven't paid much attention to."

The miles dissolve quickly and in no time, Crist has veered off onto the Santa Monica Freeway and is now driving in Los Angeles County. The three men start looking for the exit that will take them to the Guest Quarters on Fourth Street in Santa Monica.

Eventually, they locate the hotel and pile out of the car, the Love brothers toting their luggage and Davis' golf bag into the lobby. Davis registers, gets the key to suite 707, and he and Mark take their belongings up in the elevator.

Crist, knowing that Davis won't have his courtesy car until tomorrow morning, offers the brothers a ride to dinner, and after quick showers, they men head to Tony Roma's on Santa Monica Boulevard. Davis enjoys going to Tony Roma's all across the country, but not enough to stand in line for an hour waiting for a table, so he suggests a little Chinese place down the street, and Mark and Crist agree. Davis loves Chinese food, so he's satisfied when they arrive and sit down to eat.

It is a typical trendy Los Angeles bistro with about four or five tables and neon glaring from the windows. The food is pretty good. Dinner is spiced with lighthearted conversation, but it is a short evening and soon, Davis and Mark are back in their suite at the Guest Quarters, settled in front of the television. The closing ceremonies of the Winter Olympics in Albertville, France, are on, but that gets boring, so the remote control beams up the Steven Segall movie *Above the Law* on HBO. After that comes to a gory end, the lights go out.

Welcome to Los Angeles.

1 Monday

You can't play golf every day. Some of us probably wish we could, but it's not possible, nor is it healthy. For most of us, playing golf can be a humbling, demoralizing, maddening, aggravating, exasperating, patience-provoking, royal-pain-in-the-ass way to spend four or five hours. If people played golf every day, suppliers of high blood pressure and ulcer medications wouldn't be able to keep up with the demand, suicide rates would rise in dramatic fashion and our president and vice-president wouldn't know what the hell was going on with the country they run. Golf can drive you nuts. Even the best players in the world, the men who play on the American PGA Tour, get frustrated trying to get that little dimpled white ball to do what they want it to do.

At the opening of a new private country club in Victor, New York, last year, featured speaker Gary McCord, the occasional Tour player and popular CBS golf commentator, summed up golf in his typically comical manner.

"I played in Memphis a few weeks ago," he began, referring to the 1991 Federal Express St. Jude Classic. "I hadn't played in a while, so I had to get back there and rekindle, get mad again, get the adrenaline going again. I played in the Wednesday Pro-Am, shot 66, won it, so that's pretty good. On Thursday, I'm 3-under-par with two holes to go. Finish bogey-bogey for a 70. I'm a little hot, now I'm starting to rekindle. I'm thinking, 'You choking dog, I can't believe you did that.' Go out there Friday, cut day, an awful day. I'm going along pretty good, I've got three holes to go, I'm 1-under and the cut's gonna be even-par. I started on the back so I get to the seventh hole, my sixteenth, drive it perfect, hit it on the green and I 3-putt it. Now I start to remember the day before. Go to the next hole, the eighth, 3-putt it. Go to the ninth hole, a par-4, drive it down there perfect, I've got a wedge to the green, have to make a birdie to make the cut, spin it off the green back into the water hazard and make a double bogey. So in two days, I've gone bogey-bogey and bogey-bogey-double bogey and I miss the cut. I go back to my room, lock myself in for a day and a half, never come out. I never change, never do anything. It rekindled itself so quick, you can't believe it. I go from television where you don't have to worry about anything, making a nice income, do a lot of outings, life's good, lots of limos, to going back to thinking how awful this game is to play and how awful it is to play bad. I relieved eighteen years of frustration in a day and a half.

"It's a Goddamn amazing game. In golf, it takes three minutes between each shot. The ball doesn't move. If the ball moved, you'd react to it. If you were hitting it or running for it, throwing it in a hoop or catching a pass, you'd never think about it. But in this game, it sits there on perfectly conditioned fairways, it's a brand-new golf ball we get for free, we're using brand-new equipment, we're sitting there in our brand-new clothes that we get for free, and that ball sits there and says, 'Now idiot, don't hit me in the hazard. Don't hit me over there, hit me on the green. You think you can, you idiot? I doubt if you can. Especially when you're choking your guts out.' All these things go through your head because it takes three to four minutes between each shot. Now all of the vile pasts of the game start to haunt you and it comes up, and that ball's still sitting there. So by the time all this stuff occurs every three or four minutes, you're brain-dead. You can't react, you're comatose, you belong in a boardinghouse somewhere.

"You and you alone are responsible for every shot. You need an imagination to figure out how you're going to get the ball from point A to point B within your abilities. Whether it's going to be Greg Norman or Sammy Slap who hits the ball one hundred fifty yards with a ninety-yard slice, both of them have to figure out how to play the same hole. It offers a myriad of alternatives. I don't want to compare golf to life, but it offers itself a lot like life. You're by yourself and there's an awful lot of opportunities out there and a lot of ways to screw up."

Even the pros' bodies and minds need a rest. On Tour, players grind and grind to maintain their consistency, but there comes a time when you just need to relax and forget about your swing plane, your ball position and your putting stroke.

So when Davis awakens at mid-morning, he starts formulating a plan for the day that leaves little time for practicing at the course. Normally, he does not arrive at a tournament site until Monday night or Tuesday morning, but because of the proximity of Los Angeles to San Diego, he is here this morning. This does not mean he will get a headstart on preparation for this week's Los Angeles Open. This is not a day for work. He'll hit a few balls this afternoon, but primarily, it is a day to relax, get settled and get some errands done.

There haven't been a lot of days like this since Davis first discovered that playing professional golf was how he wanted to make a living.

Davis Love III was born on April 13, 1964, in Charlotte, North Carolina. On that day, his father, Davis Love, Jr., played in the final round of The Masters, finishing tied for 31st. Love Jr., then the head pro at Charlotte Country Club, had earned an invitation to play at Augusta National because he had placed in the top 16 in the 1963 U.S. Open at The Country Club in Brookline, Massachusetts. It was the second time he had played in The Masters, having also competed in 1955 at the wide-eyed age of twenty because he had advanced to the quarterfinals of the '54 U.S. Amateur. Back then, nerves, and Bobby Jones's magnificent swath of hilly Augusta terrain and glassy greens ate him up and he shot 82–85 to miss the cut. This time, Love Jr. brought a more mature, well-rounded game to Augusta and when he birdied No. 18 on Thursday, his sixth one-putt of the day, it capped a 3-under-par opening round of 69 which lifted him into a five-way tie for the lead with Arnold Palmer, Gary Player, Bob Goalby and Kal Nagle.

On Friday, his putter betrayed him and he three-putted three times to shoot 75. And on the weekend, he couldn't maintain his concentration knowing that his wife, Penta, was so close to delivering the couple's first child. He shot 74 on Saturday and 76 on Sunday to finish at 6-over 294, 18 strokes behind Palmer, who was fitted for his then-record fourth green jacket.

Ten hours after putting out on No. 18, Love Jr. was back in Charlotte with Penta and the third-generation Davis Love.

Less than two years later, the Loves moved to Atlanta, where Love Jr. took a job as head golf professional at Atlanta Country Club. He purchased a home situated on the second fairway, providing Davis and Mark, who was born a few months later, quite a backyard to play in as children.

Being the host pro, Love Jr. was able to play in the PGA Tour's annual event in Atlanta, the Atlanta Classic, and Davis would marvel at all the Tour pros as they'd swagger by behind his house on No. 2. He and Mark would sell lemonade to spectators much of the day, then go up and hang around at the 18th hole and watch the pros finish and hound them—much the same way that Davis is badgered today—for autographs, none of which he has anymore. Eventually, they would meander over to the driving range and spend hours watching their dad and the other contestants—greats like Palmer, Jack Nicklaus, Lee Trevino, Player and Johnny Miller—hit balls. Once in a while, Love Jr. would reach into his bag, pull out the smallest club in there, the sand wedge, hand it to Davis and tell him to hit a few, and the pros would watch attentively as the youngster would swing.

Growing up in this environment, it was no surprise that Davis would go on to play professional golf. He had begun walking at nine months old and swinging miniature clubs at 18 months. Love Jr. never pushed his sons to play golf, but he always made sure that they were equipped to play the game if they chose to.

"He went out of his way to make it where we didn't feel we had to play golf," Davis says of his father as he sits at a table in his hotel room, fidgeting with a rubber band. "He always made it available and helped us with it. He'd get us old equipment, or at Christmas time, if we wanted something, we'd always get it. But like when the Atlanta Flames [the team joined the National Hockey League in 1972 and later moved to Calgary, Alberta, in Canada] came to town, I wanted to play ice hockey and he drove me to ice hockey practice and bought me all the equipment and supported that as much as golf. After a couple of years, I got tired of that and I wanted to go back to golf. He didn't say, 'I spent all this money on hockey, let's play hockey.' He was real good about letting us do what we wanted. When we were young, we had a blast playing nine holes or seven holes out back, goofing around, but those were the normal kid times. If you got tired of it, you'd go play basketball or end up in the creek fishing for balls."

When he was about nine, Davis surmised that playing golf would be a great way to make a living. He saw how much his dad enjoyed the game, how good the game had been to him, and he decided to forfeit some of the fun of being a child for the sake of improving his golf game.

"My father challenged me," he recalls. "I was kind of goofing off and only giving it a half effort, but I was only nine or ten years old. He said, 'If you want to play golf, let's play. If you don't then let's do it for fun.' I said I wanted to be as good as I could be and then he started pushing me. Every time he would push me, especially when I was twelve, thirteen, fourteen, fifteen, he'd say, 'You told me you wanted to be the best player you can be.' I'd say, 'Yeah, I told you that,' and he'd say, 'Well, you're not going about it right,' and he'd get furious about it. He'd say, 'If you're going to do it, you're going to have to listen to me and do it my way,' and that was fair. He told me he'd be just as happy if I played college golf, went into business and then played golf for fun, but he said, 'I'm not going to let you try to be a pro player and not do it right.'"

When Love Jr. took a teaching job at Sea Island Golf Club on St. Simons Island, Georgia, and moved the family there in 1977 when Davis was 13, the golf training became more regimented. Davis studiously worked on everything his dad told him to, but Mark didn't possess the same desire to play, nor the willingness to learn from and listen to his father. He wasn't in any hurry to stop being a kid because it was too much fun. He stepped off the fast track his father and brother were on.

"Mark didn't like to listen to it as much as I did," Davis says, "and I put up with it a lot more and that's probably why I advanced faster as a player than him. I knew from an early age that my dad knew what he was talking about and I better listen."

"When we moved, things got a little more serious," Mark says. "I wasn't as involved in golf as Davis was as a young person, I did other things athletically such as soccer, football and basketball. Plus, I was prone to hit the beach in the summer while Davis was still playing golf or working on his game. Some guys would finish a tournament round and then go to the pool or the beach, but Davis would stay around and hit balls.

"If you made the decision that you wanted to be a good player and made that commitment, then dad had a plan for you and you needed to stick to that plan. If that's what you really wanted, then you were going to have to work for it, and Davis did a much better job at that then I ever did. It was always assumed that we were going to be good players because of our background. Any time your father is a pro, people expect the pro's son or sons to play well. Sometimes that was hard. When you were playing well, it wasn't hard because you were playing as well as everyone expected, but if you weren't playing well, people would ask, 'How can you not play better than that? Your father is a pro and you've played all your life.' Davis never really had that because he became really successful as a player his last year of high school and from then on, was at the top of every level he competed on. I never did work at it very hard because I was never at the level that he was at. I was a pretty good player, but then the talent level rose and I kind of stayed at the same level."

Love Jr. was known for his trademark yellow legal pads which he used to carry everywhere, meticulously scribbling down notes.

"I didn't realize that everyone didn't have legal pads in their house," Davis says, a smile crinkling his nose. "I just thought that's what all people wrote on. Him and his lists. There was never a work session without a list. We would practice on the range and there wasn't a time in the car ride home that you didn't hear about everything you did all the way to the house. You couldn't wait to get out of the car and into the house. Then you'd sit down to dinner and it would be more of the same stuff. It was a list of what you were working on at the time. It was my job to take it and learn it, I was supposed to read the list before I went to practice and have it in my bag so I could check to make sure I was doing everything. It was a release for him because he would get so excited, ya know, 'He's hitting it so good, here's what he did to hit it so good, and I'm going to give it to him.'

"It was almost all work. But it was enjoyable work, practicing and playing, watching videos of my swing, reading about golf, all that stuff that you have to do to learn the game. It was organized and serious. There was not as much father/son stuff, it was more teacher/student. It was a working relationship, but we probably got more out of it than most fathers and sons, just in a different way. I had so much trust in him because we worked together on so many different things. Even my schooling, he told me I had to do good in school because if I didn't, I couldn't go to college and I couldn't play college golf. Everything was based on golf."

And at times, golf became too much. It was such an integral part of Davis's life that he needed a diversion, someone to remind him that even though golf might be his career, it shouldn't so dominate his life that nothing else mattered. Enter Jimmy Hodges, another teaching pro at Sea Island.

"One of the great things that Jimmy did was he got me away from that," he says. "His whole life was teaching and being a golf pro, but he had a family and other things that he enjoyed, like hunting and fishing. He was a release for me. I could go on the range and practice and have other things to talk about, even though my dad would get mad at us. Jimmy would ask if we were going to go deer hunting and we'd talk about all this other stuff and then I'd hit a bad shot and my dad would say, 'Well, if you'd quit talkin' about hunting, it'd be better.' They were a good balance for me."

With this unique blend of coaching, Davis's game flourished in high school. His long, fluid swing enabled him to drive the ball seemingly miles past his competition and he won the Georgia state junior championship in 1981 as a junior in high school. In his senior year, playing in the Georgia state high school champion-ship at Bull Creek in Columbus, he fired a 6-under-par 66 to set a state record. It was then that the future really started coming into focus. Countless young golfers have shown great potential as youths, then fizzled in college and never made it to the pros. But Davis's talent transcended child prodigy status. It was obvious that when Davis accepted a three-quarter scholarship to play at the University of North Carolina, it was merely a stopover in the minor leagues before the inevitable promotion to the big leagues.

He won eight collegiate events, and in 1984, he captured the Atlantic Coast Conference individual title and won the prestigious North and South Amateur, both played at the historic No. 2 course at Pinehurst (North Carolina).

After his sophomore year, his father estimated that Davis could probably go out on the Tour and finish in the top 50 on the money list. After his junior year, the father felt his son could crack the top 30. That was all Davis needed to hear. He knew his dad had been there and he also knew his father wouldn't lie to him. He left North Carolina after his junior year and began playing in as many top amateur tournaments as he could in preparation for the grueling PGA Qualifying School in the fall of 1985.

Part of that preparation was playing for the United States in the Walker Cup matches in August at what is widely regarded as the world's best golf course, Pine Valley in New Jersey. The United States Golf Association selects the amateur American squad that competes in the biennial matches against a team comprised of players from England, Scotland, Wales, Ireland and Northern Ireland. The USGA picked a winner as the Americans beat the foreigners, 13–11, and Davis—despite playing with a very sore wrist due to tendinitis, which would ultimately force him to miss the U.S. Amateur the following week—was responsible for 2½ points.

Carrying supreme confidence, he was ready to tackle the Q-School. A total of 825 golfers signed up to play in the eleven regional qualifying events across the country and Davis was one of the top 162 scorers from those trials who earned a position in the Q-School finals at Grenelefe Golf and Tennis Club in Haines City, Florida, the week of Thanksgiving. It may not seem fair—especially to those who fail—but unless you are a full exempt member of the PGA Tour, the results of the Q-School finals determine a professional golfer's fate for the following season. Play well and you get to compete against the best players in the world with colossal purses at stake. Play poorly and you're stuck playing the low-rent mini-tours against guys you know you're better than. Davis played well at Grenelefe. He shot 66 the first day of the marathon six-round final and followed that with steady scores of 74-71-73. His 72-hole total of two-under 284 enabled him to be one of the 105 players who made the 9-over 295 cut. With only 50 Tour cards available, he went out and completed the tournament in 68–71 to finish in a seventh-place tie at 6-under 423, eight shots behind medalist Tom Sieckmann.

In his rookie season, he finished 77th on the money list with $113,245 and led the Tour in driving distance, posting a then-record average of 285.7 yards per drive. During a round at the Players Championship at the TPC at Sawgrass in March, Davis realized that his life's ambitions were being fulfilled.

"I was paired with Ben Crenshaw the last day and I had a really good round [67] while playing in front of a lot of people and with one of the stars of the game," Davis recalled. "That day, something told me that I belonged."

He entered '87 with his new bride, Robin, by his side and quickly proved he belonged with the big boys as he won his first PGA tournament, the MCI Heritage Classic at the Harbour Town Golf Links in April, just a couple hours up the Eastern Seaboard from Sea Island.

Later that year, he finished second in the Colonial and went on to pocket $297,378, good for 33rd on the money list. In 1988, the arrival of his daughter Alexia in June stole some of his concentration, and he played less, missed more cuts, and earned only $156,068, 75th on the money list. Still, with his awesome length off the tee helping him to overpower golf courses, and with three full years of learning experiences accrued, it was time to step up to the next level and start getting himself into contention on a regular basis. Greatness seemed just a par-3 away.

It was November 13, 1988, and Davis and Robin had just arrived at the Kapalua Bay Hotel on Maui, site of the Kapalua International, a non-PGA event that at the time featured a field of the top twenty-four PGA Tour money-winners and twenty other sponsor invitees playing for a $150,000 first-place check. For the third year in a row, Davis had been invited to participate. It had been a long flight and the first thing the Loves did was take a dip in the pool. When they returned to their room, the phone rang. Davis answered and on the other end was a minister from Charlotte who had known his mother some twenty-five years before. He told Davis that he was in Kapalua and was looking forward to watching him play in the tournament.

Davis wasn't going to call his mom for a couple of days, but he was so excited to tell her that her friend had called, he dialed her number in Sea Island.

"I called up and I said, 'Guess who I just talked to,' and she said, 'You're not going to believe the phone call I just got.'"

Just minutes before, Penta Love had been informed that the plane carrying her husband, Jimmy Hodges and the other golf pro at Sea Island Golf Club, John Popa, was missing somewhere between Sea Island and Jacksonville, Florida. The threesome, all members of the *Golf Digest* School's teaching staff, was being flown to Jacksonville in a four-seat Piper Cherokee plane by pilot Steve Worthington, and from there, were going to fly to Miami for a *Golf Digest* meeting. They never got to Jacksonville.

"There was a line of fog just over the airport," Davis explains, his features stern and his emotions firmly in check. "There's still pending lawsuits [the families of the three men jointly sued the Federal Aviation Administration], but apparently it was control tower error. They gave all the big planes the information on the fog, but didn't give the small planes information. This plane just got lost in the shuffle. I've read piles of control tower stuff . . . one plane came in and it was too foggy so he went somewhere else, another plane came in and landed and there was a couple other big jets that landed. This other guy [Worthington] got lost in the shuffle. They never really told him how bad the fog was. I guess he got too close to one of those big jets, got into the jet wash and got off track and was outside the lines."

Davis hung up the phone, and he and Robin frantically dashed back to the Maui airport.

"I called a guy named Jim Griggs, who was Joey Sindelar's sponsor when he first came out on Tour. He had a corporate jet. I told him what had happened and I told him I had to get home, I couldn't spend time waiting for a connection, I'd pay him for the gas."

Griggs, who is a member of the Tour Investments Board and at the time was chairman and president of his own company,

Financial Investors Advisors, told Davis that he'd pick him up in San Francisco and that he would fly back to Georgia with him.

Every chance he had, Davis had been calling home to see if there was any news because he needed to know, good or bad, what was going on. But the fog hadn't lifted and it was impossible for a search crew to look for the plane, so when he boarded Griggs' plane, his dad's whereabouts were still unknown. Now faced with a five-hour flight from coast to coast, he couldn't call. Griggs' plane touched down at six in the morning and the search party had just begun to comb the area where the plane may have gone down. The news came at 7 A.M. that the plane had indeed crashed, and there were no survivors.

All at once, at the still slightly impressionable age of twenty-four, Davis had lost his father, his teacher, his confidant and his coach. In addition, he had lost Hodges, his other teacher and perhaps his best friend; and a good friend in Popa. Where does one go after an experience like that? Well, for the first week or so, Davis would sit on the front porch of his mom's house with friends or other family members and just cry. Then, he realized that these three men—especially his father—had always been there, sharing their time and knowledge with him. They had given so much to him. It was time he gave something back.

"The thing that hit me the most about how I was feeling and how I was reacting to it all was that these guys gave me so much of their time for me to play golf. I can play golf and my golf game was going to be fine. I was competitive and I was going to continue to be competitive and this wasn't going to hold me back. I was concerned about losing my two best friends, and John was a pretty good friend of mine, too. And I was more concerned about their kids. All I could think about was all my little friends. I was twenty-four, I could understand it, but it's hard to tell a three-year-old that his dad's gone."

Hodges left behind a wife and three small children and Popa was survived by his wife and two children.

"The first Christmas I felt like I had to be there for the kids. Jimmy had given me so much so I had to make sure that I was doing my part. The kids are grown now and doing their own thing and right now, I'm not like their friend, I'm a celebrity that they know. But it won't be much longer before they'll want to go hunting and fishing and wanting me to drive them around and I can get back into the fun of being with them."

A memorial fund was set up to help the families and Davis says, "I guarantee you, we ended up with enough money for five college educations. Fuzzy Zoeller knew my father, but he didn't know these other two guys from a hole in the wall, he just wrote a check for five thousand dollars and said, "Here.' People all around the world who had taken lessons from my dad, people from Georgia, Sea Island, anyone who knew Jimmy or John, it was unreal. So that was one thing off my mind, that they were taken care of, and the insurance money got settled, so once that started rolling in and they were going to be all right financially and they weren't going to have to sell their houses, then I was all right."

The pain will always be there for Davis. You never get over the passing of a loved one, but what makes it so much more difficult for him is that he is constantly reminded of his dad. They are from the same world, the world of golf, and almost everyone Davis comes in contact with knew, or knew of, his dad. Many had taken lessons from his dad. His dad was gone, but in many ways, he wasn't.

"I would wake up night after night after and I'd be crying because I would dream that I was talking to my dad or Jimmy. After the first week I would never just sit down and cry. I have every once in a while since. Something will hit me and I'll cry, but for a year there, I would just wake up and be in absolute tears. I talked to Bob [Rotella, his sports psychologist] and he told me that all that time, I never got it out of my system, and now, my subconscious was getting it out, which was just as good. My mom would walk out on the golf course almost every day and cry. She wouldn't do it when I was at the house, so she'd go up in the shower and cry."

Tomorrow or the next day, he will call his mom to chitchat and at some point, she will ask him how he's playing. He will tell her, and she might give him encouragement or maybe even pass along a tip. He will hang up, and like he almost always does, he will recall the invariable phone conversations he and his father used to have.

———

22

"I miss somebody to talk to about how I'm playing every day. Nobody wants to hear it. You go in the locker room, the old story is, half the people don't care and half the people wish it were worse. They don't care, they don't want to hear how you played. They're in the business and they're trying to do the best for them. My mom listens to it, but I don't get the feedback. She's interested and she loves to talk about it, but it's not somebody who's really dying to hear about it. Now with my dad, it was different. My dad genuinely cared about every golf shot I played. He wanted to hear every shot of every round. If I went three days in a row without talking to him, it would be an absolute miracle, especially my first couple of years on Tour. He wanted to know how far it went, what if felt like, where it went. It was his way of knowing where the shots were going and what my tendencies were and he would keep track of it. That's what I miss.

"By doing that, dad helped my confidence, too. I'd tell him what I'd do wrong and he'd say, 'Well, it's not that bad. Listen to how many good things you did.' I could shoot 75 and feel lousy and he would find ninety percent of it good and he'd say, 'You were three swings away from a 68 if you had done this, this and this.' He made me have confidence in myself. Mark and I still say how many swings I was away from turning a good round into a great round or a bad round into a good round."

After his father's death, Davis figured he could make it on Tour just by implementing what his dad had already taught him, and he had done pretty well using that philosophy. In 1989, he finished 44th on the money list with $278,760 despite missing about six weeks due to a broken bone in his left wrist, an injury he suffered while playing in the British Open at Troon. He had started working occasionally with Jack Lumpkin when Lumpkin moved to Sea Island in 1989, but Davis was still relying on himself when the 1990 season began.

The problem with his wrist went away and he opened the season with a pair of strong showings on the West Coast. But soon thereafter he went into a slump and fighting through his stubbornness, he decided to seek help.

"I had been working with Jack, but it was really when I started to work with Butch Harmon [son of former Masters champion and longtime Winged Foot head pro Claude Harmon] and I started to trust myself a little more, that I was able to play better and win," Davis admits. "That summer in 1990 was when I started working with Butch, and I started playing better. Butch, in a roundabout way, teaches almost exactly like my dad. And his dad was a lot like my dad, and Jack Lumpkin used to work for Claude Harmon so he thinks like my dad. All these guys that I have around me are very similar to my dad."

He had first spoken to Butch in May in Japan. Davis, Jeff Sluman, Steve Pate and a few other Americans went overseas for a tournament, and Harmon, who had been working with Sluman, accompanied him to Japan. Davis had overheard some of the comments Harmon had made to Sluman, liked what he was hearing, and one day, asked Harmon what he thought of his own swing. Harmon's response was "I was hoping you'd ask." He gave Davis a couple of tips, and they meshed with what Lumpkin had been telling him, and suddenly, his game started coming together.

He missed a couple of more cuts, and because he wasn't exempt for the U.S. Open at Medinah, had to go to sectional qualifying in order to earn a spot in the field. He failed to make it and missed the Open, and he later missed the cut at the British Open at St. Andrews and tied for 40th at the PGA. But he was feeling better about his swing and going into The International at Castle Pines (Colorado) Golf Club, Davis could see that the work with Harmon and Lumpkin was beginning to make a difference.

That week, in the high Colorado altitude, Davis broke through and earned his second tournament victory, his first since his dad's death.

"I want to say that it [his father's death] didn't affect my golf game, but it did," he says. "I know I put a lot of pressure on myself to prove that it didn't bother my game. After I won and I went to the press room and sat down and thought about it, I realized that it was so much harder than it should have been. I went boom, boom, birdie, birdie, win and it just hit me how much pressure I had been carrying around to win a golf tournament. That made me realize that maybe it did affect my golf game. Not my shots or my putting, but I couldn't quite win because I was trying so hard to win."

He wound up the season with a career-high $537,172, 20th on the money list. He ranked eighth in driving distance (276.6), but more importantly, he was 27th in average number of putts per hole (1.776) and was seventh in percentage of holes played under par (21.7).

In '91, he soared to eighth on the money list with $686,361, pushing him past the $2 million mark in official career earnings. He was one of only thirteen players to make the cut in all four majors, and his scoring average in his sixteen rounds of play in the majors of 72.06 was seventh-best in that group (Fred Couples led at 71.00). Overall, he missed just five of 28 cuts, finished in the top 10 eight times, and won again at Harbour Town.

And now, in 1992, he is off to an average start. He finished tied for seventh in the season-opening Tournament of Champions, had a chance to win at the Hope before tying for eighth, tied for 52nd at Phoenix and missed the cut at Pebble Beach prior to his tie for 38th at San Diego.

He has hit 176 out of 264 fairways for a 66.7 percentage, only 88th on Tour, but that is better than he has ever finished in that statistic in his first six years on Tour. He has hit 249 of 342 greens in regulation, a 72.8 percentage ranking him 48th. And on the greens, he is averaging 1.767 putts per hole, good for 62nd place. With 80 birdies, he is ranked 20th, but his sand saves percentage is way down at 38.7 percent, placing him 126th.

"I'm not playing that great," he says. "I feel like my swing is real close and my putting is real close, but I'm just not scoring real well. I've made a lot of birdies, but I've been making a lot of mistakes. I haven't been putting two rounds together or four rounds together, just not playing great. It's the beginning of the year and I'm playing with new clubs, so there's always the excuse that you're getting settled in. I feel like I should have won the Hope, I had a good chance there. Last week I was six shots out and I feel like I threw away at least six shots the first two days. I'm at the point now where if I have a good week concentrating, I'll be right there. It's getting close, it's just beneath the surface."

Mark sleeps nearly an hour longer than Davis, so when he rolls out of bed, showers and shaves, Davis calls the L.A. Open transportation committee and requests that a driver bring his courtesy car over to the hotel. Within minutes, a new white Nissan Maxima pulls up in front of the main entrance, the Loves climb in, and drive to Riviera.

Both have to register, Davis to play, Mark to caddie. Davis also signs up his daughter, Lexie, for the tournament day-care center. With those minor details taken care of, they set out to find a place where they can get their laundry done. The search ends on San Vicente Boulevard in Brentwood.

Davis is told by the woman at the front counter that his laundry will not be done until Thursday. Unsatisfactory, so he barters for Wednesday and she reluctantly agrees. Then, she notices the Maxima out front with the L.A. Open logo on the side panel and decides that because he is a golfer, she can have his laundry ready by 2:30 the next day. So not only has he saved a lot of money—because when you have the hotel do your laundry, they gouge you in charges—he'll have it the next day. Good start.

Next on the list is trying to find Mark a hotel. With Robin and Lexie coming in tomorrow, Mark will be banished from the suite at the Guest Quarters. After driving around unsuccessfully, they postpone that search and head to a Harley-Davidson motorcycle accessory shop. Last October, Davis bought a Harley, and he had been looking for black leather saddle bags, but hadn't been able to find what he wanted. Until today. The shop had just taken a trade-in on a bike that had amassed a scant 500 miles. The saddle bags had a few small scratches on them, but when the shop owner offers them to Davis for about half the price that brand new ones would cost, he says, "I'll take 'em for half price."

Dutifully pleased by his good fortune at the laundromat and the Harley shop, he returns to Riviera and grabs lunch in the players' lounge. The players' lounge is for contestants and their family members. Caddies are not allowed, but Davis is discovering that he's in a unique situation with Mark.

"Is my brother my caddie, or is he a family member that's allowed in the locker room and lounge? Only players, wives and immediate family are supposed to be in the lounge. So if Mark McCumber's brother or Fred Couples's brother is in there, why can't my brother be in there? I've talked to some officials and they don't know what to do. I kind of feel bad about taking him in, but it's Monday so no one was in there."

After lunch, Davis starts to wander down to the driving range, but Mark gets there twenty minutes before him because as Davis walks down the steep hill that leads to the range, he is interrupted three times. First, a recruiter for the Freeport-McMoRan Classic in New Orleans asks him if he's going to play in the tournament, scheduled the week before The Masters. Each tournament has recruiters who try to convince the players who haven't already signed up, to play in their event. Every tournament's goal is to corral the best field possible, so the recruitment at times takes on the aura of college football and basketball recruiting. The players often seek a hiding place when they see a particular representative from a tournament they know they're not going to play in, just to escape having to say no. Again. The pitch often includes a detailed description of how much the course has been upgraded or what great condition it's in; how much fun the parties are; and how many activities there are for the players and their families in the host city. On the flip side, when a player signs up to play in a tournament, the recruiter for that event is invaluable.

"Ninety-five percent of the time, those guys are the greatest help," Davis says. "They take out their notebooks and they start checking off the list: 'Do you want to play in the Monday Pro-Am? The Tuesday shootout? Do you want a room at this hotel and how many rooms do you need? Do you want to use the nursery? Do you need a car? So they're a great help." But all that doesn't matter when it comes to New Orleans, because Davis isn't going to play, and he politely informs the recruiter of this.

As soon as he finishes that brief conversation, he is approached by a photographer who shows Davis publicity photos he had taken at Sea Island for Polo, the clothing company Davis endorses. He looks at the photos for a few seconds, then continues working his way down the hill until he is stopped by a reporter who asks him a few questions.

"He says, 'I've got a question and it'll only take a minute,'" Davis explains. "Well, there's a scale out here. One minute means ten, five is twenty, ten is about thirty. These TV people come up and say they want an interview and it'll take two minutes. Well, they can't even set up their cameras in two minutes. If it's thirty minutes, tell people it's going to take thirty minutes. If it's five, tell me it's five. I bug the CBS guys all the time. They say, 'Can I have five minutes of your time?' and I say, 'Yeah, I've got a half hour.'"

Finally, he makes it to the range, but before he hits balls, he has to do a little socializing. He walks over to Dillard Pruitt and tells him that he found saddle bags. Pruitt also has a Harley, so he's interested in every detail of the saddle bags and he wants to know where the store is so he can check it out later in the week.

Derek Crawford, one of the representatives from Ping, comes over to Davis and Davis tells him that he needs a new sand wedge this week. Davis began playing Tommy Armour irons this year, but he still uses a Ping sand wedge and Ping L-wedge. In the third round of the season-opening Tournament of Champions at La-Costa last month, he mashed his sand wedge against the lip of a trap after hitting a poor shot. He changed the bent shaft, but it hadn't looked right and after screwing around trying to figure out the problem, he just decided the hell with it and asked Ping for a new one.

"Ping is the greatest," Davis says. "If I called them up tomorrow morning and said I wanted a whole set of clubs exactly like the ones I won the 1987 Heritage with, I'd have them the next day. They keep files on every club they've ever made for me and I'm not even on their staff. If I say I want this model putter, they'll fire it out just the way I want it at thirty-four inches, three degrees loft with a smaller grip and a slightly open face. Nobody is as good as Ping at putting clubs together and having them being perfectly consistent.

"Last year, I went to the U.S. Open [at Hazeltine National in Chaska, Minnesota] and the greens were hard and I wasn't happy with the sand wedge. I called Derek and I said, 'How about getting me a sand wedge to match my L-wedge.' It was there Tuesday morning in my locker. I practiced with it and I said, 'Man, this is great, these greens are hard as rock and I'm hitting great sand wedge shots.' So I call him again and said, 'How about sending me a pitching wedge.' This is Tuesday and on Wednesday morning I get the pitching wedge. I used all three of those wedges and I finished 11th. I didn't have to ever worry that the wedges weren't exactly what I needed. I just took them out of the box and put them into the bag."

Even more incredible than Ping's ability to make clubs to precise specifications in such a short period of time is the way that Ping and every other club manufacturer spoils the pros. These guys get anything they want, and all of it is free. In fact, they get paid to play with the clubs and balls they use, they get paid to wear certain pants, shirts, visors, shoes and gloves. The average American family could live very comfortably just on what pro golfers make in clothing endorsements. Throw in equipment deals, and average American families could live luxuriously on that income. And all this money is banked before the player even tees it up and starts earning prize money. Davis' deal with Tommy Armour, which he cannot divulge, probably pays him nearly a quarter of a million dollars a year. He's not paid by Ping, but they get publicity because pro golfer Davis Love III uses their wedges and putters. So it's worth it for them to give him anything he wants.

"Every company is great about it," Davis says. "Out on the range, you'd be amazed. It would be fun sometimes to do an article on seeing how much free stuff you could collect in one week, without taking advantage and getting people mad. You can walk off with tons of stuff, and then put a dollar amount on it."

At last, he joins Mark behind a bucket of white Titleist range balls, does some quick stretching exercises, pulls out his 9-iron and starts hitting crisp shots at a flagstick about 150 yards out. It is about 3:15 and the bright sunshine burns behind his back. The atmosphere is relaxed, and players all around Davis are chitchatting and laughing. Soon, a club rep from Cleveland Classics ambles up to Davis and asks him to experiment with a few new drivers. Davis uses a Cleveland Classics driver with a persimmon head, and these new clubs have persimmon heads with metal implants in the face. Davis hits a few shots with each one, but he can't tell if they're any good because the clubs aren't made to his specifications.

"They're trying to keep the reps away from us on the range," Davis explains after the guy from Cleveland Classics walks away. "There are guys out here with absolute garbage and they're always trying to get you to try stuff. Now, the Tour is trying to keep them in a little area and they can't come out unless a player asks them for something. They [the Tour officials] are not strictly enforcing it yet so we tease guys once in a while to get back in the corral. What they don't want a guy to do is get his wad of drivers and hit each guy. They want players to come look at them, then go back and try it. It's getting ridiculous and guys started complaining.

"I'm one of the guys that they come to for drivers because they can get good feedback from me because I hit it a long way. So I do a little bit, but people have learned not to mess with me. What's nice about having a deal with Tommy Armour is that I have to use their irons, and the reps know that. Hitting those drivers didn't do me a bit of good."

For the past few years, Davis has been aligned with the Ben Hogan Company, but before the start of this season, the company informed its Tour playing staff that because of financial difficulties, it would have to cut back drastically and spend the majority of its dwindling resources supporting the club pros. While it would honor all the existing contracts, Hogan told its players that if they could get a similar or better deal with another organization, to do so. Almost all did, and only Tom Kite and David Frost on the PGA Tour and Don January on the Senior Tour remain with Hogan.

The trouble started when Japanese multimillionaire Minoru Isutani, whose computer software company, Cosmo World, is Hogan's parent company, got in over his head when he purchased Pebble Beach Co. in September of 1990. Isutani paid $840 million in the landmark real-estate deal, which included the Pebble Beach, Spyglass Hill, Spanish Bay and Old Del Monte golf courses, the Lodge at Pebble Beach, the Inn at Spanish Bay, residential homesites in Del Monte Forest and the beautiful 17-Mile Drive.

Isutani had hoped to initiate a membership plan for Pebble Beach, which has always been a public facility. But when the California Coastal Commission decided that the membership plan violated Del Monte Forest land-use provisions and the California Coastal Act, it nixed the idea and left Isutani scrambling for funds to pay off a $574 million loan he had taken out to help pay for the original purchase of the property. Isutani's Cosmo World of Nevada, Inc. filed for Chapter 11 protection in December, and two days later, Monterey County officials filed a suit against Pebble Beach Co. for unpaid real-estate transaction fees.

With all of these problems, Isutani had to drain his other companies—including Hogan, which he bought for $52 million in 1988—to help alleviate some of his debt.

"Hogan told us we were free to look elsewhere and if we found a better deal, we could take it, which was a nice thing," Davis says. "I don't know what would have happened if everybody couldn't find a better deal and they would have kept their contracts."

Among the players who left Hogan were Davis, Steve Pate, Lanny Wadkins, Chip Beck, Tom Bryum, Doug Tewell and Mark Brooks. Hogan's staff won more Tour events last year than any other company.

"They had a lot of high-dollar guys. It was costing them millions a year in retainers, and paying bonuses and all that, they had so many guys, it was just killing them," Davis says.

Davis fielded a number of offers, but settled on Armour for the simplest of reasons—he liked the clubs.

"I was in a good position because I had just had my best two years back-to-back. Fred Couples used to play Armours and I had hit a lot of balls with his clubs and I really liked them. I was comfortable with them already. When it started happening, they asked if I wanted a set to make sure I liked them and I said, 'No, I'm happy with them. If you can work the deal, I'm going to do it.'

"These are very similar to Pings and I used to use Pings so the only change for me from the Hogans was cosmetic and it wasn't tough because I had used the Pings before."

Another key part of the decision was that he liked the staff Armour had compiled.

"I had a couple of companies where I could have gotten more money, but I wanted to go with Tommy Armour. When it got to a number that I was happy with, I just told Vinnie [Giles, his agent], 'Okay, that's it, let's take that, let's not talk to anybody else.' There's something to be said for the peace of mind of it. I knew it was a company that I could live with—the people, the clubs, their marketing style—everything about it was fine. And I could live with their staff. At Hogan, we had a great group of guys. Bruce Lietzke is a good friend, Joey Sindelar is one of my best friends, Jim Gallagher is a guy who I'm getting to know and he's a great guy. We have to do commercials together or corporate outings and it'll be nice that we can all get along and we can enjoy being part of a staff."

In his bag he has the Cleveland Classics eight-degree driver, a Taylor Made 12-degree 3-wood, a Tommy Armour 1-iron and then Armour irons 3, 4, 5, 6, 7, 8, 9, pitching wedge and a 56-degree sand wedge, a Ping 60-degree L-wedge and a Ping putter.

He spends 20 more minutes hitting balls, using every club. Given perfect conditions, he says he can hit his driver anywhere from 275 to 320 yards, his 3-wood can be hit as far as 250, his 1-iron tops out at about 225-230, the 3-iron at 210, 4-iron at 200, 5-iron about 190, 6-iron about 180, his 7-iron around 168, 8-iron at 155, 9-iron at 145, pitching wedge at 130, sand wedge about 110 and his L-wedge at 75.

When he finishes, he talks briefly with some players, caddies and club reps, and then tells Mark that he's going to work out in the fitness trailer. So the brothers climb back up the hill, Mark puts the clubs in the Maxima, then sits in front of the caddie headquarters tent and reads the paper while Davis goes into the trailer to work out. An hour later, they drive back to the Guest Quarters, turn on the television and watch basketball. First up is St. John's–Providence, followed by Kansas-Oklahoma. Room service arrives at about 7:30, and the only other interruption is a pair of phone calls from Robin and one from Mark's girlfriend, Lynn. Pretty soon, the lights are out.

2 Tuesday

There is an orange ball of fire in the eastern sky, making its daily burn through the dirty air of Los Angeles. Its heat is not yet stifling, but it promises to be a hot day in Pacific Palisades, a wealthy, well-scrubbed suburb to the northwest of downtown Los Angeles, the Pacific Ocean serving as its border to the west. There are no clouds in the sky, so the sun's glare will be unimpeded when it reaches its warmest peak later in the afternoon. The eucalyptus trees that dominate the foliage are still, no wind to rustle their leaves and branches. Riviera is peaceful at seven in the morning. A few volunteers begin arriving for their day of work, a few players are already playing practice rounds, and in the fairway at No. 2, the difficult par-4 that plays as a par-5 for members, a caddie stalks from sprinkler head to sprinkler head, trying to get the exact measurements of the hole so he can note them in his yardage book. Early-risers on the range include Morris Hatalsky, Jim Hallett and Steve Elkington. As they propel balls into the sky, they have great difficulty following their flight paths because the sun is in front of them and blinding their view.

From the driving range, you look to the north and there, perched on a cliff high above the playing surface, is Riviera's clubhouse. Long ago dubbed "The Grand Hotel of Golf," it has stood stately and historical since 1927, when Riviera first opened its doors. Nearly all of the legends, men like Walter Hagen, Gene Sarazen, Ben Hogan, Byron Nelson, Sam Snead, Arnold Palmer, Jack Nicklaus and Tom Watson, have talked about their rounds over dinner and drinks in Riviera's clubhouse. It has been a playground for the stars of Hollywood and the wealthiest, most influential businessmen. Its history is as rich as the golf course it overlooks.

In the early 1920s, The Los Angeles Athletic Club produced national champions in swimming, diving, gymnastics and weight-lifting. But there were no golfers. The club had only a nine-hole putting course and driving net on the roof of its headquarters building in central Los Angeles. Anyone interested in playing the gentlemanly game went to nearby Brentwood Country Club on an arranged basis. However, LAAC official Sam Hall toured the Palisades one day, looked at the tall brush, mesquite, cactus and wild palms and pines and pictured an 18-hole golf course carved out of this vibrant acreage. What he saw excited him, and he shared his vision with LAAC vice-president Frank Garbutt. Garbutt exclaimed, "This is it, this is it," when he saw the land, and soon the LAAC purchased the 640-acre lot for $265,500 and hired George C. Thomas, Jr., to shape it into a golf course. Thomas was a decorated World War I pilot and a golf-course architect responsible for many layouts, including Bel Air Country Club and Ojai Country Club; a scratch golfer, a ranking authority on deep-sea fishing and a cultivator of prize roses, he had authored books on all of his pursuits, including *Golf Architecture in America*. Thomas later regarded his work at Riviera as his best ever, and when the club was officially opened in June of 1927, the $1 million it had cost to build the course and clubhouse and install a sprinkler system was well worth it.

In the 1930s, four polo fields were cultivated and international polo players flocked to Riviera. Tennis courts were later installed.

Through the years, the club has been one of the most prominent social gathering points in the country. Greta Garbo, Marlene Dietrich, and Gloria Swanson used to watch the polo matches; Douglas Fairbanks would bet people $1,000 that they couldn't shoot par or better; Howard Hughes, a man way ahead of his time, brought video equipment to the driving range to film his swing. In the 1940s, Riviera's land became the Spanish Revolution countryside for a film called *Blockade*, starring Katherine Hepburn and Spencer Tracy. In the movie *Forever Amber*, the course doubled as pastoral England. The Ben Hogan story, *Follow the Sun*, starring Glenn Ford, was also filmed at Riviera, where Hogan won two Los Angeles Opens and the U.S. Open within a 17-month period in 1947/48.

In fact, that U.S. Open in 1948 was Riviera's first major golf tournament. The leaders of the U.S. Golf Association had never brought its national championship further west than Cherry Hills in Denver. But based on the success Riviera had had with the L.A. Open, the USGA finally relented and came to Los Angeles. Later, the West Coast would offer the Olympic Club and Pebble Beach in northern California as hugely impressive Open sites, but southern California is still waiting for its second Open.

The only other major tournament to be held at Riviera was the 1983 PGA Championship, won by Hal Sutton with a 10-under 274, one less than Jack Nicklaus. The PGA has agreed to return in 1995.

Today, the polo fields are gone, replaced by the tennis courts and expensive housing, but the golf course remains virtually unchanged. Only the barranca that runs through the course has experienced cosmetic surgery. It used to serve as a drainage ditch during heavy rainstorms, but a cement storm drain project constructed at a cost of $1.8 million took the burden off the barranca and now its only purpose is to create havoc for any golfer who happens to hit a stray shot into it.

Davis and Mark get to the course at 8 A.M. Mark takes a seat on the bench in front of the locker room entrance while Davis hurries through a bowl of cereal in the lounge. When he is finished, he walks briskly to the first tee, Mark in tow, and sees that it is crowded, so he proceeds to the 10th tee. Just before he begins the descent down the hill, he pauses to check who is teeing off. It is Dillard Pruitt and Jay Haas.

"Hey, Dillard, can I join y'all?" he yells, and Pruitt waves an okay. Davis walks down the hill, strides up to the teeing area, takes his driver out of the bag, loosens up with a couple practice swings, inserts his tee into the lush green grass, looks down the fairway, addresses his ball, brings his club back slowly, then releases it downward in a fury of controlled motion. The clubhead strikes the ball with the face just a fraction open and the Titleist is launched on a bulletlike trajectory toward the green 312 yards away. Without hitting one practice shot, with the benefit of only a couple of swings to find some type of rhythm, he has hit the ball just off the fairway in the right rough, almost 280 yards. Pretty good start.

Davis likes to do everything early in the morning so his whole day isn't shot. The earlier he can play, the more time he has later to practice, work out, run errands, or perhaps most important, to "goof off."

"I saw Tom Kite in the locker room and I asked him what time he was playing and he said he was meeting his caddie at eight-thirty, so he wouldn't be ready until at least nine o'clock," he says. "That's too late. This worked out perfect for me because these guys [Pruitt and Haas] are doing the same thing I want to do. They're playing a little skins game and they won't be out here hitting chips shots and a ton of putts on every hole. I'm not out here to work on my swing, you can do that on the range. All I want to do is see the course and work on a few shots."

He arrives at his ball, sees that it is sitting down in the rough a bit, but surmises that his L-wedge can pick it out cleanly. He hits a high-arcing flop shot to within eight feet, then misses the birdie putt and blows a chance to win a $2 skin. While he, Pruitt and Haas stroke a couple of putts from various spots on the green looking for subtle breaks and trying to get a feel for the speed, Mark, Haas' caddie Tom Lamb and Pruitt's caddie, Norm Blount, pace off yardages on the greens and check their George Lucas yardage books to make sure the figures are correct.

Lucas is the man who has been authoring yardage books on Tour since 1976. He is a former caddie who worked briefly for Arnold Palmer, Tom Shaw and Bobby Nichols before recognizing his real purpose in life. There was a void that needed to be filled on Tour and he decided he was just the man to fill it. Another former caddie, Harry Brown, had been designing books on a part-time basis, but Lucas took over the duties full-time and today he runs his own business called Tour Yardage Books, Inc.

Driving around the country in a customized van accompanied by his faithful golden retriever, Corky, Lucas tries to visit each Tour course once every two years. The forty-one-year-old paces yardages off from tee to green and his comprehensive surveying includes yardages to the pin from almost every possible vantage point on a particular hole. Most courses have sprinkler heads that are already marked for the members, but Lucas double-checks those and if he comes up with a different number, the players always use his figure. After spending three or four days charting a course, Lucas then draws the design of each hole and indicates the various landmarks such as trees, bunkers, sprinkler heads, water fountains and bushes. Yardages are written next to all sprinkler heads and other selected sites. Lucas even provides yardages from places where players would only be if they got into trouble, or hit a terrible shot. In these instances, Lucas uses his trademark notation of J.I.C.Y.R.F.U. This acronym translates to "Just in case you really fucked up."

At No. 12, Davis walks down the fairway and looks up at the top of the hill at a huge white mansion. "That's Mel Brooks' house," he announces. "I heard a story that when he built that house, he pissed off the people behind him because he blocked their view of the golf course. So he just gave them $1 million. I don't know if it's true, but that's the story."

When the group reaches the par-3 14th green, John Cook's caddie, Andy Martinez, is pacing yardages. Davis whispers, "Watch this, when he starts walking, I guarantee you he'll flip his yardage book to the right." On cue, Martinez begins pacing and with every other step, he flips his book with his right hand as if he's throwing a frisbee and Davis just smiles.

At 16, Davis pushes a 7-iron to the right and murmurs, "Forgot to swing." When they reach the green, Pruitt is tantalized by an eight-foot putt. With a skin on the line, he misses, then tries the same putt five more times and can't make it. He walks away a little miffed.

Eighteen, one of the most demanding holes on the course, provides good humor when Pruitt hits a weak drive into the left rough, leaving himself a long, long way from the hole. Blount starts checking for yardage and Pruitt, knowing he can't reach the green, tells Blount with a laugh, "You won't need a yardage." He slashes with a 3-wood, but still ends up twenty yards short of the putting surface.

After a good drive, Davis pulls his approach to the left of the green and his ball gets stuck in the thick kikuyu grass on the hill that surrounds the green. He struggles just to get the ball on the green and after he putts out, he goes back to the hill and practices chipping from the same spot.

"That's the toughest rough on the whole course," he says.

Now, the moment everyone has been dreading: the climb up that damn hill to get to the first tee. Blount looks up at the clubhouse above, and shakes his head.

"That's the worst thing about this place," he says. "They oughta have a T-bar going up there."

The players, but more so the caddies lugging fifty-pound golf bags, chug up the hill and when they get to No. 1 slightly out of breath, they see that it is backed up with two groups waiting to hit. Davis uses this break in the action to run into the locker room to grab a Coke, and he bumps into Peter Jacobsen. Every year on the Monday and Tuesday after The International in August, Jacobsen runs a charity tournament in his hometown of Portland, Oregon, called the Fred Meyer Challenge. It is a two-man best-ball, invitation-only event that last year boasted a purse of $700,000 with the winners taking home $50,000 each and the last-place duo guaranteed $22,500 apiece. Jacobsen recently invited Davis to play. Davis thanks him again for the invitation and then the two discuss who Davis would like to play with. He and Fred Couples have talked about playing, and Jacobsen said he'd work on it.

"I'm excited to be included," Davis says. "There's a lot of money, but it isn't the money, it's nice to be included. And it's good exposure for two days. It's like the Shark Shootout or some of those other special events. Freddie and I would like to play together. We enjoy the same style of golf and we think we could do real well together. Hey, Fred Couples and me in a best ball . . . I'm good at picking partners."

The back nine went quick and Davis remarks, "Man, we flew around that side," but the front is going to be a longer haul because play is backed up. Also, Wayne Grady joins the group, so now four players are hitting shots. After the initial delay, though, play actually moves along pretty well.

Walking down the third fairway, Bill Crist comes inside the ropes to talk to Davis about the investments the two had discussed in the car ride up from San Diego on Sunday. Davis gets around to telling him that he's going to see *Phantom of the Opera* tonight and Crist tells him that he's going to enjoy it. Davis isn't so sure. "I'd rather just sit home and watch ESPN," he says.

At the conclusion of the practice round, Davis tells Pruitt and Haas he'll see them later, then walks up the hill towards the locker room, along the way stopping to sign a few autographs. Outside the locker room, an L.A. Open official pulls up in a golf cart and asks Davis if he'd like to play in the Merrill Lynch Shootout, which is beginning in about forty-five minutes. Davis knows he has to pick Robin up at the airport in an hour. But winning the Shootout means $4,000 in prize money. Hell, getting knocked out on the first hole still gets you $400. It is tempting and he considers calling transportation to have a courtesy car sent for Robin, but he eventually decides that he'd better get her so he tells the official no. He goes into the locker room, sits down on one of the benches in a remote corner, and assesses his morning tour of the course.

"For a Tuesday I thought I hit it pretty good," he says. "I'll hit it better in the tournament, but today I hit it pretty solid and pretty much the right distances so that's a good indication. You just want to hit it solid and get a feel for the golf course and where the holes are going. You don't want to think too much about the swing, just hit some shots, get a feel for the greens and see how they're rolling. I didn't hit too many bad ones. I kinda wanted to jump out there and play fast by myself, but that never happens, you can get here at seven o'clock and there'll be guys playing. At least I got to play with some friends who are fun to play with instead of someone who's real serious and hits a lot of shots. Some guys will chip and putt on every hole for ten minutes. There's plenty of time to practice, you don't need to take five hours in a practice round.

"On Wednesday, you have to shoot a score and help your teammates in the Pro-Am and be competitive, so that serves as your practice scoring day, at least for me. Tuesday is usually a fun day unless you're hitting it bad, and then you have to grind and work on it."

He takes a sip of Coke, then expresses his excitement about playing at Riviera this week.

"I think Pebble Beach and Riviera are the two best courses that we play all year," he says with conviction. "It's one of the few old-style classic golf courses that we play. We don't play many good courses, we play on a bunch of junk. I skipped this tournament for a couple of years and that was stupid. Wherever it falls in the schedule, you have to play it because it's a classic course. I started thinking I hadn't played a good course so I said I oughta go back to Riviera if for nothing else, just to play four or five rounds on it. It's silly not to play a great course like this that's well respected when the next week, you're back on another TPC course."

Davis is a fan of traditional courses that reward good shotmaking and penalize wayward strokes. He dislikes most of the Tour-owned and -operated courses in the Tournament Players Club network.

He also enjoys playing in tournaments laden with history and tradition, such as the L.A. Open.

"It's nice to have a tournament that has some history. We need to separate a few tournaments and keep them a little more sacred. I haven't played the Kemper Open ever since it moved from Congressional because I don't think I could enjoy playing a TPC course when across the street, there's Congressional where the greats have played. We left a lot of history over there. In Memphis, we left Colonial where Al Geiberger shot the 59 [in 1977]. We oughta play there every year just so we can talk about the stories of the 59. I would have hated to have been a rookie in 1991 and come out on Tour and not been able to play Colonial or Congressional or Cypress Point. You lose so much by leaving those courses. If they ever left this course, it would be a tragedy, this is one of the most historical courses and tournaments we have. You get a special feeling winning on a course like this. Things can't always be the same, but that's what makes this place so special, that it has stayed the same."

Davis stands up and arches his back to stretch it out. He looks at his watch and realizes that he has to stop gushing about Riviera because he has to pick up his wife and daughter at the airport. He runs into the players' lounge, eats a sandwich, and hears from Brad Faxon that the *Phantom of the Opera* tickets may have been given away. Brad and his wife Bonnie are going, but they weren't sure if Robin was going to come in, so they didn't hold two tickets for the Loves. This is not going to please Robin. One of the main reasons she was flying cross-country was to see *Phantom*. Davis and Mark drive, with some trepidation, to Los Angeles International Airport.

Robin and Lexie are not sitting in first class so it takes some time for them to deplane. Davis is parked in front of the Delta terminal and he starts getting antsy, but then he sees former Atlanta Hawks coach Mike Fratello walk out of the terminal, and a few minutes later, a PGA Tour official who he knew would be on the flight from Atlanta, so he knows that the plane has arrived. He gets out and goes to baggage claim and Robin and Lexie are there, watching luggage circle around the carousel, casually waiting for their bags to appear. Lexie is thrilled to see her daddy, and he lifts her up and kisses and hugs her. Robin gives him a kiss, but it's obvious she is tired from the long flight. She has been up since 6 A.M. eastern time. When the bags come into sight, they snatch them off the belt and haul them to the car for the ride back to Santa Monica.

Davis breaks the news about *Phantom*, but he cushions the blow by telling Robin that he'll work on trying to find some tickets. You can almost hear her saying to herself, you better. The freeways are beginning to get crowded, but luckily, they are traveling just before the rush hours begin. Davis buzzes through traffic expertly and within forty minutes, they arrive at the Guest Quarters. Robin changes her clothes and washes up and says she feels a little better. Mark gathers his belongings so he can move to the Holiday Inn on Sunset Boulevard near the on-ramp to the San Diego Freeway, and then the four Loves get back into the Maxima. They go to the dry cleaners to pick up the laundry, then over to Riviera so Davis can work out and Robin can sign up for the wives' activities on Wednesday.

In the fitness trailer, Davis hears that his good buddy, Jeff Sluman, pocketed the $4,000 for winning the Shootout. Davis also learns from Brad Faxon what happened to his tickets. A friend of Tom Kite's, Dr. Ernie Katsuyama, is a *Phantom* fanatic who has seen the show about a dozen times and plays host when others want to see it. He is the man who obtained the tickets, but when he heard that Robin wasn't in town yet, he gave Davis' pair to Kite's caddie, Mike Carrick. "Miscommunication, as usual," Davis says. The good news, Faxon tells Davis, is that Dr. Katsuyama can probably come up with two more for the 8 P.M. curtain-raising at the Ahmanson Theater.

Davis completes his workout, drops Mark off at the Holiday Inn, then takes Robin and Lexie back to the Guest Quarters. While playing with Lexie, the phone rings and Dr. Katsuyama informs Davis that he has two more tickets. Phew!

Davis, nattily attired in a dark-green Polo suit, and Robin, in a black evening dress, drive Lexi to Mark's hotel so he can babysit, then pick up Brad and Bonnie Faxon, who are staying across the street from Mark at the Radisson Bel Air Summit. The couples go to the theater, and while they aren't sitting together, they are only a few rows apart. Not that it matters because you can't talk during the performance. It turns out that Davis and Robin get seats five rows from the stage, in the center aisle. And Davis is wrong. The game on ESPN wouldn't have been a good option. He is duly impressed by the performance.

The only detraction to the evening is its longevity. Davis has been up since 7 A.M. and, worse, Robin since 6 A.M. eastern, so both are exhausted when the show lets out at 11 P.M. Still ahead is a half-hour drive back to the hotels to drop off the Faxons and pick up Lexie, then another fifteen minutes over to the Guest Quarters. They don't get to bed until well after midnight.

"I loved it, but I wished I could have gone tomorrow because I was so tired," Robin says. "He only did it for me because I came all the way out here. It usually takes something other than just the fact that he's missing me. I wasn't supposed to be here this week and it was kind of hard to fly all the way out just for a week, but I did it because he said he needed me, so he says. He also said that this is a great week because there's lots for me to do and we had tickets to see *Phantom* and a [Kings] hockey game. So I came."

Davis and Robin were best friends in high school and while they would occasionally go on a date, they weren't really considered boyfriend and girlfriend. When he left Sea Island to attend college at North Carolina, they remained in close contact and when he would come home, they'd go out for pizza or to see a movie together. They were just two good friends and she never pictured being married to him.

"I hated golf," she says. "I remember every Sunday going to the swimming pool and then coming home at three o'clock so my father could watch golf. I thought, 'How boring can this sport be?,' and he'd watch it on Sunday afternoons. I never thought I'd even enjoy golf, much less be married to a golfer."

But sure enough, "One day, it just hit me like a rock."

She had fallen for Davis, but when he qualified for the Tour, she thought she was going to lose him. "I thought I'd never see him again."

She was wrong.

"The next thing I know," she says as her blues eyes twinkle and her blond hair sways with a shrug of her shoulders, "there's an airplane ticket in the mail, he took me to the Bahamas, we got engaged four months later and got married seven months after that."

Ask any Tour player to name the hardest thing about playing professional golf and he won't say a five-foot putt for par or carrying a 3-iron 200 yards over water. He'll tell you it's the constant traveling and the lonely times being away from his family. Earning as much money as today's players do would seem to more than make up for those inconveniences. But to most, including Davis, it doesn't.

The life of a Tour player is not normal. Football players leave their families eight times during the regular season, and are usually gone just one night. Hockey, baseball and basketball players spend half their seasons on the road, but the other half, they're at home. For pro golfers, there are no home games, unless they happen to live near a course that the Tour plays on. A pro golfer's season is one long road trip. If a player decides to compete in thirty events a year, that's not thirty days that he's away from home. That's thirty weeks.

"This is a very tough business when you look at the fact that we start in January and finish in December," says 1991 U.S. Open champion Payne Stewart, a husband and a father of two children. "There is no off-season like the team sports. I mean they have three or four months off where they can go rest and do whatever they want. We have to create that time on our own schedule and I think the hardest thing that people don't realize is traveling thirty weeks out of the year. We're away from our homes, our families, living out of a suitcase. Try it for a few years and people will realize how hard this job really is."

Mark Calcavecchia takes the approach that the traveling is a necessary evil.

"We get used to traveling out here, it's part of our life and part of the Tour so there's no use complaining about it," he says. "I told my wife [Sheryl] when we first got here that there's going to be plane delays and there's going to be cancellations, we're going to get hung up in some town some night, it's going to happen. She used to get bummed out if planes were late, but that's just normal stuff and now she's become a pro at it and she's a good traveler. I don't think of it as a hassle or a pain in the neck. It's like waking up in the morning and brushing your teeth, it's just something you do."

Davis feels the same way. And if he has to travel, he'd rather do it with his family than do it alone. To him the obvious hassles of being on the road with a family—lugging suitcases from city to city, dealing with airports, hotels, restaurants, trying to find your way around strange cities and trying to keep your wife and daughter entertained—are easily outweighed by the fact that he can spend time with Robin and Lexie. Not to mention that Robin can do little things that make his already hectic days less congested, enabling him to concentrate on his livelihood.

"I'm a lot more comfortable when they're here. It's actually easier for me to have her with me once we get to a tournament because I can ask Robin to pick up my laundry when she gets back from the mall or she can mail letters for me or whatever. She can do little things to help me and then I can stay as long as I want at the golf course. She helps me so much and she doesn't get enough credit for it.

"It's not a normal life. Robin's not home cooking dinner when I get home from work. We can't have dinner, put the baby to bed and live a normal life. You have to go out to eat all the time and if Lexie wants ice cream, you can't just go to the freezer, you have to go to the ice cream store and get it. Planning is the big thing. You have to plan everything out the day before and say 'OK, tomorrow we'll go out to dinner with Billy and Jody [Andrade] and we'll take Lexie to the zoo the next day,' things like that.

"You can complain about it and say, 'Man, my family is here and I don't have enough time to get done what I have to do and my little girl wants to go to the zoo and I can't practice and I can't rest.' I mean you can complain about everything, but you've got to have a good attitude about it and say, 'I'm lucky that I can fly my family here, I can afford to pay for an extra hotel room or a small suite for a week, and they can spend the time with me rather than me being here by myself.' I think anybody that says having their family here is a disadvantage has a bad attitude. I love having them here. It'll be hard for me when Lexie starts school and Robin will have to stay home more, because I'll miss them."

Having his family with him certainly hasn't been a detriment to his play. On the contrary, while some players may get distracted because their families are with them, Davis has actually played better when Robin and Lexie are with him.

Before they were engaged, Robin accompanied Davis to Tour Qualifying School at Grenelefe in the fall of 1985, something about which his parents openly expressed their disapproval.

"Back then we were just dating so she had to have her own

room because that was against my mom and dad's ideals of two young people who weren't married," Davis says with a smile. "It was against their wishes, but then I qualified for the Tour and my dad said, 'Maybe that wasn't such a bad idea.'"

Indeed. Robin was sort of a good-luck charm for him.

Shortly after Tour School, Davis was invited by Mark Rolfing— who runs the Kapalua tournament—to compete in a similar special event in the Bahamas the first week of January in '86.

"It was really nice of him to do that," Davis says. "I had finished seventh in the Tour School so people had heard of me a little bit. We went down there with the money I won at Tour School and I almost won the thing, finished third and made about twenty-five thousand dollars, and that was enough to get me started on the Tour. My dad was going to sponsor me, but then he didn't have to. I made [$113,245] official money and then [at the end of '86] Mark invited me to play at Kapalua. It was another forty-man field and I finished second in that and made about seventy thousand dollars. I made over one hundred thousand dollars off the Tour and she had been with me, so my family admitted that I was right and I was playing better when she was with me. She's seen just about all my successes except the International [in 1990]. She missed that because her sister was getting married."

There are times when Robin gets fed up with being on the road and sick of watching golf, when she longs to return to Sea Island and be more of a mom than a Tour wife. But she admits that she likes traveling with her husband, and once Lexie starts school and she won't be able to do it as much, she concedes that she'll probably find herself missing the jet-set life.

"I think I can probably go for two weeks at the most before I start missing him," Robin says. "And the baby misses him pretty much from the moment he leaves. When it's time to go to bed at night, she wants her daddy there. So it's going to be hard when Lexie starts school because I'll be home more and then I'll really appreciate the time out on the road with Davis. I think we take it for granted now because it's there if I want to go and if I don't want to go, I don't. But when I want to go and I can't go, then I'll really want to be out there with him. I love this life, I wouldn't trade it for anything else in the world, and I hope I'm here on the Seniors' Tour, too."

She does acknowledge, though, that life on the road contrasts with life back in Sea Island. There is a vast cross-section of personalities on the Tour. The players come from all over the country—some from different countries—and it is interesting to see how they co-exist as a group despite all their cultural differences. Davis is one of a large group of players who enjoys fishing and hunting. Snow skiing is also a popular pursuit. Many just simply list all sports as their hobby; Fred Couples loves old Mustang cars; Ben Crenshaw is into golf history and golf-course architecture; Steve Elkington enjoys character drawing; Brad Faxon is interested in sports psychology; Bruce Lietzke is into hot-rod cars; Australian Wayne Grady likes cricket; Brian Claar lives—and usually dies—for the Tampa Bay Buccaneers; Mark McCumber enjoys going to the movies; Wayne Levi follows the stock market; Donnie Hammond pursues astronomy; Rocco Mediate collects trading cards; Tom Purtzer follows auto racing; Joey Sindelar collects golf clubs; Jeff Sluman likes to bowl; Mark Brooks and Payne Stewart enjoy cooking. Like their husbands, the wives are diverse. So when they get together on Tuesdays and Wednesdays of tournament week to have a baby shower, go to a fashion show, go to a luncheon, see a taping of a television program or whatever activity the tournament has lined up for them to participate in, the melding of the various personalities is a show all by itself. Robin finds herself acting differently in the presence of other Tour wives than she does with her friends in Sea Island.

"This life is totally different than the one I have at home. When I'm with my old high-school buddies back home, it's so silly to say this, but just the language we use, like 'Hey, girlfriend, how are ya.' Out here, you say, 'Hello, how are you doing.' We'll go out for happy hour back home, but I would never think of drinking like that on Tour. This is more uppity than it is at home. With my closest friends out here—Bonnie Faxon, Jody Andrade, Marie Lohr, Jennifer Mudd—we've had girls' night out maybe three times in the last two years and we had a great time, but it's like the next day, everything goes back to the way it was. I'm more relaxed at home. Out here, it's like you're trying to keep up with everybody else."

Robin can do without trying to keep up with anyone. It's not her style. She characterizes herself as the type of person who is fun and feisty and can get along with anybody. Besides, while she counts many Tour wives as good friends, her best female buddy of all—at home or on the road—is Lexie. You would think caring for a three-and-a-half-year-old little girl for weeks at a time on the road, setting up home base in a different hotel and trying to get her to adapt to ever-changing environments would be a perilous task, but Robin shakes her head from left to right when posed that question.

"It's not hard at all to take her, I only pack one suitcase for her. And she's a little friend to me because she's there all the time. I never have a dull moment. Of course she started traveling when she was three weeks old, so maybe that's why it's not so hard, I'm used to it. But when we have a second child, I think things will change then."

Lexie is still too young to understand exactly what her father does and why she spends so much time away from home. She is also too young to appreciate all that she has seen and experienced.

"For a kid growing up, it's a great way to see the world and get to do fun stuff," Davis says. "She's been to more zoos than most kids will get to in a lifetime. You try to think of fun stuff so she won't be bored so she ends up getting to do more fun stuff than most kids. She goes to the nurseries on Tour and the people try so hard to make the kids happy so the parents will be happy and then the dads will come back and play the tournament again next year, so they really take good care of us. I'll tell ya, when I was little, like seven, eight, nine years old, and I got to go to a tournament with my dad, that was the most fun for me. I got to stay in a hotel, I got to eat in a restaurant, I got to go to the golf course and watch dad play golf. That's something that I'll never forget. I try to make it fun for my little girl and as she gets older and understands it, she'll have more and more fun in the summer being out here."

Her life-style makes her different from most children her age,

48

but Robin is trying to impress upon Lexie to keep her life on the road separate from her life in Sea Island.

"Right now she's so little, but it'll be interesting when she gets older and she understands the way she's being brought up," Robin says. "I think it'll be interesting when she's with her friends. I want her to always know that she's not better than anybody else because she travels and sees the world and does things that none of her schoolmates do. I want her to be able to keep the two lives different."

Already, that has been difficult. Lexie still hasn't grasped that her little friends that she sees on the road, like Melanie Faxon, Katherine Crenshaw and Nicole Pate, can't come home with her to Sea Island.

"She talks about them when she's at home," Robin says. "I think she's starting to understand that these friends live in other places and we all meet in one place to be friends, but one time we went home and she demanded on going to Melanie Faxon's house and I couldn't explain to her that Melanie doesn't live where we live. She just went into a rage and I had to put her in the car, drive to someone's house and show her that the car wasn't in the driveway and they weren't home. I couldn't make her understand."

Other than the occasional excursion to a stranger's driveway, the Loves lead a perfectly normal life at home. Their brand-new home that backs up to the fourth green and fifth tee of the retreat nine at Sea Island Golf Club is aptly described by Robin as their "dream house."

"I love it and we will fill it up with children one day," she says. "I'd like to have a lot more furniture in it than there is right now, but Davis put me on hold."

As you enter the property, you wind around a circular concrete driveway that leads to the three-car garage on the right and the front entrance of the house to the left. In the garage resides Davis's Harley, his extended cab Chevy pickup, and Robin's car, a Cadillac Seville that Davis won the use of for one year last November, when he finished first in the season-finale Merrill Lynch Shoot-Out. Also in the garage is what Davis calls his "tackle shop," an area where he keeps all of his fishing gear, as well as old golf clubs, a lie/loft machine so he can check the measurements of his clubs, and a vice that he uses when he re-grips clubs. The outside of the house is covered by gray-stained Shaker town cedar siding, trimmed in white. There are white posts that extend from the ground up to the second story, supporting the roof that covers the front porch. As Davis says, "It's a house that looks like it should be on a beach."

Passing through the front door, you stand on beautiful hardwood floors that extend into the dining room and living rooms. Right inside the entryway, there are two big trophy showcases with glass shelves displaying many of the various trinkets, trophies and crystal that Davis has won or he and Robin have purchased. The living areas face the golf course out back, which is visible because most of the back of the house is windows. The first floor has a whitewashed, soft look and an open, airy feel. In the kitchen with its Mexican tiled floor and granite countertops sits a black and white couch.

As you move to the second floor, white carpeting and cream-colored walls dominate until you get to the theater—a huge room featuring a meeting-room-sized TV screen built into one wall with a big-screen projector that descends from the ceiling. The surround-sound Sony stereo equipment is based here, but speakers with individual control pads are in most of the main rooms of the house, so Davis and Robin can operate the system without having to go into the theater. Robin has added her own personal touch to the room by painting the walls white and the ceiling dark-purple. There is a purple paisley print U-shaped couch, a big white chair, and a blue chair. The walls are tastefully decorated with modern impressionistic paintings, many by Andrea Smith, Robert Nelson and Guy Buffet, all of Hawaii, and other pieces from local artists including Mildred Hughey, who is well known in Georgia. There are also four large bedrooms and two baths upstairs.

There is plenty of outdoor play space for Lexie, even in the back, because only the fifth tee is close to the yard. The fourth green is about sixty yards away so she is not in danger of errantly struck golf balls.

When he's at home, Davis spends most of his time "goofing off." He goes deer hunting and fishing and now, he plays around with his new toy, the Harley. Sometimes, he can get too far away from golf and Robin has to remind him which activity pays the bills.

"She's learning when to push me to practice, she's learning what to say and what not to say," Davis says. "She doesn't meddle in golf very much, but if I get home and I have a week off and I go fishing on Monday and Tuesday and Wednesday, she'll say, 'I think you better take a day off from fishing and at least let Jack Lumpkin watch you hit balls.' She'll remind me that I'm getting a little carried away with goofing off, and I need that."

Robin says Davis is a great husband and father and she admires the way he manages to leave his golf game at the golf course.

"He never brings home golf. When he's away, I talk to him probably twice a day, and he almost never talks about golf. Sometimes I'll ask him, 'How did you play?' and then he'll go through the whole round with me, but if I don't ask, he'll just say, 'Oh, I was hitting it good, but I just scored bad,' or something like that.

"There isn't a whole lot that I don't like about him. I like the fact that he doesn't get upset about anything. I think it has a lot to do with the way he grew up. He never raises his voice, he's never upset, he listens very well. He's very understanding. He's a great person who'll do anything for anybody. He's pretty stubborn and pretty argumentative. If he thinks different from your opinion, he's going to tell you. He gets that from his mom. I'm glad he was my best friend before he was my husband. It makes a difference. He knew me and I knew him for a long time before we got married."

3 WEDNESDAY

The explanation is simple, really. We are at a posh country club, and furthermore, a posh country club in southern California. For this reason, no one even bats an eye this morning when a man walks onto the driving range dressed in slacks that look like they were used as a couch in a previous life. Why people wear clothes like this to play golf—better yet, why companies make these clothes—is a mystery that may never be solved. Ugly clothes and country clubs go together like peanut butter and jelly. And very often, the outfits amateur golfers wear look very similar to peanut butter and jelly mixed together with Grey Poupon, mayonnaise, ketchup and relish.

The pros used to dress like this back in the '70s, when plaid bell-bottoms and floral-print shirts were vogue. Thankfully, the pros have come around these days; they dress rather stylishly. The main reason for their improved appearance is that most get paid to wear a certain brand of designer apparel, and no company is going to outfit one of its human billboards in distasteful attire.

Unfortunately, no one is paying the amateur and advising him on how to dress. Mister Sofas and Chairs actually thinks he's hip. Somebody should tell these guys that only Payne Stewart looks good in knickers, only Ben Hogan looked proper in a porkpie hat and only Jack Nicklaus and Arnold Palmer could be excused for wearing offensive-looking garments.

Incredibly, clothing isn't the worst of it this morning on the overcrowded range. How about some of these swings? One middle-aged man winds up with his graphite-shafted Big Bertha driver, does a funky little hitch near the top, then swings harder than José Canseco would at a slow curve. The ball starts out straight and on a low plane, and you think hey, maybe that swing isn't so bad. But then the ball starts fading to the right and continues to fade until it turns into a full-blown helpless banana-ball slice. By the time the ball hits the ground and stops rolling, it has traveled about 200 yards, 100 straight and 100 to the right. Yeah, that swing was pretty bad. He tees up another one, eyes his target, which is most likely the unreachable—for him—50-foot-high mesh screen at the end of the range 250 yards away, then returns his focus to the ball positioned in front of his saddle-shoe golf spikes. He is frozen in concentration, probably 15 swing thoughts speeding through his brain. Take it back slow, not too far past parallel, keep the right elbow close to the body, keep the left foot planted, don't jerk the club down with the hands, get the hips out of the way, follow through high, make sure the belt buckle is facing the target. He's probably mentally worn out before he even starts to swing. Finally, up comes the club, and down it goes at dragster speed. Big Bertha meets Top Flite XL, and Top Flite XL meets ground. It's a hot shot to the shortstop, otherwise known as a wormburner. Pity his playing partners today.

Down the line a bit, there's a guy who has just hit a ball straight up in the air, which would be understandable if he was using a sand wedge. Sadly, he has a driver in his hands and a look of disbelief on his face as he casually peeks around, hoping that no one has seen what he has just done. Another guy battles a pull-hook, another swears at a slice, there's another ground ball, but that one gets through for a base hit. Divots fly everywhere and you start to wonder if the range can survive this assault from the high-handicappers. Their swings are ineffable, yet they all think they know what the problem is, so they try to correct it, succeed, but do something else wrong and the results are unchanged.

Suddenly, you spy a short guy with blonde hair hit an iron that is truly artistic and you think maybe there is hope. You walk in that direction to get a better view, but then you realize it's Ben Crenshaw. To be fair, there are a handful of amateurs who are hitting the ball reasonably well. But there aren't many and besides, those guys take it too seriously and aren't any fun.

It is Wednesday, Pro-Am day on the PGA Tour. It is a day where the pros do some grinning, but a lot more bearing. The top forty-two players from the previous year's money list who are at the tournament (top 52 when daylight saving time begins) and 10 sponsors' choices (usually the defending champion and other fan favorites who aren't already qualified from the money list) are paired with four amateurs for a day that sometimes is more exasperating than coming down the stretch on Sunday battling for the lead.

The players understand Pro-Ams are a must if they want to continue to play for enormous prize money. These sponsors and their clients are the people who make those purses possible. But six-hour rounds with a bunch of guys who generally hit two shots for every one of theirs; who, no matter how awful a shot may be, will insist on saying, "Good shot"; and who feel the need to share every experience they've ever had at this particular course or in a previous Pro-Am, can be a test of patience even a saint would find difficult to endure.

On top of that, Davis is tired. *Phantom* was phenomenal, but as he arrives at Riviera at 7:30 for an 8:15 tee time, he looks like a man in need of a couple more hours of sleep. His taupe-colored pants and white Polo shirt look impeccable, but his eyes are like slits and he can't stop yawning. He was going to pick up Mark at the Holiday Inn, but didn't feel like dealing with the morning traffic on Sunset, so he called his brother and told him to take a cab, and Mark still beat him to the course.

Davis had considered calling the tournament and begging out of the Pro-Am, but without a viable excuse such as illness or injury, skipping Pro-Ams isn't very smart. Players who blow off a Pro-Am are penalized a portion of their retirement money.

The Tour's retirement fund is based on how many tournament cuts a player makes. When he makes fifteen cuts in a year, he is awarded fifteen retirement credits and then any cut he makes after fifteen, he gets two credits. When a player has made seventy-five cuts in his career, he becomes fifty percent vested in the retirement fund and when he makes one hundred, he becomes completely vested. The players' share is determined by how many credits he has built up during his career. Davis survived twenty-three cuts last year so he earned thirty-one credits, and because he has made more than one hundred cuts since joining the Tour in 1986, he is fully vested. Thus far, he has accumulated close to two hundred credits. He can start collecting on his investment at the age of fifty. However, as a way to make sure that the players who are eligible for the Pro-Am play, a credit is taken away if they skip out.

"You're tired and you don't feel like playing, but you don't want to screw around with your pension," Davis says.

In the locker room he says hello to one of the attendants, then sees the first- and second-round pairings posted on a bulletin board and notices that he has drawn a very interesting group—this year's leading money winner and two-time titlist, John Cook, and long-hitting, legend-growing-by-the-day PGA champion, John Daly. As he walks over to his locker, one thing comes to mind: Because he's playing with Daly, who is the hottest name in the game these days thanks to his unlikely PGA victory last August, the galleries following the group tomorrow morning and Friday afternoon are going to be huge and almost certainly rowdy.

In his locker, he finds a package from Butch Harmon containing separate envelopes with the names of Jeff Sluman, Hal Sutton, Dillard Pruitt, Fred Couples, Robert Wrenn and Ben Crenshaw, as well as his own. Inside the envelopes are pictures of each player's swing with notes attached. Harmon has sent the package to Davis with instructions to pass along the envelopes to the other players. He sleepily walks around and wedges each envelope into the horizontal vent of the various players' lockers, but keeps Wrenn's because Robert isn't playing here this week.

Breakfast fails to revive Davis, but hitting a few short irons on the range at least opens his eyes a crack more. Derek Crawford, the Ping rep, comes over and asks Davis what he thought of *Phantom* and Davis nods his head, overcomes another yawn and says, "Great." Yesterday, he had told Crawford that he'd rather sit home and watch a game. Today, he knows he was wrong and Crawford, who had seen the show in New York, says, "I was like you. I was like, 'Where's the beer and the popcorn?' I thought it was going to be three hours of 'Oh, man.' But it was great."

Davis goes back to hitting balls, this time with his driver, and while he's swinging, another club rep tells one of the many Mike Tyson jokes making the rounds. "What's the only thing that makes Mike Tyson cry after sex?" Blank stares all around before the rep delivers the punch line. "Mace." That draws laughter from everyone, as does the look on Fred Couples' face a few moments later when George Willets, a club repairman who works for Taylor Made, pulls the head off Couples's Ping putter. The putter hadn't felt right to Couples; he slapped it on the ground a few times and heard a rattling inside, so he summoned Willets to have him take a look at it. Instead of bouncing it on the ground, Willets shook it with his hands and couldn't hear anything. He looked at Couples as if to say, "What's the problem?" Couples reiterated that something was wrong, so Willets put his left hand on the grip and his right hand on the head and pulled the head off.

"Hey, I've gotta tee off in five minutes!" Couples says frantically, and Willets just sort of rolls his eyes and tells him to calm down. He walks back to the Taylor Made trailer, puts the head on and within five minutes, before Couples is even done on the range, the putter is back in his bag, good as new.

Couples tries to explain his anxiety to Willets. "Well, I had to tee off in five minutes and you pull my putter apart." Willets shakes his head and laughs lightly.

Davis completes his abbreviated warm-up, walks past Couples and says, "Nice putter," then he and Mark leave the range and wander to the 10th tee, his starting point for what he anticipates is going to be a long day.

P ro-Ams are typically the same," he says. "The guys are so excited to be out there and they're so serious, they want to win. They remember every year how they were doing. They're so into it and you have to get a little bit excited and remember that this is their big day and if you're miserable, you're going to ruin it for them. Every once in a while you get guys who know people that you know or they like to talk about things like fishing or hunting and you get some pretty good guys, but for the most part it's just your average Joe who likes to play golf."

Davis ducks under the gallery ropes and onto the 10th tee and introduces himself to his playing partners, four employees of ARCO: executive vice-president Jim Middleton; public relations and advertising honcho Steve Giovanisci; George Babikian, who is the president of the products division for the refining and marketing sector; and Jim Morrison, who is an executive vice-president, chief financial officer and a member of the board of directors. They each shake Davis' hand, express their excitement to meet him and after some general chitchat, it's time to play.

The announcer presents Davis to the gathered crowd and he acknowledges their applause with a wave, then bends down to tee up his ball. He can't help but yawn again as he goes through his practice routine, but when he settles over the ball, he looks interested and ready and he hits a drive into almost the same place he was yesterday morning during his practice round, about 280 yards down into the right rough. The fans are impressed, though he isn't. He comes over to Mark, hands him the driver, then stands with his arms folded across his chest to watch his partners hit.

First up is mild-mannered fifty-five-year-old Middleton, a 7-handicap from Pacific Palisades. The best amateur in the group plays a nice drive into the fairway. Up steps Giovanisci, whose personality is as vivacious as his yellow pants. The fifty-six-year-old native Philadelphian, now living in La Cananda, also hits a decent drive into the fairway. The senior member of the group, happy-go-lucky sixty-four-year-old Babikian of Palos Verdes Estates, isn't real happy when his drive ends up just beyond the fairway bunker in the right rough. But his position is great compared to Morrison's. The sixty-two-year-old, who lives in San Marino, tops the ball and it rolls feebly for about forty yards before stopping in the rough to the left, just ahead of the tee box.

Because everyone is so spread out on the hole, Davis and Mark walk alone down the fairway, stopping occasionally to watch all of the shots. You have to pay attention on Pro-Am day because you never know where a ball is going to come flying from next. Davis executes a nice flop shot with his L-wedge and he is left with a seven-footer for birdie. But he doesn't need to make it when Babikian rolls in a 15-footer from the fringe for a natural birdie, which goes on the scoreboard as an eagle for the team because of his handicap. Davis high-fives Babikian, watches him celebrate with the rest of the guys, then says, "I hope they do that all day. I hope they don't need me." Davis, who has to play out every hole because he is required to post an individual score, misses his birdie attempt and taps in for par.

Standing on the next tee, the 11th, Davis peers down the fairway and yawns as he observes the players in Mark Brooks's group scattering shots all over the landscape. "This is going to be a long day. And what gets you is all the standing around."

The team settles for a disappointing par at 11, then goes to the 12th tee and poses for its team picture, which will be copied and mounted on separate plaques and presented to each amateur at the end of the day. Things are backed up at 12, so Brooks' group is still waiting to tee off when Davis's entourage arrives. After a couple of minutes, Brooks hits his drive, then walks down to the front tee box and talks to Davis while his partners hit. Three of their shots are flameouts into the right rough and one is hooked into the left rough. Yet as soon as each ball is struck, one guy says, "Good shot." Anything that gets airborn is a good shot, apparently.

Despite the fifteen-minute delay, Davis cranks a perfect drive. As he walks away, Babikian tells him, "Great shot. Just think how far it would have gone with a metal driver."

Davis thanks him, but doesn't bother explaining that it wouldn't have gone any further with a metal wood. He's a traditionalist so he's a bit biased, but he doubts that balls travel greater distances when hit by a metal wood.

"I think it's a myth," Davis says. "Some players might hit it farther with a metal wood than a wood wood, but when you look at who you'd want to drive your golf ball, most people would pick Fred Couples. Fred drives it as long and straight with a wooden wood as anybody would with a metal wood. I can't think of anybody, except Paul Azinger, who would really impress you with his distance and accuracy with a metal wood. To me, it feels like you can work the ball a lot better with a wood wood.

"I've tested a lot of metal drivers, but I can't find one that I can hit consistently in both directions. You have to have confidence that you can turn it both ways off the tee and I just don't feel as if I can do it as good with a metal. I will always find one that I can aim down the left side and hit sliders with, but I can't find one that I can aim down the right side and be sure I can draw it. The draws always turn into snap-hooks. Besides, my driver is so good that until I'm forced to play something else, I don't think I'll find anything better. As long as this one's in one piece, I'll keep using it."

Davis theorizes that the biggest problem amateurs have when it comes to equipment is that they don't have the right paraphernalia to fit their game. They seem to buy whatever is hot on the market. Right now, primarily due to John Daly's success at the PGA last year, large-headed drivers like Callaway's Big Bertha or Wilson's Whale are the must-gets. For a while after Jack Nicklaus won his sixth Masters title in 1986 using a MacGregor putter with an oversized face, everyone had to have one.

"People get trapped up in clubs like Pings, Armours, Hogans," Davis begins. "It makes no difference if they aren't fit properly. Buying golf clubs is the same as buying a pair of pants or a suit. They have to fit your needs. People shouldn't buy Tommy Armour 845s with x-shafts because I use them. If they buy them, that doesn't mean they're going to play like me. Joey Sindelar uses Tommy Armours with s-shafts, and he hits it as far as I do because the s-shafts fit his game.

"The most important thing about golf clubs isn't the size of the head or the brand name, it's finding a shaft that fits the way that you play golf, getting them the right length and lie and with the right grip size. The name on the club means nothing. If people want to buy Lynx clubs because Fred Couples is using them, fine, buy 'em, but make sure they fit your game. I would say use Tommy Armour's because I use them and like them, but go to a pro, let him fit you and buy the shaft that you need in them. Don't buy my shaft. There's probably fifteen people on Tour who can hit shafts like mine.

"I have to use extra stiff shafts because of my clubhead speed and the strength I have hitting the ball. Someone who swings slower and less aggressively, if he has a stiff shaft, his ball's going nowhere but right. You want the clubhead and the hands to get to the ball at the same time, so if you have this shaft that's incredibly stiff and you swing slow and you can't bend it, it's not going to come back to the ball in the right place. Or if you swing real fast and you have a whippy shaft, it's gonna go all over the place. It's how fast or hard you swing. Other guys swing real steeply and they need a shaft that flexes further up the shaft. A guy that swings real level through the ball needs one with a little kick at the bottom to get it up.

"I can't use Jeff Sluman's clubs because they don't fit. There's not very many sets of clubs on Tour that I can't play well with, but in order to be consistent, through years of trial and error, I found out that this is what I need. That's what people should do. Find something they can play with."

The same goes for balls. As far as Davis knows, only he, Payne Stewart and LPGA star Beth Daniel use the 90 compression Titleist 384 low-trajectory ball in tournament competition. The LT ball spins less, which means its flight pattern is lower than other balls and when it hits the ground, it rolls farther. On a calm day, the LT ball isn't going to stay in the air and won't travel as far as other balls, but that lost distance doesn't affect Davis, Stewart or Daniel because they're long hitters and can keep up with everyone else and in most cases, still outdrive the competition. But on a windy day, they really have an advantage because the less spin on the ball, the less the wind will affect it and the farther the LT will travel.

"There's not very many guys who can use the ball I use and get any distance out of it because lower trajectory balls always want to come back down," he explains. "That's why I use it, because I hit the ball long enough so I need a ball that gets out of the air. Most amateurs need a ball that stays in the air longer.

"The first thing the amateur ought to look at is durability, because at twenty or twenty-five bucks a dozen, that's a lot of money. That's why people use Tour Editions, Pinnacles, Top-Flites, because they last longer. The next thing they ought to look for is a durable ball that has some feel and touch. The more durable it is, the harder and bouncier it is and it won't stop as well. You have to find the right balance, like a Titleist 384 DT. The soft balata ball that the players use, when you hit a full solid wedge with it, it scuffs the cover so that doesn't make much sense for a guy with a new set of Pings to be buying a dozen balls a day to play. For most people, it's economics and the best deal might be the bonus pack of Top-Flites at Wal-Mart or the deal the guy in the pro shop is running that week.

"A lot of it is preference. If they want distance, get a hard surlyn-cover ball; if they want a ball that's easier to chip with and they can afford to go through a bunch, get a soft balata ball. My mom likes to use Pinnacles, but I try to get her to use Titleist DTs because I think she can chip and putt better with them, but it's hard to get her to give up that extra ten yards. Nobody on Tour uses any ball to hit it farther. They use a certain ball for more control, a lower trajectory, a higher trajectory, less spin or more spin. Nobody says, 'I'm going to change balls because this one goes farther.'"

Even perfect equipment wouldn't help Jim Morrison today. He hits his second shot into the barranca that runs in front of the 12th green and continues down the left side past No. 12 and all along No. 13 on the back side of the property. Morrison is in the section of the ravine that is next to the green. He climbs down and surveys his options and makes the mistake of trying to play it from there. He takes a mighty cut, hits the middle of the ball and sends people scurrying as it flies over the green, bounces on the cart path and clangs off the electronic scoreboard.

At 13, Morrison's drive finds its way behind a garbage box. He moves the box, takes out his 3-wood and promptly hits his ball into the good ol' barranca on the left. This time, he wisely stays on level ground and doesn't bother trying to finish the hole.

"This is a tough course for people who can't hit it straight," he muses, before explaining what he was trying to do back on 12. "I was thinking that I'd have to hit it real hard because it was in deep grass and it just came flying out of there. Wrong time to hit one of my beauties."

Morrison used to caddie when he was a kid, then began playing the game and loved it, but marriage, family and work afforded him little time to play and he put his sticks away for about twenty-five years before picking them up again a decade ago.

"I like to get out here and do a little walking, it's a change of pace and you can get your concerns off your mind," he says.

Morrison likes playing in Pro-Ams, but unlike many other amateurs out here, he doesn't get a huge thrill out of roaming the fairways with a PGA pro, which is a refreshing attitude. After all, the pros are just ordinary guys who happen to play a game very well. "It's no big deal," he says.

On the 14th tee, Davis makes a sloppy practice swing and after he hits his drive on the par-3 hole, Mark tells him to make his practice swing more useful.

Walking from the 14th green to the 15th tee, Davis tells Babikian, "This is a tough hole coming up," to which Babikian replies, "Show me an easy one." Babikian then makes reference to Davis's pairing with John Daly for the first two rounds of the tournament. "That should be interesting, two of the longest hitters on the Tour," he says, and Davis comes back with "Yeah, he's two of 'em."

Babikian is really having a good time. He has hit some good shots and has also helped the team with a nice putting touch that has racked up a few birdies.

"Golf is a fun game for me. I'm not good enough to challenge course records so it's fun," the 16-handicapper says. "Once in a while you hit a great shot or have a great round and that keeps you coming back."

Babikian has played in a lot of Pro-Ams, and what strikes him is the way the pros stay patient with their inferior partners.

"They give you tips and they help you with your putting and your swing. They're all nice guys. I've never played with someone who was a sour puss. Maybe there are some on Tour, but I've never played with one."

Tomorrow, he and Giovanisci are flying to Augusta, Georgia, for a weekend of golf at historic Augusta National, home of The Masters. "That is going to be an honor," he says.

Giovanisci hears Babikian talking about Augusta and he

comes over and chimes in: "What a thrill that's going to be for a golf nut. I just hope I play a little better than this."

Giovanisci has been struggling to get his game together today, probably because unlike Morrison, he always gets a kick out of playing with the pros. "I think for an amateur golfer to be on one of the greatest courses in the United States with these players is always a thrill, except when you stink," he says with a chuckle. "I've been playing in this about eight years. The first year, I played with Sam Snead. It was a thrill for a while, but Sam's not a real thrilling guy. Davis is a nice guy."

Giovanisci thinks he's going to come around today, though, because the original excitement is behind him and now it's just like another day of golf.

"Playing with the pros isn't as much fun as you'd like it to be because they're serious and they're working on their games. The Pro-Am is more of a thrill to think about than it is to play in because you end up picking up on a lot of holes unless you're playing real well and making all the shots for your team. Which I'm not today."

After Davis finishes the front nine and makes the dreaded climb up the hill, he runs into the locker room to get a Coke and to see if his new L-wedge has arrived. Sure enough, it is sitting in his locker. He grabs it, jogs back out to the first tee and puts it in his bag. "Gonna cheat a little in the Pro-Am," he says with a wink. Players cannot replace any equipment during a tournament round unless it was accidentally damaged during the course of play. For example, a scuffed ball or a club that gets bent when a player hits a rock in the ground while swinging can be replaced. A club that is thrown into a lake in anger or snapped in half over a knee in frustration cannot be substituted. But in the Pro-Am, the rules get bent a little.

The boys from ARCO are scoring pretty well and as they make the turn and play the first few holes on the front, they begin to notice that they are creeping up on the leaderboard. Thus far, they hadn't really mentioned their overall team score, but now that they see that they have a chance to place high in the standings, a little more meaning accompanies each shot.

Standing on the tee to the brutal par-3 fourth, it is brought to their attention that the hole is sponsored by ARCO. "This hole is gonna be good to us," Babikian says. It isn't. They only manage a par.

At No. 5, Middleton wonders why amateurs get nervous playing with the pros.

"It's kind of strange, people like us, we've been all around the world and done a lot of things, yet you come out here and you feel butterflies. It's because they're so good and we feel a little bit less than."

Like Babikian, Middleton is impressed by the way all the pros he has played with have handled themselves in Pro-Ams.

"I've always found the pros to be very pleasant, they have to put up with a lot with the amateurs, but they're good about it. Davis is a great player and he's been fun to play with. It must be hard for him to concentrate, but he's obviously working on his game and doing what he has to do."

No one looks nervous on the fifth green. Morrison rolls in a 50-foot putt for par, Giovanisci curls in a 20-footer for par, and Middleton completes the hat trick by draining a 20-footer, but his is for birdie and with his handicap, the net score is an eagle-2 and now the team is in serious contention for first place. Davis can't keep up with his teammates. He misses a 20-footer for birdie.

A par is obtained at the sixth, and then golf strikes back at seven, and Giovanisci is its victim. He pushes his tee shot into the right rough and the ball gets lodged in a pine tree about three feet above the ground. When he locates the ball, he ponders his predicament while the rest of the group bites back laughter. When he's ready to hit, he holds his club straight out like a Samurai sword, takes it back parallel to the ground and swings as if he's holding a baseball bat. Strike one, as a branch gets torn away while the ball remains untouched, snickering at him. Giovanisci looks to the sky and asks, "Why me?" He gathers himself for a second try and this time he hits a foul ball which in this case isn't bad because at least the ball is out of the tree, albeit only two feet from the despicable pine. Unfortunately, his woes are far from over. His next shot hits the limb of a tree about forty yards in front of him and shoots straight down and his fifth hack is a fat blooper that lands about fifty yards short of the green. Mercifully, he calls it quits and tells his caddie, "Pick it up, partner, I've had enough. I'm ashamed to finish."

While Giovanisci's ball goes into his pocket after five swings, Davis' goes into the hole after three. He chips in from just off the left side of the green for a birdie to get the team to 14-under-par, which is one shot behind the current leaders.

At the eighth tee, Giovanisci relives his nightmare.

"Boy, I sure have some damned luck at this L.A. Open," he says shaking his head. "One year, my tee shot on the first hole hit a tree about ten yards from the tee and it stayed up there and I was shot for the rest of the day."

It happens to the pros too, though, and Davis shares an incident from the Greensboro Open a few years ago.

"I hit a drive way up into a pine tree, way up, and it didn't come down, so I asked a few of the marshals to see if they could find it, and they told me they weren't going up there. I had my spikes on so I went up the tree. I found four balls up there, plus my own. After I identified mine, I took an unplayable lie, dropped, then I hit it on the green and made the putt for par. The same marshal is there every year at that hole and every year when I play it he asks me, 'Do you remember the time you hit that ball up in the tree?' and I tell him, 'Well yeah, because you keep reminding me.'"

Giovanisci recovers from his experience and makes par at eight while the team scores a net birdie to get to 15-under and a tie for the lead. But they can't make birdie at nine, so 15-under probably isn't going to be good enough to win.

As the group collects its mounted pictures in front of the scorer's tent, Davis shakes all of their hands, says goodbye, and they wish him well this week.

It's over. He has survived another Pro-Am, and even managed to take away a good thought from the round.

"I was kind of bored and kind of tired at the start, but after playing a few holes, Mark told me at 14 about my practice swing and he said I needed to practice like I was swinging at the ball, try to tighten it up a little bit and make my practice swing meaningful, and that really helped," Davis says. "I thought I hit it really well after that. Standing around for so long, it's hard to say you hit bad shots when you hit one and wait ten minutes. I'm real happy with the way I hit it though. I'm hitting the driver more on a line and lower. I hit a lot of irons close today, hit a lot of crisp shots. I felt a lot better about it today. I'm real close to being where I want to be with my full swing."

Davis sits down in a chair behind the driving range, watches players hit shots into the cloudless blue sky, and he talks about the role of the Pro-Am in his tournament preparation.

"It's hard because you want to be concentrating on your game, you want to be working and getting something out of it, but you want to make sure that your amateurs are having fun and you're helping them. It's a conflict of interest, I mean they're always doing crazy things, like the one guy, Steve, who hit the ball into the tree. Things like that happen a lot. They hit it in garbage cans or purses, they do so many crazy things that you get used to it. I've seen just about everything. I've seen them hit scoreboards, I even saw one guy hit one of those cars out on a lake that they display on some par-3s where if you get a hole-in-one, you win the car. You can start getting frustrated when they say, 'good shot' on every shot even when you're hittin' it terrible, and you can get a pretty bad attitude so you have to laugh most of it off and remember that they're the ones who are ultimately paying for the tournament. And I thought it was a good day considering that I didn't get enough sleep and I was kind of tired and didn't really want to be out there. I thought the guys I played with had a good time. They were tied for the lead when they finished so they had to be pretty pleased with that."

Davis' performance in a Pro-Am is rarely a reflection of how he plays in a tournament. An example of this is Davis's putting this morning. It looked like he was struggling with the putter, but he explains that he really wasn't.

"In a Pro-Am, when they've made a birdie, you just kind of feel like picking yours up and gettin' out of there because they're off running around and having fun," Davis says. "You just don't concentrate as much. I hardly ever play good in a Pro-Am unless I have a bad team and I'm carrying them all the way, then I'll shoot some low scores. When a guy knocks in a 40-footer for a three-net two, yours doesn't matter. I've been working on trying to stay more steady on my putts and the ones that they needed me to make, I felt like I made, and that's what counts. When I was concentrating, I felt like I made them.

"The biggest thing you want to do out there in a Pro-Am is get used to the speed of the greens because they'll be pretty similar on Thursday morning. I thought they seemed slow today, I kept knocking putts by. As far as my stroke, my main emphasis on that comes in the morning before an actual tournament round. I'll go through my routine on the practice green, I'll hit some putts and that's when I get my confidence, not from how I putted the day before. Basically all I do to warm up before a round is putt across the green, like 30- and 40-footers, so I can get used to the pace. I learned that from Ben Crenshaw's putting tape. It helps you to get the feel for the speed. You don't worry about your aim, don't work on knocking in 4- or 5-footers. All you want to do is get into your stroke. That gets your stroke and feel warmed up and that's all that putting really is."

Davis twirls his new L-wedge in his hands, stands up and takes a practice swing with it. "Gotta get this checked," he says, looking at the head of the club. He walks across the range and climbs the portable steps leading into George Willets's Taylor Made club trailer.

He greets Willets with "Hey, George," then asks him to check to make sure the lie and loft of the wedge is correct. Willets inserts the club into his lie and loft machine and tells Davis the measurements.

Willets, along with Dave Rennie, are the club repairmen that the pros rely on the most. This week, Rennie isn't working so Willets has been besieged with players requesting swing weight checks, grip changes, club adjustments, lie and loft checks and in Fred Couples' case this morning, replacement parts. A native of Atikokan, Ontario, Willets has been on the PGA Tour for four and a half years, after spending nearly two years on the European Tour.

Willets attended a golf business college in San Diego and to help meet his expenses, he had to get a part-time job, preferably golf-related, so he could supplement his education with on-the-job experience. He found a little golf shop in Vista, California, that needed help and worked there while he went to school. He made a number of contacts at Taylor Made while doing some repair work for the company, and in early 1984, when Taylor Made moved its operation to Carlsbad, California, it offered him a job.

Willets says club repair work "is like anything else. It's a trade, like bricklaying. You could learn the fundamentals about it, but you don't learn half the problems until you start doing it and learn by watching and doing it yourself."

The trailer, carrying more that $50,000 worth of equipment and machinery and powered by a two-ton cab that runs on an 8.2 diesel General Motors engine, is Willets's home in between truck stops as he journeys all around the country to the various PGA tournaments to provide a vital service to the players.

"Truck Stops of America, that's me," Willets says. "Everyone else on Tour collects frequent flyer miles. I collect gold stamps from Truck Stops of America and after 30,000 of those points I get a free alarm clock."

The trailer is custom built and houses a lie and loft machine; a swing weight scale; equipment for club sanding, finishing and polishing; metal wood bending vices; and basic vices which provide Willets an extra set of hands to perform tasks such as grip changing. It also contains more than 600 clubheads—irons, woods, metal woods and putters—of various swing weights, lofts and lies; shafts of virtually every swing weight and stiffness; and a wide selection of grips. The machinery runs on a 12.5 kilowatt generator and there are a pair of exhaust fan/air conditioners in the roof. Willets estimates that to build and stock this trailer, as is, would cost about $100,000, and that's not counting the golf equipment or the cab, which Taylor Made bought used for about $35,000 in 1987.

To the players, every last penny is worth it, and they appreciate the effort Taylor Made and the other companies have put forth to help them.

Neal Lancaster walks in and asks Willets to change the grip on one of his clubs, and Willets performs the task expertly. First, he cuts off the old grip with a knife, then applies a cleaning solution to take off the tape that was wrapped around the shaft. The tape gives the grip extra width the way Lancaster likes it. Other players wrap tape around certain parts of the grip to make it thicker for the right hand or left hand. Once the shaft is clean, he retapes it, puts fluid on the tape and inside the new grip so it will slide onto the shaft easily, and then slips it on. In a couple of minutes, Lancaster's grip has been replaced.

"I do a lot of work with Neal and I know exactly what his grip size is and what he's looking for in a golf club," Willets says. "He'll come in and say, 'Here, make me a driver,' and he doesn't even have to stick around because I know what he's looking for. I know what length he needs, what kind of shaft, how much lie and loft. I keep a book that has all the players' lies, lofts, shafts and grips. I'll see between eighty and one hundred guys consistently and from working with them every week, you know what they need."

A few moments later, Mark Carnevale enters and asks Willets to check to see if his irons are all the same swing weight.

"All the swing weight is is a balancing factor to keep everything consistent throughout the set of clubs," Willets explains. "Basically, you use a fourteen-inch fulcrum. Now with a sand wedge that is thirty-five inches long, the clubhead might weigh three hundred grams. If you go to a club that is a half-inch longer, in order for it to have the same swing weight, you'll need a lighter head. In half-inch increments, it's approximately seven grams lighter as the club gets longer. So, off the top of my head, by the time you get to a 3-iron, it might be 236 grams in the clubhead.

"Now, a graphite shaft is lighter than a steel shaft, so you have to increase weight in the head to maintain the same swing weight. That's the whole advantage of going with graphite, there's about ten more grams of weight in the head and with that little bit more mass behind the ball, sometimes it's easier to hit the ball farther."

Next into the trailer is Howard Twitty, who like Davis, wants a lie and loft checked. To measure the lie, you rest the sole of the club on a horizontal plane, then measure the degree angle to that horizontal plane. For example, a player who addresses the ball in an upright stance might have a lie degree of 58, while a player who addresses the ball in a more standard position might have a lie degree of 53. Loft is the angle of the clubface measured from an imaginary vertical line. For example, Davis' L-wedge is 60 degrees, so this club produces a high, short shot. His 3-wood is 12 degrees, so it produces a shot that flies much lower and much farther.

"I check my lies and lofts pretty regularly to make sure the lies are right for my setup and that the loft is right for the distance that the ball is going to go," Davis says. "As long as those are right, I'm fine."

And the players are meticulous about these numbers. The loft Davis prefers on his L-wedge is 60 degrees, but when Willets measured it earlier, it came out to 59½, so he bent the shaft until it read 60. In doing swing weight checks, if the weight in the head is just a gram or two less than what it should be, Willets will apply a small piece of lead tape to the back of the iron to even out the weight distribution. It seems inconceivable that such a minute change could make a difference, but to the players, it does.

"If I took a set in to Dave Rennie and one club had a swing weight of D1 and one was D2, he wouldn't say they're fine, he wouldn't send me out to play with them," Davis says. "If he was building me a set and I asked for all D2s, every one of them would be D2. You want them all the same. What Dave does for me is he might take maybe ten sets of shafts, wedge thru 1-iron, take all of them out and find me a perfectly matched set, then do another set. One might be 109 grams, one might be 111, so he separates and matches them. He knows the weight of each shaft for me, that's why he's so important to me.

"Sure you can argue between 59½ degrees and 60 on the loft of a wedge, but if you have the capability to set it there, then set it there. A lot of it is peace of mind. But you have confidence in the set that you know is perfect."

Club perfection is not a big deal to Fred Couples. A club rep could give Couples four different 5-irons to hit, all made with different shafts, and then ask him which ones he likes. He might pick out two, but he wouldn't be able to explain why. He wouldn't talk about swing weights or shaft flexes. He'd just say that the two he picked felt the best. But Couples is in the minority.

"These are the greatest players in the world," Willets said. "I'm effectively changing the weight of the club by a couple of grams, that's not much, but a lot of it is confidence. If he knows that his clubs aren't all the same, it's like a mental block. Even though it's one swing weight and the normal person can't tell, he knows it. That's where my role as psychologist and bartender comes into play out here. At this level, these guys all have pretty much the same ability, but when the bell rings Thursday morning, something happens. There's something about a certain guy's heart or confidence that makes him better that day and if it lasts the whole week, he wins."

Amateurs invariably play with the same set of clubs no matter what course they're on or what the conditions are. The pros do not, and this fact is what keeps Willets the busiest during the week.

"This is one of the weeks where we'll build a lot of golf clubs to suit the course," Willets explains. "This week, there's not a lot of fairway woods, but there are a lot of long iron shots, so we'll make a lot of railers which are 16- to 19-degree fairway woods that are good out of the rough. So a player might take his 2-iron out of his bag and put in a railer that we make for him.

"There's always something to do out here. If it's very wet, guys will need to carry the ball farther so they'll go to drivers with more loft. In Texas or Hawaii with the wind blowing all the time, they want to keep the ball down so they use less loft. It's actually quite interesting. It's a science. A guy can give me a Taylor Made 9.5-degree loft driver and I can make it a 5 or 6 just by bending it closed or a 10 or 11 by bending it open. And with the lie and loft machine, I can change them without guessing. It's probably the most valuable piece of equipment we have."

The pros have men like Willets and Rennie to make sure that their clubs meet all of their precise specifications. But what about the amateur who walks into a pro shop, a golf store or the sporting goods section of a department store and buys a driver or a set of irons off the rack? What are they getting in terms of lie and loft?

"I can speak for Taylor Made, and because of the quality control of Taylor Made, a club that says 8.5 or 9.5 out of the factory you can pretty much guarantee it'll be within a half degree plus or minus. The lies, the standard is 53 or 54 degrees. Of course you can order them or buy them in different fitting centers with different lies, but the lofts are generally pretty standard."

Twitty needs some more work done on a club so Davis leaves Willets to his craft and makes his way to the fitness trailer.

If there is anything on Tour more important to the players than their equipment, it is their health. And their health has never been better thanks to the Centinela Fitness trailer.

Dave Stockton, who served as the United States Ryder Cup team captain in 1991, described the way players dealt with physical problems before the fitness trailer became a part of the Tour in 1984: "What you did was keep playing until it hurt so bad you had to withdraw," he told *Golf* magazine.

Those days are over.

"We've been rated as pretty much the most important thing on Tour, ahead of the club vans, courtesy cars and free phones," says one of the full-time physical therapists, Paul Hospenthal.

When the trailer debuted in 1984, it was staffed by Centinela Hospital trainers and sponsored by Diversified Products, which manufactures home workout equipment. Centinela began sponsoring and staffing a trailer on the Senior Tour in '86, then took over all aspects of the PGA program in '88 when DP directed its sponsorship to other Tour programs.

The door is open and when Davis walks in, he is greeted first by Mike Ploski, the other therapist, and then by Hospenthal. Just inside the doorway to the left are two stationary bikes, one being ridden by Steve Elkington, who looks like he's peddling through the French Alps on one of the stages of the Tour de France. Against the left front wall is a rack of light free weights. To the right of the entrance, there are two versa-climber machines, one occupied by Mark O'Meara, whose gray t-shirt is so wet, you'd think he was halfway up Mount Everest. Straight ahead, situated in the center of the forty-five-foot-long by twenty-four-foot-wide (when parked and expanded) trailer is a multistation weight set where players can do leg extensions, hamstring curls, pectoral exercises and bench presses. Along the back wall are three treatment tables; in the back left corner is the medicine storage area, where over-the-counter drugs and other supplies are kept—as well as the trailer's all-important stereo system and video tape library, which currently numbers more than one hundred movies.

A sign on the wall above one of the cabinets reads: "Fitness Center advice—answers $1, answers that require some thought $2, correct answers $4, dumb looks still free." Players used to have plenty of quizzical looks when the trailer first started following the Tour around. Golfers had always been told that muscle mass was bad for them because it inhibited the fluidity of their swings. And to a degree, that is true, but the Centinela therapists aren't promoting heavy-duty weightlifting.

"That's kind of been a stigma in golf, that if you lift weights, you'll lose your touch, but actually, I think you improve your touch," Ploski says. "Just with the accruement of muscle fibers that you don't normally use, you can improve your touch as long as you do low-weight, high-repetition things. These guys aren't bench-pressing three hundred pounds. What they do is more for endurance training, and the players have found that it helps their game. Steve Elkington's not power-lifting, but he has doubled his strength twice, a four-time improvement, and I think he's gone up a club-length in how far he hits the ball. A lot of players do that. It's real common to see a player play really well for the first couple of weeks after they start working out."

Davis concurs: "The guys that are going for bulk, like football linemen, are doing something different. We're going for strength and stamina. I've talked to Roger Clemens and he's told me when he's doing work on his arm, he's only using five-pound dumbbells. The guys in here say that if you do the Centinela program, that's all you need to do for any sport, unless you're trying to get bigger."

Davis changes into blue shorts and a white t-shirt and after doing some stretching exercises, he positions himself on a versa-climber and begins rhythmically pumping his arms and legs up and down. In the back, Hospenthal gives Brad Faxon an electronic stimulation treatment for his back, while Elkington has taken to the floor for sit-ups.

"We see a lot of shoulder and wrist injuries, but the majority of injuries we see are to the back," Ploski continues. "Probably eighty percent of the injuries are spine-related. It's the repetition of the golf swing. These guys are out here sometimes ten to twelve hours a day swinging, and it's an abnormal motion from a flexed posture like that. It could be a flexibility problem or disc problem. What we do is put guys on strengthening programs, like trunk, abdominal and hip rotator strengthening, things that will help support the spine. It's more of a preventive thing, and then if the problems persist, we'll have the tournament doctors take a look and they can prescribe medication. Acutely we'll use things like ice, electrical stimulation to decrease swelling and manual mobilizations to get things moving properly. But we're not doctors, we're here to supervise their exercising."

Hospenthal finishes treating Faxon and comes over to the storage area and sits down.

"When I first started a few years ago, they didn't have the concept of how they could fit this into their day, or how necessary it actually was," Hospenthal says. "More and more, guys are fitting their workouts in. Last year at the Tour Championship, twenty-two of the thirty guys that played were regulars in here. The younger players see that and they wonder, 'How come the leading money winners are going into the trailer? What's going on in there? Is that something we have to be doing?' And a lot of the older players are seeing the financial success they can have on the Senior Tour and they're thinking they have two or three years before they get out there, why not start coming in here and getting in shape. Look at the Senior Tour, the guys that are doing well are the ones in better shape, the guys who haven't aged as much."

Ploski chimes in, "Look at Ray Floyd. He has really learned that he can lengthen his career by staying fit. He's forty-nine years old, but he's still competing with these twenty-five-year-old players, so when he gets on the Senior Tour, I think he's going to tear that up."

The twenty-nine-year-old Ploski, whose black hair is prematurely turning gray, got his undergrad schooling at Wabash College in Indiana, then earned a masters degree in exercise physiology from Temple and a masters degree in physical therapy from the University of Indianapolis. He worked as a physical therapist in a private practice before joining the Centinela team on the Tour three years ago. Hospenthal, a twenty-six-year-old who looks younger, is in his second year working in the trailer. He obtained an undergrad degree in physical therapy at Puget Sound in Seattle and attended graduate school at Western Michigan on a fellowship to become an athletic trainer. He also has a certification for strength and conditioning. They agree that the greatest satisfaction they derive is when they can get a physically ailing player back in shape, and then watch that player do well.

They reel off a number of cases such as Jeff Sluman placing second in a tournament after almost having to withdraw; Steve Elkington, Chip Beck and Fred Couples all experiencing problems with some type of injury, but going out and winning tournaments thanks in large part to the treatment they received in the trailer.

"That's a lot of fun, to see a player you've been working on all week do well and maybe win," Hospenthal said. "It's also been nice with players who have had long-term problems, guys like Bill Glasson, who's had back problems for two years and his game has been nearly nonexistent; Payne Stewart had a major problem with his neck; Dan Pohl had to have major back surgery. You spend months and months and months and then they're able to come back and be successful.

"We had so many first-time winners last year, and basically, those are the guys that are using the truck. It's starting to pay off. One of the reasons is we allow them to swing to their best potential because they don't get fatigued as easily, they don't have to worry about injuries all the time. These guys are out there all week. It gets to Sunday; they have a lot of mental pressure, but they're in shape and it doesn't bother their body. Their bodies are still fresh, they're still strong and, consequently, their minds are as well, so their concentration is better."

One of the most important services Centinela provides is the use of its Biomechanics Laboratory in Culver City, California, which is the leading physical research facility for golf in the world. Dr. Frank Jobe, the medical director for the PGA Tour, team physician of the Los Angeles Dodgers and one of the leading orthopedic surgeons in the world, and his associate, Dr. Lewis Yocum, have developed scientific exercise programs specifically for golfers.

"We put tiny electrodes into their muscles, have them swing a club and through that, we can see exactly what muscles are and aren't being used in the golf swing," Hospenthal explains. "It was done with baseball pitchers and swimmers and now we're working with golfers. We now know what muscles are being used and to what potential. At the hospital [in Los Angeles], we have the Centinela Fitness Institute and every year, players can come in and take a physical designed specifically for them. Ear, nose, throat, heart, blood pressure, eyes, body fat, and we do a golf analysis by taking high-speed film to show them how much their shoulders and hips turn and we can relate that to other pros. We also offer a service to amateur golfers where they can take the same physical and compare their attributes to the pros. It's voluntary, but the more successful players are the ones who have taken advantage of it. We have twenty-five to thirty guys doing it this week because we're here in Los Angeles."

Like the club vans, the fitness trailer serves as a place for the players to get away from the hustle and bustle of Tour life. Davis comes in to work out, but once in a while—especially when Robin is not out that week—he'll stop in and watch a movie or just converse with Ploski and Hospenthal or with whomever happens to be exercising at the time.

"This is the only place the players can really go to get away," Ploski says. "In the locker room, media people and club reps can get in there. We generally don't let anyone in here except the players, not even the wives. It's a nice place to get away. We have about one hundred different movies and during rain delays guys will come in and watch movies or listen to the stereo. We develop friendships and a camaraderie with the guys."

Billy Ray Brown gets off the phone after confirming a haircut appointment and catches a little flak from the other players. He

76

ignores the insults and tells Ploski he'll be in to work out tomorrow.

"These guys are great," he says, referring to Ploski and Hospenthal. "They have the hardest job in the world. Look at how many weeks of the year they're out puttin' up with our bullshit. We come here late sometimes and they have to fit us in, and they always do. I've had some back problems for years and they've helped keep my back in good shape. I've been one to have a few beers and eat the wrong foods and I was never one to work out, except for a little running once in a while. But these guys have kept me playing in times when I probably shouldn't have been playing. They really stay on you because they don't want to see you suffer."

Davis completes a twenty-minute battle with the versaclimber, and sweat is pouring from his body. He's running a little behind schedule, so he decides to cut off his workout. He talks to O'Meara and Faxon for a few minutes while he cools down, and then he walks over and asks Hospenthal when they'll be packing up on Sunday.

"Early," Hospenthal says.

The West Coast portion of the Tour schedule concludes in Los Angeles and the Florida leg begins next week. This is the longest trip that the trailer has to make all season, more than 2,100 miles, and for a nice change of pace, Ploski and Hospenthal will be allowed to fly while Centinela hires a driver to get the trailer to Miami.

The long hours aren't a problem for Ploski and Hospenthal, and the constant travel, for a pair of single guys who aren't yet tied down to families, isn't bad either. But driving a truck week after week can get a little annoying.

"Yep, I came out of graduate school and went into truck-driving school," Hospenthal says with a shrug. "They always said, 'Do well in school or you'll end up being a truck driver or a ditch digger.' Well, I worked construction all during school and now I'm driving a truck."

Davis towels off, slips back into his golf clothes, and decides to wait until he gets back to the hotel to shower, rather than do it in the locker room. Mark already has the clubs loaded into the car, so Davis takes the keys, starts it up and off he goes, first to the Holiday Inn to drop Mark off, then to the nursery to get Lexie, and finally, back to the Guest Quarters for a shower and a much-needed nap.

At about 7:30, Robin arrives back at the room after a busy day of shopping on glamorous Rodeo Drive in Beverly Hills.

The family orders room service for dinner, and spends the night relaxing in front of the television. It is a very early evening, because a 7:40 tee time comes around awfully fast.

4 Thursday

Every great athlete experiences it. Joe Montana before he takes the first snap, Roger Clemens before he throws the first pitch, Wayne Gretzky before he first touches the puck, Michael Jordan before he takes the first shot. It is fear. The fear of losing, the fear of failing. If they had not been fearful, they would never have become Joe Montana, Roger Clemens, Wayne Gretzky or Michael Jordan. God-given talent, practice, intelligence and desire all play a major role in the making of a great athlete. But it is fear that sustains him, that pushes him to be the best that he can be.

Davis can hit a golf ball 300 yards, he can make five-foot putts for par, he is smart and he burns with desire. But every time he steps up on the first tee to start a tournament round, he is fearful. And because of fear, he has become one of the finest players in the world. Once that first swing is complete and the ball is flying down the fairway, the fear disappears, just as it does once the football is in Montana's hands and he's reading a defense and looking for a receiver; just as it does once Clemens has blazed a ninety-five-mile-per-hour fastball past some overmatched batter; just as it does once Gretzky feathers a perfect pass to a streaking winger; and just as it does once Jordan has defied the laws of gravity and slammed the basketball through the hoop. In the end, for the great athlete, fear is always a loser to the talent, practice habits, intelligence and desire, but that initial battle with apprehension will always be waged.

In forty minutes Davis will be standing on Riviera's 10th tee feeling the fear as the butterflies flutter away in his stomach. But right now, maybe because it is barely seven o'clock in the morning and the butterflies are still asleep, Davis is not nervous. He sits down at a table in the players' lounge and as he ingests a bowl of cereal, he talks about Harley-Davidson motorcyles with Dillard Pruitt's wife, Fran. Davis isn't nervous because he hasn't had the time to think about being nervous. Like Davis, Dillard is also teeing off at 7:40, starting on No. 1. Unlike Davis, Dillard did not get off to a late start back at the hotel. He has eaten leisurely and is now down at the range warming up.

When Davis finishes eating and talking about Harleys with Fran, he goes to his locker, puts on his golf shoes and walks to the practice putting green, where Mark is waiting for him. After a few putts on the crowded carpet, Davis says hello to Steve Pate and asks Pate about the putter he used last week to win at San Diego. It is the same putter that a club rep had asked Davis to take a look at yesterday. Pate shows him the club, Davis compares it to his Ping putter, and he is deeply involved in this conversation until he hears a caddie say that it's twenty-five minutes past seven. Holy cow! Davis gives Pate back his putter, jogs down the hill and onto the range and quickly tries to get loose by hitting a few wedge shots.

Only when Davis sees one of his playing partners, John Daly, just getting to the range does he realize how late he is this morning. Daly is famous for being behind schedule, hitting only a few balls and then running to the tee. Daly, dressed in a red shirt, tan slacks, white Reebok Pump shoes and his customary cigarette dangling from his lips, takes his Wilson Whale driver out of his bag and the crowd standing behind the ropes surrounding the range begins to murmur in excited anticipation. Daly and his driver may be the most exciting match since José Canseco showed up at Madonna's New York apartment early one morning last May. Daly's driving prowess has been the talk of the golf world since his stunning victory last August in the PGA Championship at Crooked Stick in Carmel, Indiana. The fans salivate as he tees a range ball, coils the large-headed club way around his neck with an enormous upper body turn, then whirls the titanium shaft around and mashes the ball into the next zip code. While the fans cheer Arsenio Hall–style, Daly drags on his cigarette, bends over and tees up another one.

No one knew who John Daly was. He was just some chunky pug-faced rookie with a punky blond haircut who hit the ball off the tee as long as he hit it sideways. In the Tour stats, he was No. 1 in driving distance, but No. 185 in driving accuracy, which pretty much summed up his one-dimensional game prior to the PGA Championship. As the ninth alternate for the PGA, he hadn't even bothered to go to Indianapolis for the tournament, figuring there was no way he'd get into the field. He was back home in Memphis—having one day earlier purchased a new red BMW that he really couldn't afford—when the phone rang on Wednesday afternoon. It was a PGA official telling him that if he could get to Indianapolis by Thursday morning, he might get to play in the season's final major. Nick Price was expected to be the sixth man to drop out because his wife was about to deliver the couple's first child. Sixth alternate Bill Sander was injured, seventh alternate Mark Lye didn't want to play without a practice round and eighth alternate Brad Bryant wouldn't be able to play because of an illness in the family. Daly and his then-fiancée, Bettye Fulford, packed up the BMW and hit the road for the eight-hour drive.

Daly arrived in the middle of the night and found a message waiting for him at his hotel that Price had indeed bolted town. He got a couple hours of sleep, then went out and pummeled the Pete Dye–designed monster called Crooked Stick. Without ever having seen the course, Daly shot 3-under 69 to stand two strokes behind Masters champ Ian Woosnam and Kenny Knox. Wasn't this the same hellish layout that Jack Nicklaus had said was the hardest course he had ever played? Wasn't this the same course where Ben Crenshaw and Curtis Strange each shot 81 and withdrew? Wasn't this the second-longest tract ever used for a PGA Championship? Yes, yes and yes. But long courses had never intimidated Daly, even when he was missing cut after cut earlier in the year. He was as long as ever on Thursday, but the difference was that he was hitting it straight. It was obvious that if he could keep it in play off the tee, his "grip it and rip it" philosophy was going to serve him very well.

On Friday, the bludgeoning continued with seven birdies and an eagle for a 67, giving him a one-stroke lead over Bruce Lietzke.

By the time Saturday morning dawned, the Daly legend had been born. A nobody two days earlier, he had become the fan favorite and media darling. Here was a guy that every golf fan could relate to. A self-taught player with a swing that would get ridiculed by almost every teaching pro on the planet. An unassuming guy with a go-for-broke, knock-the-flagstick-down style whose lone swing thought was "Kill." When he did something good, he showed emotion, and when the crowd cheered for him, he cheered back at them.

"I feel like I can relate to the fans because most of the fans are just like I am," he said. "I didn't have anything handed to me. I wasn't treated with a silver spoon or anything. I just went out and fished balls out of the pond, never had a pair of golf shoes until I was fifteen, had one glove at a time and wore it for a month or two until it was all full of holes. I think that's what the fans like about me."

With the CBS cameras focusing on his every move Saturday, he shot 69 to widen his margin to three shots over Knox and Craig Stadler. And on Sunday, with the galleries flocking to him in Palmeresque fashion, he brought it home in 71 for a 12-under total of 276, three better than Lietzke, thus completing one of the most unlikely victories in the illustrious history of the sport.

Last year, he stormed away from Riviera when a parking attendant, not knowing who he was, refused to allow him to enter the players' lot. He vowed never to return to the Palisades. But he is back because he knows the Los Angeles Open is a tournament the top players rarely skip. And this year, there have been no problems parking. There isn't a soul on the grounds who doesn't know who John Daly is.

There will be two huge galleries today at Riviera. One will be following Daly, and the other will be keeping pace with Tiger Woods, the local high school junior who at sixteen years, one month and twenty-eight days of age, will become the second-youngest player to ever compete in a PGA tournament. Davis is prepared for the throng of fans. He knows the crowd is going to be distracting, and he also knows that it's going to be much worse tomorrow afternoon, so he tells Mark that this will be a good warm-up for that.

Despite the short warm-up session, Davis is not concerned. He knows he's hitting the ball well, and he feels good about his game. It's just a matter of going out and playing.

"One thing my dad had a hard time understanding, and he was finally getting a handle on it before he died, was how I would try to forget everything we had worked so hard on and just go play golf. I was trying to get rid of all my mechanics on the golf course, all my swing thoughts, just get all of the junk out of my mind and just go play the game. When he finally realized that he had done that when he went and played, he said, 'Yeah, maybe you're right.'

"If I go out and mentally play a good round, there's no reason why I shouldn't hit the ball good. Now, you can be perfectly prepared and things still might go wrong, but if I go out and have a good routine and a good attitude, I ought to play well. There isn't anything I can do different with my golf swing between now and Sunday that's going to make me play that much better. It's all just going out and playing and not trying to be mechanical and working on my game."

John Cook and his caddie, Andy Martinez, are already at No. 10 when Davis gets there with Mark. Seconds later, the fans begin clapping as Daly and his caddie, Greg Rita, enter the arena.

As the players and caddies pick up their pin sheets, score-cards and local rules sheets, a woman from the Darrell Survey Company performs her Thursday ritual of taking inventory of every single piece of equipment and item of clothing each player possesses. She checks to see what type of ball they're playing, what clubs they have in the bag, what kinds of shafts and grips are being used, and what brand visor, glove, hat, shoes, shirt, pants and socks they're wearing.

"It's for the manufacturers," Davis explains, "and it's also to check up on guys. If a guy is under contract to use 12 Tommy Armour clubs for example, they find out if he's using 12 clubs. If they have a guy under contract to play a Maxfli ball and he's playing a Titleist, it'll show up. They know their business pretty good and you help them a little bit if you change things by telling them what changes you've made. I usually tell them what my shafts are because not many guys use my shaft."

Once she has completed her checks, the announcer alerts the players that it is time to play. Davis, Cook and Daly all wish each other luck, and then Cook steps up and inserts his tee into the ground.

"Ladies and gentleman, from Rancho Mirage, California, John Cook," says the announcer, and Cook, dressed in light gray and blue plaid pants and a white shirt, acknowledges the applause with a smile and a wave. He stares down the length of the hole and his eyes focus on the green. At 312 yards, the par-4 10th can provide lots of drama because the long hitters try to drive the green in search of birdies and eagles. Cook isn't a real long hitter, but he's going to go for the green here.

In George Lucas' yardage book, he refers to the 10th as "par fun." But if you hit a bad drive, you might be in one of Lucas' J.I.C.Y.R.F.U. areas. This is only "par fun" if you hit it straight. A pushed drive to the right can be big trouble because the tiny green is protected by a bunker, and chipping over that bunker and holding the green is extremely tricky. A pulled drive to the left can hide behind a set of palm trees.

"It's a strategy hole and when you pick your way to play, you better hit it there or you can turn an easy birdie into a hard par by putting it in the wrong place," Davis says. Davis will try to drive it whenever the pin isn't back right, and when it is, he'll hit an iron long enough to carry the far edge of the fairway bunker two hundred yards out, which will leave him a wedge to the green. The green is thirty-four yards deep and the pin today is twenty-three back and five from the right edge, slightly back right, but assailable. On Sunday, it will be twenty-nine back and four from the right.

The crowd becomes silent as Cook addresses his ball, then groans slightly as they see him swing through a little quickly and pull the shot to the left of the green.

"Ladies and gentlemen, from Memphis, Tennessee, John Daly," and the gathered spectators greet him warmly and you can hear fans yelling, "Long John!" and "Kill!" However, there are a few moans and hisses when Daly pulls out his 1-iron, eschewing the driver. The fans want the big club, but Daly does not oblige. He's going to play it safe and try to chip and putt for a birdie. It turns out to be an imprudent choice as he snap-hooks the iron way to the left.

"Ladies and gentleman, from Sea Island, Georgia, Davis Love III," and the applause meter goes back to Cook's standards as

Davis steps to the tee dressed in blue pants and a white shirt with red horizontal stripes. A slight breeze is at his back, so he hesitates at first to take his driver, thinking that maybe a 3-wood will get it there. However, this early in the morning, he isn't sure he can power a 3-wood that far, so the choice is driver. He hits almost the exact same shot as Cook, a pull to the left of the green.

The fear is gone for all three and the game has begun. As they walk down the fairway, their footprints linger in the light covering of dew that hasn't been evaporated by the bright sun.

After Daly hits a pitching wedge from the left rough onto the green, Davis gets to his ball and finds it on top of a small folding chair, a rather inauspicious beginning. If a ball is leaning up against something like a rake on the side of a bunker, you mark it, take the object away and if the ball moves, you replace it. But if it's sitting on top of something, you put a mark as close as you can to it, then drop the ball to that mark, which is what Davis does. The lie is not bad, and after a little traffic directing to move the crowd back, he settles over his chip shot, takes his time planning where he wants to land the ball, and does a good job to get it within ten feet of the hole. Cook follows with an even better chip to four feet.

Daly two-putts for his par, Davis's putt bounces a little on its way to the hole and misses to the right so he taps in for par, and Cook drains his four-footer for birdie. As they walk to the 11th tee, Davis asks Mark what happened on his putt and Mark says, "It jumped right as soon as you hit it."

"That green is always kind of bumpy because it's so little and it can't handle all the traffic on it," Davis says. "I hit a good putt, but Mark said it bounced a little. When I hit a putt, I'm not like most guys who look up. I'm almost going the other way. I'm still looking at the ground. On a two-footer, I don't see it until it's almost in the hole. A lot of time I'll ask, 'What did that ball do?' because I won't see it, like on that one. That's the best way to putt, keep your head still and don't look at it."

Davis looks relaxed, unaware that for a Thursday morning there are a lot of people following his group. He is thinking about his routine, about making good swings and good decisions, which in turn should produce quality shots. The butterflies have cooled their wings, but now, he has to remind himself that every shot is important and even though he is relaxed, he cannot get lackadaisical.

"The exciting pressure comes at the end of the tournament when you've got a chance to win, but you have to put some type of pressure on yourself on the first day, on the first hole to get yourself to concentrate," he explains. "You've got to find a way to get yourself excited at the beginning of a round and then if you're playing well, it's going to get your attention at the end. I think the most incredible thing about a guy like Michael Jordan or Wayne Gretzky, or somebody who's the best at what they do is that they find a way every game, every night, to get themselves interested and concentrating. Obviously, Michael Jordan is one of the best athletes there is, but how does he do it every night? He has to find some way to get himself excited to play against the Miami Heat. He knows the Bulls are going to be in the playoffs in two months, and that's when it really counts. And that's the thing about Thursday. The shot you hit on Thursday that you weren't concentrating on is just as important as any shot on Sunday. You have to get some pressure going when you start and once you get into contention, then it's easy to feel the pressure and get yourself to concentrate."

The 11th is a true par-5. It is 566 yards and even Davis has to hit a huge drive to have a chance of reaching the green in two shots. Almost always, he'll be short and will need to hit a little L-wedge, sand wedge or pitching wedge on his third stroke. The green is basic with no discernible features and players with good short games can make a slew of birdies.

Daly pulls out his driver for the first time and he gets the crowd into an uproar as he crushes one down the left side of the fairway. Davis reminds himself before he tees off that it's going to be like this for the next two days, so he has to avoid slipping into a driving contest with Daly and just stay within his own swing. He does that here, hitting his driver right down the middle, although it comes up ten yards shy of Daly.

Davis has never played with Daly before so what happens in the next few minutes really surprises him. Davis hits an excellent 3-wood and leaves himself a sixty-five-yard chip shot from the middle of the fairway. Daly takes a 1-iron and nearly knocks it on the green.

"I was amazed," Davis says. "He hits a 1-iron farther than my 3-wood and that doesn't happen to me ever. Usually if a guy outdrives me, I'm usually past him on the next shot on a par-5 like that. That was kind of amazing."

Davis pitches with a sand wedge to one foot and taps in for birdie. His plan to land the ball fifteen feet in front of the hole and let it slow down naturally as it rolls back to the pin works perfectly.

"I knew it wouldn't check up. From the fairway you plan on one big bounce, then a little bounce and it stops or slows down pretty quick like that one. It's funny, you watch Ken Venturi on TV say, 'Watch this ball, it'll take one big bounce, then a little one and stop,' like he's magical or something. Every ball takes a big bounce and a little bounce then rolls or stops. It's hard to get a golf ball to bounce three times. That always cracks me up."

Daly makes a six-footer for birdie, right after Cook, who had wedged to fifteen feet, made his second birdie in a row.

Mark walks over to Davis as Cook is pulling his ball out of the cup, and Davis says to him, "I wonder why John Cook's the leading money winner on Tour this year."

People were calling John Cook the next Jack Nicklaus back in the late 1970s. After all, he was born in Ohio like Nicklaus, went to Ohio State and became an All-American like Nicklaus, won the U.S. Amateur like Nicklaus. Hell, he was even blond like Nicklaus. But no one is like Nicklaus except Nicklaus.

"I came out real young, twenty-two when I started, married with a child and I had to be husband, father and professional golfer all at once at twenty-two plus be the next Jack Nicklaus," Cook says. "It wasn't easy and it didn't get any easier."

He played decently—but below his and everyone else's expectations—as a rookie on Tour in 1980, finishing 78th on the money list. In '81, he won the Bing Crosby National Pro-Am at Pebble Beach and played very well in the U.S. Open at Merion and while Cook certainly wasn't the next Nicklaus, it looked like he was going to be a very successful player.

A decade later, that prediction is finally coming true. He won in '83 at the Canadian Open, then injured his wrist and spent the rest of the '80s battling the injury as well as self-doubt.

"It was not easy, I struggled a lot the first four or five years," he says. "The first year wasn't a whole lot of fun, I didn't play that well, I expected to play better than I did. The second year was a lot better—I won a tournament, I finished in the top 10 four or five times, I almost won the U.S. Open and I thought I had adjusted. But the next three or four years became really tough.

"More and more people said, 'You ought to be doing this and doing this like so-and-so does,' and while I never got wrapped up in it, I kept listening and I started wondering, 'Am I really doing the right thing?' I was doubting myself. There were a lot of people who thought I could play and I knew I could play, but I just hadn't shown myself anything. My inconsistency was driving me nuts. I'd have a good couple of weeks and then I couldn't find it for a few weeks, then I'd come back and play well. The ups and downs were tough to take.

"I think that was a result of the way I was. I didn't know if I should be home, and if I was home, I felt like I should be playing. I couldn't correlate it very well. Once I decided that I was going to do what John Cook needed to do, not what someone else said I needed to do or be like anybody else, that's when I started to believe that I was doing the right things. It started to turn around in '86. I started doing the things that I wanted to do and my priorities definitely got straightened out. They may not be priorities to other people, but once I started figuring out that golf was down the list a little ways and I realized that once I became a good husband and father, then I could feel good about playing, I had a lot more fun playing the game. I needed to take charge of it and I did it because I stuck to those guns, it gave me the confidence to progress in the right direction."

His priorities righted, he won The International in '87, but the wrist injury only got worse and he suffered through a dismal '88 season before finally deciding to have surgery in May of '89, effectively wiping out the rest of that year.

Cook started 1990 with a fresh attitude, played well all year and won a career-best $448,112 and had four top 10 finishes. In '91, he topped that with $546,984 and eight top 10s, but he remained stuck on three career victories until the first six weeks of this season, when he won twice.

"I have no explanation," Cook says of his fast start in '92. "The only one I can give you is that I had been home from Sunday of Kapalua [in November] and I didn't leave the house until I flew up to Pebble Beach the Monday before the tournament last month. I came out rested and ready to play. Growing up I never played twelve months out of the year, I always needed some time off, and that's a good time to take off, November and December. I started getting ready just after New Year's, hit some balls, played every day and that was it. Things just fell into place. I've had some good breaks and I've taken advantage of good opportunities that I've had and I think now when I get close, I feel like I have a pretty good chance. I made a commitment to myself that if I'm going to start winning again, I'm going to have to go out and win. I'm not gonna get to that point and wait for something to happen, I'm going to go ahead and try to win the golf tournament. That's what I've done. In the last rounds that I've played with a chance to win, I've stayed aggressive and shot at every flag. It kept me going."

His aggressive play was never more evident than at the Hope, when he steamrolled his way through a five-man playoff. He and Gene Sauers each birdied the first two extra holes to knock out Mark O'Meara, Tom Kite and Rick Fehr. On the third, Sauers was in tight with a 7-footer for birdie, so Cook, figuring he had to make birdie, did so from the fringe by chipping in from twenty feet. Sauers did indeed make his putt, prolonging the playoff. On the fourth extra hole, the short par-5 18th at Indian Wells, Cook missed the green to the left with his second shot while Sauers stuck his approach 40 feet from the hole. Cook had to get up and down for birdie and he did better than that. He chipped in again, this time for eagle, and when Sauers missed his eagle putt, Cook's four-year winless drought had ended.

Three weeks later in Hawaii, Cook avenged one of his most frustrating defeats ever. In '91, Cook began the final round of the Hawaiian Open with a one-stroke lead, but high winds got the better of him on Sunday and he skied to a 75 and lost to Lanny Wadkins by four shots. This time, he entered the last day tied for the lead with Paul Azinger, then dusted the Zinger with a 65 to win by two.

"I remember while Lanny was up on the podium, I was already going through my round, trying to figure out what happened," Cook told *Gold World*. "I wanted to learn from that, and I did. I learned a lot last year. I'm tougher overall. I think I'm a better player than I was last year."

One look at the current money list proves that statement.

All three players make routine two-putt pars at the par-4 12th.

The par-4, 422-yard 13th doglegs to the left with out-of-bounds looming on the left and eucalyptus trees flanking both sides.

"For me the temptation is to hook it around the corner, but the trees are so big, anything left gets sucked into the trees. So if there's no wind, the play is probably a 3-wood to the corner and then a 5- or a 6-iron to the green," Davis theorizes. "I've even hit 1-iron when the fairways are fast. You just keep it in play, hit to the middle of the green and feel lucky if you can get a good birdie putt. It's a big green, but it's a long hole and a bad drive leaves you a very tough shot in."

Davis decides to go with his driver and he hits it well, but not as good as Daly and Cook. It's rare, even with the low trajectory ball, that he is outdriven by both of his playing partners.

"John [Cook], when he slings one, he hits that turnover and run drive, so he's going to outdrive me once in a while," Davis says, "because my ball won't always go as far with a driver, although it will usually go further with the irons. I was telling Mark, it's amazing when I go on the range after a good driving round and those 384 range balls feel so juiced up compared to my LT ball, they just take off."

Despite being outdriven, all Davis has left is a pitching wedge. Before he hits, he checks the trees up around the green and sees that the wind is blowing right-to-left so he tells Mark that he's going to play the wind, but Mark warns him not to play too much. He listens to Mark, doesn't start the shot as far to the right of the flag as he was going to, and sure enough, the breeze blows it about eight feet left of the hole. He looks at Mark and Mark just shrugs his shoulders and smiled an "I'm sorry" smile.

The putt is slightly uphill, Davis aims for the right-center of the cup, his ball reacts on command and drops in for his second birdie and Mark is off the hook. "To me," Davis says, "uphill right-to-left is the easiest putt to make."

Play gets backed up at the par-3 14th and while he waits, Davis is perplexed by what club to hit. The hole plays a little downhill, but that is made up by the fact that it usually faces the wind. The green is shallow, only twenty-two yards deep, but it's very wide and the most difficult pin placement is back right on Sunday. It's a little narrower back there and the pin is hidden by a trap. Today, his yardage is 177 and the pin is tucked in the back just five yards from the right edge. He knows it plays downhill, so he considers an 8-iron, eventually decides on the seven and as soon as he follows through, he says, "Damn, get it wind, get it." The wind doesn't knock it down, it hits the right edge of the green and kicks off the back, coming to rest in matted rough twelve feet off the putting surface.

"That one could have bounced a little better," he says. "I was trying to slide the seven in there against the wind and get it real close, which I guess is what I always try to do, but I should have just ripped the 8-iron left of the hole and taken a 20-footer uphill."

His chip shot is difficult. The terrain is uphill to the fringe, then flat for a few feet before going downhill to the pin, "kind of a doopsy doodle." He tries to hit the shot into the hill with his sand wedge so it will roll slowly down, but it sticks in the slope and never gets to the decline. Now, he is left with an ornery downhill 15-footer breaking left to right, which is not a fun putt to have for par. He gives it a good run, but puts a little too much speed on it and it curls around the left lip and winds up two feet beyond the hole. He makes that for bogey, dropping him back to 1-under-par.

The par-4, 447-yard 15th is a bitch. The driving landing area turns to the right and the rough comes down off the trap on the right, so if you cut the corner of the trap a little too much, your ball will get hung up in the rough. The play is to take the drive down the left side and cut it around the corner for a shorter shot in. When it's against the wind, you can hit as much as a 4- or 5-iron into the green. Even a good drive leaves you with a tough approach because you lose some control and accuracy with longer irons and this is a green that demands a tight shot because it is divided by a deep swale. Hitting to the wrong side of the green and having to putt through the swale is an unenviable position to be in.

Davis hits a good drive out over the corner, then hits an 8-iron that lands ten feet left of the pin and backspins down into the swale, leaving him a difficult 25-footer. He rolls the putt two feet past, but this is not two routine feet. It is downhill with a slight left-to-right break and suddenly, what should have been an ordinary par has become an endeavor. He takes his time, bears down and strokes the putt into the center of the cup.

"You've bogeyed the hole before, you hit two pretty good shots on this hole and now you have this tricky little putt for par, those are the ones that can turn a round around for the bad," he says. "You miss that and now you're really pissed off because you're back to even par. Those kind of things shouldn't ruin your day, but they can. A bogey, then a three-putt after you've hit good shots can really piss you off. You just have to relax and not even think about it, and I didn't until after when Mark said, 'That was a good putt,' and I said, 'Yeah, I guess so.'"

Daly gets to two-under by rolling in a 30-footer at 16, and a marshal says, "He must have practiced his putting, he was awful yesterday in the Pro-Am." Davis and Cook two-putt for par.

Davis calls the 580-yard 17th "a forever par-5. If I kill two shots, I might be thirty or forty yards in front of the green." The second shot is strategic because a fairway bunker resides on the left side about 110 yards short of the green, so the decision is to lay up short of that and hit a pitching wedge, or try to clear it and set up a sand wedge or L-wedge. The green is large and slopes back to front with a ridge that runs horizontally, splitting it into two tiers. Being on the same level as the pin, preferably with an uphill putt, is imperative.

Davis unleashes a big drive down the middle of the fairway. He then aims his 3-wood second shot at the trap on the left with the intent of fading it back to the middle. However, the ball draws, which is an unusual movement for Davis's 3-wood, and it winds up on the mound in front of the bunker, presenting him with an awkward stance.

"I thought it was in the trap, but it was just hanging outside the edge. I had to either stand with a real open stance or put a foot in the bunker. So in that situation, I really couldn't hit a sand wedge from sixty-five yards because standing so open or with a foot in the bunker, it would have been hard to put any spin on it."

The green is forty yards deep and the pin is nineteen yards back and five from the right edge positioned just above the ridge. Davis decides to try to hit a low 9-iron that will bounce into the ridge and hop up onto the second level where the pin is. He opts for the open stance rather than putting his left foot into the bunker, takes a three-quarter length backswing and punches down on the ball. It comes out low as planned, hits below the ridge, then dribbles up to the second tier and stops seven feet to the right of the flag, just as he had hoped.

He takes his time reading the putt, aided by Mark, and he sees that it will break about two inches to the left. It does, and the birdie gets him back to 2-under.

Daly had hit a sand wedge to within three feet and after Davis putts, Daly rolls in his birdie in an attempt to move to 3-under. As a threesome, Davis, Daly and Cook are 7-under through eight holes.

"It's nice when they're playing good, too," Davis says. "You're kind of rolling along, you're not waiting on a guy who's struggling, and its more fun because they're in better moods and the crowd's more into it."

One of the finest finishing holes in all of golf is Riviera's uphill, par-4, 448-yard 18th. In the yardage book, George Lucas calls it a "par 4.38." The fairway is elevated and located on the other side of a big valley and it can't be seen from the tee so Davis says, "The key is picking out a good target to aim your drive at and you have to have confidence to hit it there." Ideally, you want to be on the left side of the fairway and that will leave the players a long- to mid-iron, if the wind isn't blowing. The shortest club Davis can remember hitting into this green is a 6-iron. More danger awaits around the green. It is narrow and surrounded by a natural amphitheater, and anything pulled left onto the hill presents an almost impossible up and down. The kikuyu grass is scraggly there and it sticks to the club. Once you're putting, it's a straight-forward surface. "When you're finishing on Sunday, it's a hard one to finish. It's just a great hole."

Davis is really in a groove with his driver and at 18, he picks out his target on the hill straight ahead and hits another good drive. When he gets to his ball in the fairway, he notices that the wind isn't blowing in his face as much as it was on the tee. Mark tells him he has 209 to the hole, so with the wind dying down, he chooses a 4-iron, hits it a bit low and the ball runs to the back of the green and stops on the collar of the fringe, twenty feet from the hole.

"You have to take your putter up abruptly on that putt so you don't get hung up in the fringe and you have to be careful on those because you hit down on the ball when you do that and if you hit it too hard, it can really take off. And I was a little downhill to begin with so to get that to tap-in range was a good putt," he says.

Daly and Cook also 2-putt for par and after the players drop off their 9-hole scorecards, they trudge up the hill to the first tee. The huge scoreboard that overlooks the 18th green shows Buddy Gardner on top at 4-under with Daly and Jay Haas at 3-under.

The first hole is a 491-yard par-5 with the tee about 80 feet above the fairway. It is a hole that the players will often have eagle putts on because a drive into the middle of the fairway will leave a long- to mid-iron to the green. "You have to drive it straight, because the rough is scraggly and there are lots of trees. It's a pretty easy hole if you can drive it straight," Davis says. The green is shaped like a horseshoe with a big bunker that cuts into the middle, so when the pin is behind the sand, it's difficult to get it close.

It is about 9:45 and the terrace that overlooks the first tee is already crowded with spectators sipping on adult beverages. Daly makes his way through the crowd and they root him on until he disappoints them by taking his 1-iron out of his bag.

This is not the same Daly who won the PGA. Back then, he hit driver on virtually every hole and sometimes, it seemed, because the crowd was telling him to do so and he felt a responsibility to please them. But today, and throughout the first seven weeks of the season, he has pulled back and has tried to manage his game better. Davis thinks a lot of it has to do with his new caddie, Greg Rita.

"Greg's going to be good for John, he'll make a difference," Davis says. "He's already made a difference."

Rita is a veteran who has enjoyed much success on the Tour. He is probably best known for having caddied for Curtis Strange during both of Strange's U.S. Open victories at Brookline in 1988 and at Oak Hill in Rochester in '89. He hooked up with Daly at the start of the year and it is obvious that he has been a good influence on the guy they call "Wild Thing."

"Greg is probably the best caddie I've ever had," Daly says. "We haven't been playing bad, we just haven't had any real good rounds. I've been under par all the way back through the Hope. We're so close to getting it going, and the reason I have shot better rounds is because of Greg. He's keeping me in there, he's keeping me focused, there's no giving up in him and there's no giving up in me. The guy has caddied for Curtis Strange for six years and won a couple of Opens. He's one guy I don't want to lose as a caddie. I think we're a good team. The other caddies and players have told me that once you're in contention, he can win golf tournaments for you and I can't wait to get into that situation."

On this hole, a short par-5 that's reachable in two, Davis is surprised by Daly's club selection, however. "Before, he was too aggressive and now, it seems like he's too conservative."

Daly yanks the 1-iron into the left rough and he mutters, "Fuck," as he gives the club back to Rita.

95

Davis hits another excellent drive, right in the middle of the fairway, leaving him 220 yards to the hole.

Davis and Cook walk down the hill together and the two discuss why Daly hit 1-iron and like Davis, Cook is also surprised. "I don't understand why he hit 1-iron with the wind blowin' in," Davis says. "It didn't make sense to lay up, but again, he may not have confidence in that driver and it's out of bounds pretty quick left, so a lot of guys see that. Maybe he thought he could still reach the road. Come to think of it, he probably could, but that's not bad, you get to drop it in the fairway." The road that runs through the fairway is 320 yards from the tee.

The discussion proves rather meaningless after Daly muscles his ball out of the second cut of rough with his trusty 1-iron and it ends up on the green, thirty feet to the left of the pin. It is an impressive shot and the fans surrounding the green let Daly know it.

"I have a 3-iron. He must have been thirty yards behind me and he just whips a 1-iron up there pin high," Davis says. "I guess it really doesn't matter where he hits it off the tee, he can knock it up there from anywhere. He was as close to making eagle as anybody."

The hole is cut in the middle of the green, five yards behind the bunker that intrudes into the center of the putting surface. It is a tough pin to shoot right at, but Davis loops his 3-iron around with that very intention. As he follows through and watches the flight, he tells his ball to cut, but it doesn't listen to him and although he reaches the green and will have a putt for an eagle, it's not one that he can expect to make, a downhill 18-footer breaking slightly to the right.

Before Daly and Davis attempt their eagle putts, they must wait for Cook. After an errant 4-wood second shot missed the green to the right, Cook stubs his chip from the deep rough and barely gets it on the green. He mumbles something to himself, then marks his ball and stares at his twenty-two-foot birdie putt while Daly prepares to stroke his eagle opportunity. Daly misses, but taps in for his third birdie in four holes and he walks back to Rita with a share of the lead at 4-under with Buddy Gardner.

Cook misses his birdie attempt short, which frustrates him

further, but rather than walking up and mindlessly knocking the two-footer in for par, experience warns him to mark, take his time and let Davis get his putt out of the way.

Davis tries to ease it down the hill aiming for the left edge, but he doesn't play enough break and it slides underneath the hole so he strides up and taps in for birdie to drop him to 3-under. Cook takes a long time studying his putt before confidently making it.

The par-4 second hole is the exact opposite of the first. It's 459 yards to an elevated green and par is a very good score. The drive has to be in the fairway for any chance of getting to the green in regulation. A marginal drive at No. 2 will most likely force the player to have to get up and down to save par. "The second hole is a par-4 and it's harder to make four than the first hole, which is a par-5," Davis says. "You hope to get a putt for a three and you're happy if you make four. Ideally, you want your drive on the left side of the fairway and that leaves you a mid-iron approach. But on that hole, middle of the fairway and middle of the green, get your four and get out of there is great."

Today, the trees have been mercifully moved up about twenty yards, so Davis puts his driver away and chooses his 3-wood because the fairway ends at about the 300-yard mark and with the tees up, he can reach that area of rough with his longest club. However, that proves to be the least of his worries. He swings poorly and he begins moaning, "Get down, get down, bite, bite," as he sees it heading for trouble on the left side. His ball skips through the rough, hops over the cart path and ends up against a tree, which gives him no chance to shoot for the green.

Daly again chooses the 1-iron and grumbles, "That's weak," as his ball gets up in the air too much and winds up on the right side of the fairway, still 206 yards from the hole. Cook then pushes his drive into the right rough, and although the gallery cheers the shot, Cook knows it's not going to end up in a convenient location and he grimly says, "Damn it, get down."

They are three solemn-looking men as they stride down the fairway, all thinking about how difficult it's going to be to get out of here with a four. When Davis gets to his ball, he realizes that four would be an incredible score. He has no other play but to use his sand wedge and chip it back into the fairway sideways, which he does, leaving himself the chore of trying to get up and down from 168 yards. Following Davis's chip out, Cook hits a marvelous 4-iron punch under the tree limbs that carries all the way to the hill in front of the green, stopping about twenty feet short of the putting surface. The crowd gives him a big ovation and his caddie, Andy Martinez, smiles approvingly. Daly misclubs himself and leaves a 5-iron fifteen feet short of the green.

Davis and Mark check the pin sheet and see that the green is thirty-three yards deep and the hole is carved six yards on and six from the left edge. Davis requests the 6-iron and tries to forget about the additional pressure he has added to this approach because of his wayward drive. He goes through his normal pre-shot routine and this procedure works. His swing is a beauty and as his ball soars through the air, Davis knows it. The ball hits on the front of the green, right in line with the pin, and rolls to a stop eight feet below the hole. He waves to thank the crowd for their applause, but there is no smile on his face. There is still work to be done.

Daly and Cook each pitch on to within four feet of the cup, and then Davis takes a look at his par-saving putt. He sees the line quickly and rather than belabor, he steps right up and intrepidly rolls the ball at the hole. However, he pulls it just a touch and it kisses the left edge and refuses to drop. The bogey brings him back to two-under and he tosses his putter underhanded at his bag as he walks to the left side of the green to watch Daly and Cook save their pars.

"I hit a perfect 6-iron, right at it, eight feet below with an uphill putt and I just thought there was no way I was going to miss it," Davis says. "It was on line, but I didn't hit it solid. The green was a little bumpy, but if you hit 'em solid, they'll go over those bumps and go in. If not, the bumps seem to affect the ball more. I'm playing it not to break and it broke because I didn't hit it solid. I was a little mad, but you go on, you get over it. That hole's a par-4½ anyway, and I know there's a long way to go."

The par-4, 441-yard third is usually played into the wind, leaving most players a mid-iron and for the big hitters, a short iron into a green that is hidden behind a trap. The fairway is very wide and hard to miss, but the key is the second shot. Most of the green is blocked by the bunker, so getting a precise yardage for the approach is vital. It also plays a bit downhill, so that has to be taken into account during club selection.

As he settles over his ball, Davis is thinking about his drive on No. 2 and by worrying about pulling one left again, he pushes this one into the deep rough on the right and now he's a little irritated with himself. He had been hitting his driver well all morning and now he's starting to struggle so as he watches Daly and Cook tee off, he tries to conjure up some good swing thoughts in his mind in an effort to get himself back on track.

His lie in the rough is not bad, so from 162 yards with a slight breeze in his face, he takes a 7-iron. Coming out of the rough, though, he can't get the shot to check up and it runs off the back edge of the green and into the fringe about fifteen feet behind the hole.

Daly had hit a poor pitching wedge from 127 yards that left him a 25-foot birdie putt, and he was away, but he asks Davis if he wants to get on the green and Davis takes him up on the offer.

"I really wasn't hurrying, but I kind of went through my routine a little quick," Davis says. "I hit the putt and I said, 'Man, that's right on line, but it's not going to get there.' But it kept trickling and trickling and just fell over into the hole. I had about three feet of fringe to get through and normally I would have chipped that, but I had kind of a bad lie. It looked like someone had chipped from there before and the grass was fluffed up and I didn't like the looks of it.

"Usually out of the fringe when it looks rough, you ought to chip it because it takes away the chance of a bad bounce or the ball not coming out as fast as you think. It's more consistent to chip and run. Most of the guys out here are just as good chipping with an iron as they are with a putter in that situation. But on this one, something told me that putting was the smart play. So that was a nice break after getting a bad one the hole before. Somebody said yesterday, all golf is is luck and 50 percent of it is bad. I guess that makes a lot of sense."

Daly walks over to check his line and Davis jokingly says with a smile, "Thanks for letting me go ahead and make that," and

Daly replies, "Sure, no problem." Cook 2-putts for par and after opening with 2 birdies, he has parred 10 in a row. Daly runs his first putt four feet past, then misses the comeback and takes a disappointing bogey that drops him into a tie with Davis at 3-under, two strokes behind Keith Clearwater who has moved to 5-under, followed by Buddy Gardner and Mark Wiebe at 4-under.

One of the two things has to happen in order to enjoy success at the arduous par-3 fourth; you have to hit a great long iron or fairway wood off the tee, or your short game has to be sharp. Ben Hogan once called the 238-yard fourth "the greatest par-3 hole in America." It is a brutally tough test, especially when the wind is blowing into the players' faces, which it usually does. What makes it so demanding is that a large bunker fronts the green, so you can't hit a bump-and-run type of tee shot. The ball has to fly the trap and then somehow hold the green. Getting a 3-wood or 1-iron to check up is asking a lot, even of the best players in the world. It's almost like a short par-4 where you try to drive the green and if you miss, you try to get up and down for birdie, only here, you're getting up and down for par. "You're trying to birdie it, but you're awful happy to make par," Davis says.

It's 225 yards to the hole today with a slight breeze blowing into his face so Davis elects to use his 1-iron, but he can't get the ball to stop when it hits the green and it runs to the back fringe, sixty feet from the hole. Cook doesn't catch a 4-wood solid and he just manages to carry the front left bunker, twenty-five yards short of the green. And Daly pushes a 2-iron way right into the deep rough. All three are going to have to rely on their short games.

Daly hits a superb sand wedge from about thirty-five yards that rolls forever on the green, honing in on the hole like a missile to its target. It stops one foot short and after the crowd settles down, he taps in for par. Cook lofts a sand wedge right at the flag, the ball bounces once, rolls about ten feet and banks off the flagstick and drops into the cup for a birdie. The crowd roars again as he pretends his right hand is a gun, points it at the hole and squeezes the trigger, smiling all the while. It's a tough act to

100

follow, but Davis provides the encore with a bump-and-run 9-iron pitch that runs out of gas a foot and a half short. "Just far enough away where you have to look at it," he says. He makes that to save par and now all three players are three-under.

A new tee has been constructed at the par-4, 419-yard fifth. It's lower and has been shifted about twenty yards to left so the trees on the left side come into play as the fairway bends to that side. "Against the wind, it's a driver, and if it's downwind, which it usually wouldn't be, I'll just hit 1-iron down there under the limbs of the trees," Davis says. The right side of the fairway is the place to be, because the slope of the terrain will take the ball to the middle and leave a short-iron approach. A pulled drive is big trouble because the fairway ends and drops off about twenty feet into a valley with two big birch trees blocking the green.

One after the other, all three pull their tee shots and wind up down the hill off the left side. Davis is in the worst shape. He had considered hitting 1-iron off the tee, but chose instead to aim a 3-wood down the left side and try to fade it into the middle. The ball stayed straight, rolled over the edge of the embankment and rather than going all the way to the bottom like Cook's and Daly's, it stuck on the side of the hill in ankle-high rough with the large birch blocking his approach alley to the green.

The safest play would be to chip it forward and down onto the fairway and try to get up and down for par from there. However, after studying his options, he decides that if he catches it cleanly, he can aim to the right of the green and hook it back to the hole. The pin is twenty-one yards from the front edge and six from the right. He chooses his 9-iron, chokes down on the grip and then tries to balance himself on the steep incline. Once he feels steady, he stares at his target, then at the ball, then at the target, and finally back at the ball, all the while, flexing his knees to maintain his equilibrium. With the ball way above his feet, he takes a baseball-like swing, hits it fat and although the ball misses the birch, it only travels about 120 yards and plops down in the fairway about 50 yards short of the front of the green.

"You have to plan on hitting behind it because you almost

always do in that situation for some reason," Davis explains. "I was putting it back in my stance to make sure I didn't hit it fat, but sure enough I hit behind it. You have to lean into the hill so you don't fall backwards, and that's why I chunked it. I would've been lucky to get it on the green from there. All you really want to do is make sure you hit it straight because if you quit on it and let the club go with the hill, you'll snap hook it and it won't go anywhere."

Cook and Daly both manage to miss the tree with excellent punch shots and both wind up on the green with makeable birdie putts.

Mark tells Davis he has seventy yards to the hole, which is a little bit out of L-wedge range so Davis takes out his sand wedge. He has a good lie and plenty of green to work with, so he tries to loft the ball onto the surface and let it run back to the hole. However, he doesn't hit it far enough and it checks up and stops thirty feet short.

"It wasn't a very good shot, and now I'm really mad because I've got a 30-footer for par all because I didn't think real well off the tee. I had just made a birdie to get back to 3-under and now I have this."

He hits a decent putt, but having to play nearly six feet of break, he feels fortunate just to get it to within one foot for a tap-in bogey. Daly drops his putter to the ground and looks skyward when his 9-footer hangs on the left edge and stays up. Cook then rolls in an 8-footer for his second birdie in a row, dropping him to 4-under for the day.

A course that proudly beats its chest and basks in its tradition should not have a hole like the 168-yard sixth. It seems out of place at Riviera. Dead smack in the middle of the green is a sand trap, which means if the pin is on one side and you hit a bad drive to the other side, you've got big problems. You either putt around the trap to set up another putt, or you chip it over the sand. "The main thing is getting your yardage to the back left pin," Davis says. "The right pins aren't that hard because you almost can't hit it left of the trap when the pin is on the right because it's so far over there, but it's real easy when it's back left to come off it and hit it down the right of the bunker. It's one of those ones where you pick a club, hit it and not worry about the trap. It's been the subject of a lot of talk, but it's been there forever. If they had come in and redone the green and put the trap in, then that would be ridiculous. I still think it's ridiculous, but it's always been there so you have to learn to live with it." Davis says if he has to use a wedge on the green, he will. "Hey, they put the trap there so they have to live with a few divots in the green. Anyway, you can pitch it off there pretty easily, it's just like a tight lie in the fairway."

The pin is on the right side of the bunker, six yards in from the right edge and 13 back. Davis's yardage is 166 and when he watches Cook hit a 6-iron that lands right by the hole, he knows an easy 7-iron is the ticket. Even coming off a bogey, he feels confident here and his swing is proof as his ball comes to rest two feet from the cup. After a quick trip to the Port-A-John, Davis rolls in his birdie to get back to 3-under while Cook and Daly two-putt for par.

The par-4, 410-yard seventh is a tough driving hole because the fairway has a big hump in the middle and it drops down so you can't really see the landing area, then doglegs to the right. If it's playing downwind, Davis will usually hit a 3-wood or 1-iron to set up an 8- or 9-iron approach. The green presents trouble because it's bowl-shaped and hard to hit if you're in the rough. But a good drive will give the players a birdie opportunity and as Davis says, "You have to take advantage of the holes you can hit a short iron to on this course."

Davis chooses 3-wood and hits it perfectly down the left side. Daly hits a 1-iron and he gets away with a bad swing because his ball goes straight and winds up on the flat portion of the hump in the middle of the fairway.

As they begin to walk off the tee, Davis asks Daly, "Was that kind of fat or did you hit that good?" and Daly answers, "Yeah, it was fat. These clubs aren't stiff enough; I can't hit it solid with them."

Daly then explains what he's been going through with his clubs. He used Pings to win the PGA Championship, but at the end of the season, Wilson offered him a five-year, $5 million contract to play their Ultra irons, and he signed the deal. He sent his Pings to Wilson and asked them to make an exact copy for him, which they did, but he wasn't sure how stiff his shafts should be.

"It's hard for a guy like that who hasn't played for a long time and hasn't had the freedom to use a bunch of different clubs and expand his knowledge and figure out exactly what he likes," Davis says. "He's probably played Pings since he came out and hasn't messed around with anything else, so it's probably hard for him to tell Wilson how stiff to make his clubs. They aren't near stiff enough for him and he knows it. It was a mistake and he said they're working on getting him some new shafts. That's his problem hitting the 1-iron, his shafts aren't stiff enough swinging that hard to keep it in the fairway. Every one of his shots is high and loopy looking and I told him. I wasn't trying to give him advice, but he brought it up. A big ol' strong guy like that ought to have shafts that are too stiff rather than not stiff enough."

Davis pushes an 8-iron approach, but the shot turns out better than he first thought and when he gets to the green, he sees he's only eight feet away from another birdie. However, he doesn't play enough break on the putt and settles for a routine par, as does Daly. Cook, on the other hand, has to fight to get his par. After running his first putt two feet past, it takes him more than two minutes to get the ball into the hole as a relentlessly annoying bee badgers him every time he sets up to the ball. Finally, the bee flies away, the giggling crowd quiets and Cook rolls in his putt.

The par-4, 368-yard eighth is short, but tight. The key is to hit something into the fairway and play a short iron to the green. The fairway doglegs slightly to the right and another option is to blast a driver around the bend to set up as little as a sand wedge, but the risk of blowing it through the fairway and into trouble on the left isn't worth it. "The trees are so big, it's hard to fit it around the corner," Davis says. The second shot plays a little uphill and it's a pretty big green for a short hole. Eight is another one where you want to have a good yardage and if you do, you would expect to make birdie.

The pin today is way back, twenty-eight yards deep on a

green with a depth of thirty-four yards, so Davis doesn't think it's worth trying to fade a driver around the dogleg. He hits a 1-iron solidly to the right side of the fairway, then a 9-iron from 127 yards that lands right next to the hole and dribbles past about six feet. As he prepares to putt, a photographer takes a picture and the click disrupts him so he backs away from the shot. He looks at the line again, repeats his routine, and calmly rolls it in for birdie to get to 4-under.

"The photographers don't realize how fast I'm going to putt it," Davis says. "When I make that practice stroke, I hit the putt right after that and I'm gone. A lot of times, guys make their practice stroke, but then they take their time before they hit the putt. As long as it happens when I'm in the middle of my routine, I'm all right because I can regain my composure and start over. It's when they do it when you're hitting the putt that drives you nuts. Mark told the guy to be quiet. He has to work on his terminology a little bit and say, 'Don't take a picture, please,' or 'Stand still, please.'"

Some of the shorter hitters on Tour have trouble driving at the par-4, 421-yard ninth. A big bunker cuts into the middle of the fairway from the left and you must hit about 255 yards to clear it. With Davis' length off the tee, it's not a problem, and the big fairway that lies behind the bunker is easy to hit. The approach is uphill to a green that is shaped like a football with the points in front and in back. The green, always one of the faster putting surfaces on the course, is another two-tier job and you must get your ball to the proper level or a 3-putt is very possible. Yesterday, while putting on the practice green, Tom Kite said, "These greens will drive you to drink, so my theory is that every member at Riviera is an alcoholic or at least in AA." He must have been talking about the ninth green.

Davis pushes his drive to the right side of the fairway, Cook hits his in the middle and then Daly, using driver for only the fourth time all day, rips one long and straight and the large gallery roars. As they start to walk, Davis asks Daly if he can look at his driver.

"It looked crooked to me," Davis says. "He said he was trying to take some loft off of it so Tommy Armour bent the shaft. It looked pretty bent to me. Sometimes you can take a wooden driver and bend it right where the shaft goes into the head and it won't look bent, but that thing looks like someone wrapped it around a tree. Tommy's big on bending stuff over his knee, he and J. C. Snead are known experts at adjusting club lofts with their knees."

Davis inspects the club further, then hands it back to Daly. "I like those titanium-shafted Whales. I've been trying to get one without as much loft, but everything they make seems to have a lot of loft. I need one with about six degrees because you can hit it so high with a metal wood. My wood driver is about eight degrees, which isn't much for a wood wood."

All three players hit their approach shots within 12 feet of the hole. Davis hits an easy 8-iron from 137 yards, but he ends up 2-putting for par, as do Cook and Daly.

As he walks to the scorer's tent to review his card, Davis notices that Keith Clearwater and Buddy Gardner are both in at 6-under 65, so his 67 puts him right near the top of the early leaderboard. Cook also signs for a 67 while Daly autographs a 68.

"It was a pretty solid round," Davis summarizes. "I figure I only hit a few bad shots and the drives on two and five were the only ones that cost me a shot. Swingwise, only two bad ones all day. I didn't hit a whole lot of approach shots close, but they were all pretty solid and pretty much in the right places. All in all, a pretty good day on a hard golf course, but it played as easy as this course can play. There really wasn't a lot of wind."

And the crowd wasn't bad, either. Daly managed to fire them up occasionally, but it never got to the point where it was terribly obnoxious. In fact the worst part wasn't the rowdy cheering after he'd smoke a long drive. It was listening to the fans bitching when he didn't use his driver.

"Yeah, they weren't that bad, but I heard them hissing, though, especially at 1 and 10 when he hit 1-iron," Davis says.

John Daly is learning what fame costs. Ever since he won the PGA Championship and was thrust into the unforgiving spotlight, his life has undergone a massive upheaval. Some of it—like a 10-year exemption on the Tour and the peace of mind that comes with that; mega-dollar contracts with clothing and equipment manufacturers; his likeness splashed across the covers of golf publications and on golf instructional videos; interviews; book offers; TV appearances; endorsement deals—has been splendidly flattering and, for a self-proclaimed country boy from Dardanelle, Arkansas, just plain fun. But fishbowls are not opaque, and living inside one has left Daly naked to a probing media and inquisitive public.

All his life he had been a survivor. His father, Jim, was a nuclear engineer who was forced to bounce around the country, so the Dalys lived in California, Virginia and Missouri before finally settling in Dardanelle before John's senior year in high school. He decided to stay near his family when he went to college, choosing the University of Arkansas, where he became a two-time All-American. After he turned pro, he couldn't crack the difficult Qualifying School, so he spent a year on the South African Tour, then a season on the Ben Hogan Tour, and during this time, he was married and divorced. Playing poorly, battling depression and almost out of money, he won the Ben Hogan Utah Classic. That gave him a reprieve and he went on to finish ninth on the money list, then returned to Q-School and earned his PGA Tour Card.

But just like everything else in his life, his rookie season had been anything but a breeze. He was spinning around in circles with no clear path to follow, trying to find his game, trying to find his niche in the world of big-time professional golf when suddenly, on one of the sport's grandest stages, it all came together at the PGA. For four days he was the best player on the planet. It was as if God had dropped a compass in his pocket.

Trumpets blared the arrival of golf's great hope. Out of obscurity, here was the long-awaited hero that fans had been starving for since Jack Nicklaus, Lee Trevino, Johnny Miller and Tom Watson stopped winning everything in sight in the '70s and early '80s.

Anyone who saw Daly's victory in the PGA remembers his then-fiancée, Bettye Fulford, running onto the 18th green and giving him an all-world hug after he had wrapped up the tournament. What a heartwarming story, we all thought. Young down-to-earth guy, about to get married, struggling to keep things together, bursts through the door of opportunity and wins a major. Another "Only in America" tale.

For three months, he was hotter than the sun. CBS asked him to hit golf balls on an airport runway to see how far they would go. A former football placekicker in high school, he was offered the opportunity to kick field goals in a National Football League exhibition game by then–Indianapolis coach Ron Meyer before the idea was nixed by the Colts front office. In Denver, the Broncos let him kick at their training camp. Also in Denver, Karsten Solheim, maker of the Ping clubs Daly used to win the PGA, flew in just to meet him; Daly got pulled over by Denver police and all the cops wanted was his autograph. Back home in Dardanelle, virtually the entire town showed up for John Daly Day. In Memphis, where he now resides, he was named an honorary member at Chickasaw Country Club. He was invited to play in the Skins Game with Nicklaus, Payne Stewart and Curtis Strange. And by year's end, he was offered obscene appearance fees to play in Japan and Australia.

He was larger than life, larger than even his prodigious drives. And then, the compass went a little haywire and the fairytale turned out to be just that. We found out that Daly was not from the cloth that heroes are cut. In fact, he was a most ordinary twenty-five-year-old man. His idea of fine dining is burritos for breakfast, and burgers, fries and a Coke at any other time of the day. He likes to go out and have a few beers with his friends, he smokes, he swears. Basically, he acts the way most men his age act. But he was no longer just any twenty-five-year-old with a few vices. Now he was a celebrity, a major tournament winner, and everywhere he went it was lights, camera, action. He wasn't ready for it all.

Just before Christmas, the engagement was called off when Daly suspected that Fulford was on a gold-digging excursion. He learned that she was ten years older than he thought she was, and that for the entire time they dated, she was not divorced from her second husband.

108

He told *Golf World*, "It was pretty obvious she was after me for my money. I don't deserve it at all. The whole thing makes me look really stupid. You date a girl for a year and a half and you think you know enough about her to marry her. It's sad. I just can't believe a woman could be that mean, that crooked."

That wasn't the end of it. Last month, Fulford said she was pregnant and announced that Daly was the father. She filed a $1 million breach of contract suit and warned that a paternity suit would be upcoming. Her suit said that Daly had promised to share the proceeds of his golf career with her and support a child they had planned to have together. Daly responded by saying he didn't think the child was his, but if it was, he would fight for its custody.

Fulford, for whatever reasons, dropped the suit two weeks later and while Daly was obviously pleased, the aroma of the whole incident still lingers.

"I'm glad everything is dropped and all, but it was hard those three or four weeks," he says now as he drags on a cigarette in the locker room. "That's all I can say. I'm happy she dropped everything, hopefully it will bury itself and hopefully we can get on with our lives and go from there. Some of the questions that were asked, I just said, 'No comment.' My personal life is my personal life, it shouldn't be with the media and the fans. We're out here to play golf—that's what the media should ask about. It seemed like when I went to tournaments, that's all they wanted to talk about was the situation with Bettye. Why not talk about golf, that's why we're here. You don't see everyone involved in Jack Nicklaus' personal life or Tom Watson's. That's why I hope it's all behind me and now we can get back to golf."

What Daly is too young to remember is that when Nicklaus and Watson first hit the big time, people wanted to know everything about them, too. However, their extracurricular activities were downright boring, not nearly as juicy as Daly's.

With the Fulford incident preying on him, he made a spectacle of himself overseas. In tournaments in Jamaica and Australia, he played terribly, signed incorrect scorecards (perhaps purposely) in both places, and was disqualified. However, he got to keep the appearance money. His past problems with drinking became public knowledge and a rumor surfaced about an incident that occurred while he was in South Africa. Allegedly, he incurred heavy gambling losses at a casino and took out his frustrations by trashing his hotel room.

In the normally sterile environment of professional golf, Daly was like a chemistry experiment gone bad and in this world full of celebrity worshippers and *National Enquirer* readers, Daly's personal life, his excitingly erratic style of play and his reputation for being a party animal drove him to the top of the gossip columns. His rock-and-roll audacity didn't fit with the symphonic style of the grand old gentleman's game and the conservative followers began questioning whether Daly was the right man to be promoting as the heir to the heroes' throne.

In actuality, Daly never wanted to be a hero. But like it or not, unless he totally crashes and burns, Daly will walk through life—be it on the fairways or on the streets—with a huge, yet selective, microscope hanging above his head. Everything he says and does will be noted and unfortunately, the magnification will focus on the scandalous, not the staid. And why? Because he's a celebrity and people want celebrities to be interesting and controversial. That burden is what Daly continues to have trouble adjusting to.

"I think it's very unfair," he says. "I've had a lot of problems in the past, but it's something that I'm done with. Now, if I'm in a bar having two or three beers with my buddies, somebody will see me and say I'm wasted. I went into a bar in Palm Springs a few weeks ago and I was in there about ten minutes and the next day I hear somebody had said, 'We saw Daly and he was smashed.' I was there ten minutes. If somebody sees me drinking a beer, they think I've had a case. In college, I was like anybody else and I probably exceeded my limits of drinking beer, but I had fun in college. I don't mind that type of past, but I don't like people starting rumors when they're not true."

Davis has heard those rumors, and he doesn't know if they're true or not, but he does know why they have been unearthed.

"I had heard he was a pretty wild guy before," Davis says as he sits on a couch in the players' lounge, Coke in one hand and a bowl of cream of broccoli soup steaming on the table in front of him. "I don't know if he's any different now, I just think he gets a lot more attention for what he's doing. Before, he's missing the cut every week and no one's paying attention. If he wanted to go out and party, nobody cared. Now all of a sudden, he's so popular, everyone's watching him and when he goes out to the bar with his buddies, it ends up being thirty people rather than two or three.

"Today, he impressed me. He really didn't hit it that good, but he shot three-under. He had some patience and he was under control. If he can get that much out of his game and play like that all the time, he's going to do really well. I think he must be learning to calm down. I've heard some wild stories, like that he hits on the run and doesn't try, throws clubs, hits his driver on every hole, all that stuff, so I was prepared for anything. But I'm going to judge him on what I see him do and if he plays like he did today, then I'm going to have a lot of respect for him and enjoy playing with him.

"Ya know, I also definitely think a lot of the reason why some of the guys out here talk bad about him and pick on him is because they wish they were the ones who jumped up to stardom so fast. It's always that way, you see the superstar guys not getting along with a whole lot of people out here because a lot of guys resent them. I just think the world got going a little too fast for him and it's hard to keep up and if he keeps playing good, it's not going to slow down for him."

The only advice Davis can offer to Daly is "Good luck." Davis is leery of being a "superstar." He wants to be a great golfer and he wants to win major tournaments, but he has seen what fame and fortune can do to a person. Daly is just the latest example. He points to fellow Tour player Greg Norman and his college buddy, Michael Jordan, as prototypes.

"If I got to the point like Greg Norman, and I had played real well and gotten to be a huge celebrity, I would cut back endorsements to cut back my time. If I won the U.S. Open and The Masters, I would take what was easy and not run myself all over the place. If I could make $5 million doing a certain amount of stuff or I could make $10 million doing a larger amount, I'm going to take the $5 million and be satisfied and learn my lesson from Greg Norman and Michael Jordan.

"Sure Michael's the biggest star in the world, but if he didn't want all that, he could have not done Wheaties or Coca-Cola or Gatorade, not done a lot of it that's just money. He could have stayed away from the huge celebrity status and just been an awesome basketball player. If you push yourself to do everything that people want you to do, you'll build it up to where you can't stand it. It might run Michael out of the sport because he won't be able to take it anymore. I couldn't do what Michael does. I'd go berserk. If I couldn't say, on the spur of the moment, 'Let's go eat here' because I'm such a big star, I couldn't stand that.

"I've told my mom, my wife, my brother, my friends, if I get that famous, remind me that I said this, that I'm not going to do all that crap. Say Greg Norman is making $4 million a year. Why work that much harder to make another $2 or $3 million, why do it? I don't want to be a huge star. I want to make enough money so I can enjoy what I like to do, and I want to win a lot of golf tournaments. I'm happy with what I've got. If I win two majors, I'm not all of a sudden going to throw out all of my contracts and try to go out and make ten times as much money just because it's the thing to do. If someone says, 'All we want to do is use your name and we'll pay you $1 million a year,' fine, use it, but don't make me do commercials. You see Michael everywhere. Maybe guys feel like they have to dominate everything, maybe that's why they're so good, I don't know. I don't want to be as popular as Greg Norman. If I get as popular as Jack Nicklaus because I won twenty majors, fine, that's the way I want to be popular or famous. I don't want to be famous because I won a few majors and I went into the commercial end of it and got so famous, I couldn't stand it.

"I don't like it [fame]. That's why I live in a small town, that's why I go fishing. People say, 'How can you spend so much money on a boat?' or 'Why do you sit up in a tree and hunt all day?' Well, that's what I like to do. When I go hunting, it's the best time in the world for me. I can sit up in a tree for four or five hours, nobody bothers me. I don't have to think about golf, I don't have to think about TV cameras. It doesn't bother me so much when I'm on TV and I'm doing an interview or whatever, it's just that that's not the way I want to live my whole life. I like to just go and enjoy myself. When you have a set schedule all week long, you're always under scrutiny or pressure and being paid attention to all the time. I like to be home and playing with my little girl or hunting or working in my garage and being left alone."

Davis pauses to taste his soup. He then begins talking about Jordan and what he thinks of his friend's much-publicized desire to join the PGA Tour when his basketball career is over.

"I mean, there it is again," Davis says. "Michael doesn't need to play on the PGA Tour. But Michael's so competitive, he doesn't want to be just a good player, he wants to do whatever the biggest thing is and that's play the PGA Tour. If I could sit down and talk to him, I'd say, 'Michael, there's no reason for you to play the PGA Tour. It's a hassle, it'll drive you crazy. If you came out on the PGA Tour, it would be a madhouse for you. Why not try to get as good as you can, play the U.S. Amateur, the Porter Cup, the Sunnehanna, the North-South, all the big amateur tournaments, and wherever you're living, play the state amateur.'

"He can play all summer long in amateur tournaments—and they'd love to have him—and he could play in the AT&T National Pro-Am, the Bob Hope Pro-Am, Kapalua, Disney World, Las Vegas, he could play probably ten celebrity Pro-Am PGA Tour events plus the amateur circuits, and have a great time. He'd never have to go to the press room in a structured sense, he'd obviously get a lot of publicity, but it would calm down after he left the NBA. So I think that's what a guy like Michael Jordan would enjoy doing. Guys that are good golfers ought to look at amateur golf. There's something to be said about amateur golf over pro golf if you have the money and you don't need golf to make a living.

"Besides, there are thousands of people who have enough talent to play on the PGA Tour, but they won't make it. Everybody that has a 4-handicap wants to play the PGA Tour, but they're just not going to do it. Your name doesn't help you at all out here and a few people have found that out pretty quickly. Their names got them some exemptions on the Tour and the Senior Tour, but pretty soon that's going to run out if you can't play.

"I don't know if it would be much fun for a guy like Michael Jordan to have to go to Qualifying School with all the media hype. He can play and play really well in a normal day of golf, but he just doesn't realize the jump it's going to be in pressure and publicity, even if he is a great amateur golfer. The media is going to drive him nuts. Obviously, he doesn't need the money. Even if he was the best player on the PGA Tour, he couldn't make as much money as he could just being Michael Jordan, the person, after basketball. When he quits playing basketball, he's not all of a sudden going to quit making money, he's probably going to end up making more because he can spend more time doing other things. He'd be taking a pay cut if he came out on the PGA Tour."

Who would have thought ten years ago that Jordan would even be contemplating a career in pro golf? Certainly not Davis. He reminisces on how he first met Jordan when the two were student-athletes at the University of North Carolina, and how Jordan got his start in golf.

"I was a friend of Buzz Peterson's, who played guard on that team," Davis says, referring to North Carolina's 1982 squad, which won the NCAA championship in the Superdome when Jordan—just a freshman—hit a fifteen-foot jumper in the closing seconds to beat Patrick Ewing's Georgetown Hoyas. "Buzz and I would go out and play a lot of golf and Michael and Buzz were roommates. When Buzz would come home from class, he'd go out and play golf and Mike would say, 'Well, I'll just tag along.' He'd drive in the cart and him and some of his buddies would bet on Buzz or me or whoever the group was. That's how he first got exposed to the sport, by going out and watching. Eventually he'd start taking a club out of someone's bag and hit a shot or two or he'd putt some, and he started getting more and more into it.

"We were always trying to get t-shirts or sneakers from the basketball and football players, and I'd trade balls or whatever. I gave Michael a set of irons and I told him, 'When you get some good stuff, you trade me.' Buzz had some old woods that he gave him and I gave him some shag balls. Buzz and Michael started playing together and they played a lot."

Davis remembers that Jordan soon became proficient at ball striking, but his greatest talent was bending the rules.

"Michael got better at hitting the ball than he did at understanding the game. He didn't understand par or the rules or the etiquette. We would always try to teach him the rules and how to play, but he was so competitive, he just wanted to play and win and get the ball in the hole. If he hit one in the woods, he didn't want to go in and look for it, he wanted to throw one down on the edge of the woods like the woods were a lateral hazard. It was like the tree line was staked off and you got to drop. I can always remember seeing his big ol' arms dropping the ball over his shoulder. We always teased him that he didn't want to go in the woods because there were snakes in there.

"I'd tell him that I'd give him three shots a hole, but he had to play by the rules. He'd say OK, but after two holes he'd be breaking all the rules. Brad Daugherty [now an All-Star center for the Cleveland Cavaliers] played a lot, which was kind of funny, seeing a seven-footer out there. He loved it, but we couldn't find any equipment to fit him. We had a great time when we played. It was more just going out and having fun. Michael and Brad didn't go and beat balls or anything; we just got out on a cart and played. We had more fun drivin' the carts around and yellin' at each other than we did playing.

"I remember lots of golf cart races and almost having some serious accidents. I remember we turned one over in a big hilly fairway. I'm thinking, 'This is stupid. This guy is going to be a star and he's our whole basketball team and we're out here turnin' golf carts over. This is crazy.'"

One humorous tale involving Jordan remains Davis' favorite Jordan story to this day.

"He always liked to hit everyone else's clubs, ya know, try this putter or someone's driver or 3-wood or sand wedge. He always thought—and I'm sure he still does because most handicap golfers do—that if he could get a better club, he could get a better game. He always wanted to hit my drivers because he swung so hard that all he could hit were my real stiff clubs. One time he hit my old MacGregor driver that I'd had for years and years. It had been broken a few times and reshafted and it had seen a lot of use. We're playing one day and Michael said, 'I'm going to use your driver,' so he hit it off No. 1 and he hit it pretty good so he said, 'I'm gonna use this all day today.' On No. 2, he hits it and the head just split down the middle, the shaft broke and it went flying and he turns to me and says, 'You did that on purpose. You tricked me into using it because you knew it was gonna break.' I'm like, 'Mike, that driver's worth about $500, it's a classic club. I don't break it on purpose.' He was embarrassed more than anything. I got it fixed and was back playing with it in a week and the whole time he was like, 'He did that on purpose. It was time for it to break.' Ya know, there's never a time for a club to break.

"Anytime that story gets brought up to him, he always says that I did it on purpose, that it was a trick. Back then, he had no clue what a 1959 MacGregor driver was. It was just a club to him. That was the funniest thing because everyone on the golf team was like, 'Oh man, Michael broke Davis's driver.' I still have it. Someday I can say Michael Jordan hit this driver so hard, he broke it. Now, the club's probably worth eight hundred dollars and not because it was hit by me or broken by Michael Jordan."

Davis used to keep in touch with Jordan, but with Jordan's fame rising faster than the national debt, the North Carolina alums have drifted apart.

"I've played with him a few times since and our paths cross every once in a while and we catch up a little, but relationships between athletes are kind of strange. I have lots of friends in other sports, but I never get to see them. Anyway, calling Michael is like calling the president. He's got a network of how you get in touch with him. His first couple years, I called to see what was going on and we kept in touch, but it's just gotten harder and harder with my schedule and his schedule. It's hard to keep up with his phone number much less keep up with him, his phone number changes every couple of weeks. It's just one of those things as you go on from college, you lose touch with your friends, no matter what you do. I haven't even been able to keep in touch with my golf team friends, except John Inman, who's on Tour. It's just a natural progression of moving on to different things. It's hard for me to feel like I should pick up the phone and interrupt his busy life just to see what's going on. I tell friends of his to tell him that I said hi or congratulations and we'll send messages back and forth between people."

Jordan may have been a clown on the golf course, but Davis remembers him as being a very congenial, together person around campus and a confident, hard-working competitor on the hardwood.

"He's always been an extremely nice person to everybody. He was a fun and exciting person to be around because he was so competitive with everything he did and he's still that way. He had a lot of self-confidence, even in college. He acted very grown up, very mature. I think that's one thing about Michael and Buzz and our crowd, we enjoyed being around each other because we were more serious about our sports than most guys were in college. It's nice to be around people with attitudes like that, people who are driven. It helped me being around him, watching how hard he worked at basketball and how confident he was on and off the court; how much he thought of Dean Smith and how much Dean Smith thought of him. It was just fun being around that atmosphere."

Davis has also palled around with another of the most visible athletes in America, Boston Red Sox pitcher Roger Clemens.

"He's another guy who is very interesting to be around," Davis says. "He's even more intense than Michael. He's more driven and he has an incredible amount of self-confidence. Probably to an extreme where he thinks that everything he does is right, but you see that in successful athletes. They think they're always right and never wrong, no matter what they're doing. He just thinks that everybody else ought to be doing it his way and that's why Roger is so successful. I enjoy being around people like that."

Davis finishes his soup, gets up to get a sandwich, then returns to the couch and the subject of having to deal with fame comes up again.

"Roger is the type of guy who thinks that if he's been wronged, he's not going to back down. I've seen Roger in public a lot. And if I was Roger Clemens, I'd punch a lot more people than he has. If I was as big as Roger Clemens, I'd have punched them for him. People just get so obnoxious with a big celebrity like that. And Roger is not like Michael Jordan. If I go up to Mike and say, 'Hey, let's go to Friday's and have a beer and get something to eat,' Michael would say, 'I can't do it; I can't get into that situation. Let's try to find someplace where I know the restaurant and I know the owner and we can get a place where we can be by ourselves.' Whereas with Roger, if I said, 'Let's go to Friday's and get a beer,' he'd say, 'All right, let's go.' And if you get Roger

Clemens in a restaurant or a bar, people are going to come up to him and talk to him and ask him why he threw at so-and-so or why he gave up that home run or why he hit that off-duty policemen, and then they're going to ask for his autograph.

"It's amazing, you'll be in a restaurant and they'll have no idea that Roger Clemens is coming and all of a sudden they have baseballs and pictures. Roger said it happens all the time. How can people be sitting in a restaurant and have a baseball? I guess they run down the street to Wal-Mart and buy all the baseballs and then come back. It's a madhouse. We were sitting in a restaurant one time, my family and his family, and people just come up and interrupt conversations. They want to sit down, want him to sign everything, it gets crazy. Then if he bumps into somebody, they want to fight.

"He's one of the nicest people around. If you called him up and said, 'Roger, I need you to do something,' he'd do it. He's just an intense competitor and he doesn't want to compromise his life-style or his kids' life-style. He's not going to say, 'Kids, we can't go to Disney World because the fans are going to bother me,' he's not going to do it. He's going to put on his shorts and his cap and sunglasses and he's going to take them to the park. That's just the way he is and you have to admire the guy for wanting to lead a normal life. And I'll bet at least once a year, Roger is going to get into an argument or a fight or a shoving match or something, just because he's not going to back down from at least trying to be a normal person. He has all this money and all this fame, but he's still just a down-to-earth guy from Texas who plays baseball."

Davis spends the next hour in casual conversation with a number of players while Robin spends time with some of the wives. Finally, at around three o'clock, he tells Robin to take the car, drop off Mark at the Holiday Inn, then pick up Lexie at the nursery while he goes to the fitness trailer to work out. She asks how he's going to get back and he says that he'll catch a ride with Jeff Sluman. She walks with him to the trailer, gives him a kiss, then she and Mark and Colyar Persons get in the car and drive off.

Robin has purchased the *Phantom of the Opera* tape and she

inserts it into the deck and turns the volume up, and then she and Colyar talk over the music while in the backseat, Mark just minds his own business and relaxes.

The nursery is full of action as little munchkins are busy playing with toys or coloring. Lexie sees her mother and runs over and hugs her leg, then Robin lifts her up and gives her a kiss as Mary Ann Isley, who is acting supervisor of the nursery, greets Robin.

Isley's daughter Deborah owns Friends Forever, a child-care company based in Phoenix that the L.A. Open has contracted to provide nursery services for the players' children. Friends Forever has been present at the Phoenix Open for six years, but Deborah Isley has started to branch out and this is the second year her company has come to Los Angeles.

Isley provides high chairs, strollers, toys, books, tables and chairs while the tournament provides suites in a hotel and enlists volunteers to help take care of the children. Mary Ann Isley is here to supervise because Deborah is a schoolteacher back in Phoenix and can't get to Los Angeles until tomorrow night.

Nursery set-ups on Tour vary from site to site, but Robin flatly states that this situation is one of the best there is.

"I wish they were all this good. They do a great job here," Robin says.

Robin has difficulty convincing Lexie that it's time to go, but she eventually succeeds and they drive back to the Guest Quarters. Meanwhile, Davis finishes chugging away on the versa-climber and he and Sluman, accompanied by Jeff's father, George, leave Riviera for the day.

At about the same time, Wayne Levi is led into the press room to discuss his opening 7-under-par round of 64, which has him in the lead.

For Levi, this is a breakthrough round. He had won four tournaments in 1990—an unheard of accomplishment these days on the competitive PGA Tour—and became only the fifth player in history to accumulate $1 million in earnings in a single season. He was the unanimous choice for Player of the Year. But as much as

119

everything went right in 1990, everything went wrong in 1991. Levi fell from second on the money list to 87th. He switched from Wilson clubs to Yonex and never quite got comfortable with his new irons. He placed in the top 10 just three times, missed more cuts than he made and admitted that he became lackadaisical, thinking that his great play in '90 would simply carry over to '91. It didn't.

However, thus far in '92, thanks to a hot putter that has him second in the Tour's putting statistics, he has won $76,312, more than a third of what he took home in all of '91.

"My wife [Judy] told me, 'You ought to be ashamed of yourself the way you played last year,'" he says in the press room. "It was kind of embarrassing because I never put anything together. She told me to just go out and play solid and keep making the cuts and there was no reason why I couldn't pick up where I left off in 1990. You probably need someone to tell you that, someone as close to you as your wife."

Levi, who just turned forty last week, has never been one to beat balls on the range for hours and hours. Unlike many players on Tour, Levi's whole life does not revolve around the golf course. Winning is everyone's goal out here, but when Levi can leave a venue with a healthy chunk of change, all has not been lost if he hasn't won. He wouldn't be happy never winning again, but taking home six figures a year is a nice consolation prize.

He enjoys his time at home with his wife and four children; he likes sitting on his couch at his home in New Hartford, New York, watching sports on TV; and he follows the stock market as avidly as an analyst on Wall Street. In the past, Levi played golf when he felt like playing and he never seemed to have any direction or career goals. He won eight times in his first eight years (1978–85), then went five years without a victory—and golf became a job. He spent more and more time away from the Tour, his head buried in the financial section of the newspaper.

Then in 1990, his putting stroke caught fire and coupled with his typically strong tee-to-green play, Levi put together a stunning campaign. He also realized that winning was fun and to compete on today's Tour and continue to win, he had to start putting more time into his game. He rededicated himself to golf and while things

Davis Love III and his brother Mark line up a putt. *(Gary Newkirk/ALLSPORT)*

Site of the Los Angeles Open, Riviera is one of the most beautiful golf
courses in the world. *(Top photo, Mike Powell/ALLSPORT; bottom, Gary
Newkirk/ALLSPORT)*

Davis chats with PGA Tour Commissioner Deane Beman. *(Gary Newkirk/ALLSPORT)*

Davis chips out of the rough, with the ever-present television cameras nearby. *(Gary Newkirk/ALLSPORT)*

Tom Sieckmann displays his unusual putter.
(Gary Newkirk/ALLSPORT)

John Cook. *(Ken Levine/ALLSPORT)*

John Daly grips it and rips it. *(Stephen Dunn/ALLSPORT)*

Fred Couples. *(Gary Newkirk/ALLSPORT)*

Sandy Lyle and his wife/caddy, Jolande. *(Gary Newkirk/ALLSPORT)*

Late in the final round, Davis follows the flight of the shot. *(Gary Newkirk/ALLSPORT)*

Friends and rivals, Couples and Love share a moment during the tense final round playoff. *(Stephen Dunn/ALLSPORT)*

didn't work out in '91, he appears to be back on track this season.

"I've changed my attitude," he says. "I had been kind of slack. I'd play a week, take two weeks off, play a week, take three weeks off. But I'm getting too old to come back here and pick up where I left off like I used to. The guys are just too good and the overall strength of the fields is so much better."

This afternoon, he began with a birdie on one and a bogey on two, then hit approach shots to within five feet on five, six and seven and made all three birdie putts to get to 3-under. A bogey at eight was offset by a birdie at nine, and then he birdied 11, 12, 14 and 18 on the back.

"It was a pretty solid round," he says. "I kept the ball in play. It was one of the better rounds I've had this year with my irons and I rolled the ball well on the greens."

When play concludes, Levi's 64 is still the best score of the day and it puts him one ahead of Keith Clearwater, Buddy Gardner, Doug Tewell, Mark Carnevale and Chris Tucker. Tom Sieckmann is alone in seventh at 66 while Davis is one of nine players tied for eighth at 67.

It is another simple evening for the Love family. Davis spends about an hour catching up on some mail. He fills out a couple of forms for future tournament housing, pays a couple of bills, takes care of his British Open entry form, looks at some of his fan mail and signs some trading cards that have been sent to him and puts them back in the self-addressed envelopes that have been included.

The plan is to go to one of the local shopping malls, then go for a bite to eat, but as Robin and Lexie are getting ready to go, Davis gets involved watching his alma mater, North Carolina, play Florida State. He tries to stall Robin so he can watch the rest of the game, but she doesn't bite so he turns off the TV and takes the family to the mall.

Davis and Robin purchase a couple of outfits for Lexie at Gap for Kids, then they buy her a school set to go with the wooden train set she had received for Christmas. Now, Lexie has had enough shopping and she wants to go back to the hotel so she can play with her new toy. Mom and Dad manage to keep her interested in staying out long enough to eat at a small diner, but Lexie isn't completely happy until she gets back to the room and unpacks the school set. Davis turns on ESPN and sees that the Tar Heels got smoked, so in retrospect, going shopping saved him some aggravation.

By playing in San Diego, Davis has screwed up the original schedule he had mapped out prior to the start of the season, so tonight, he and Robin begin to revise. When they decide on a plan, they then figure out what details have to be taken care of, such as airline schedules, housing, nursery and transportation.

When all of the technicalities are sorted out, Robin puts Lexie to bed, then turns on the TV and settles in for a big night on "Knots Landing" while Davis flips through a telephone-book-sized catalogue of Harley-Davidson after-market add-on parts that Dillard Pruitt has given him.

There is never a mention of the golf tournament all night long. Davis hears that Levi is leading and that he is three shots behind, but it does not matter. He played well today and that's what's important. Being close to the lead is only a bonus. There is a long way to go, and his only concern is to go out tomorrow afternoon, maintain the same type of rhythm he had today and hit good shots. Then the score will take care of itself.

5　Friday

Earlier in the week, Jim Murray, the esteemed columnist for the *Los Angeles Times*, addressed a subject that has been perceived to be one of the problems plaguing today's Tour: The absence of a true superstar, someone who is a dominating player as well as a captivating personality.

Murray has been covering the L.A. Open for decades and he reeled off some of the past winners of the historic tournament such as Macdonald Smith, Harry Cooper, Bobby Cruikshank, Craig Wood, Jimmy Demaret, Tommy Bolt, Byron Nelson, Ben Hogan and Sam Snead. He forgot Arnold Palmer, Lloyd Mangrum, Tom Watson and Lanny Wadkins.

In recent years, rather ordinary players such as Ted Schulz, T. C. Chen, Doug Tewell and David Edwards have been victorious at Riviera, prompting Murray to write: "Either the L.A. Open has changed or golf has. The game has become as formless as a county fair claiming race. It has gotten so you know what to expect. The unexpected."

Davis wants to know what's wrong with that.

"If you went to every tournament when Nicklaus, Palmer, Trevino and Player were playing, you could go to Vegas and bet $1 million that one of those guys was going to win and at the end of the year, you'd have $30 million," Davis says. "These days, you could guess who's going to win in every tournament and you might not get any right unless you put Fred Couples down for every one and you might get two right. There's so many good players now.

"Fred has dominated over the last eight months, he's been in the top 10 almost every tournament, but he's only won twice, B.C. and Memphis. He played great in the majors, but he didn't win any of them. Nobody will argue with you that he wasn't playing the best. You take a Nicklaus stretch like that and he might have won two majors and three or four others because the competition wasn't as good.

"There was a quote I saw where Nicklaus said that if Fred and I had played back when he played, we would have won all the time because we hit it so much farther than everyone else, we have great short games, there weren't as many great players back then and the courses were different. These days, you have different guys winning all the time because there are so many great players."

Looking at the first-round scores from yesterday provides a shining example of the depth on Tour today. Riviera is a supreme test of golfing skill, yet Levi had a 64, five men shot 65, a total of 55 shot in the 60s and 88 players were at par-71 or under.

"You can play on the hardest course in the world, but someone is still going to shoot 6 or 7-under," Davis says. "I don't care where it is, unless the wind conditions just won't allow it. And still, on a day like that if the average score is 78, someone will shoot 2-under. There's too many great players."

The age-old argument is that today's players aren't as good as yesterday's. You look at the scores that win in tournaments that are played on the old-style, traditional courses like Riviera and they aren't much different than they used to be. And then you take into account the modern equipment today's players use and the immaculate condition the courses are in ("Their fairways are better than some of the greens we used to play on," Sam Snead has said) and right away, the claim is made that the old-timers had to be better if they could shoot the same scores with lousy equipment on poorly maintained tracts.

"People are missing the point on scores," Davis says. "The winning scores aren't that much different, it's just that there's the winning score and then there's two guys at the next number and three at the next number and four at the next number. There's so many more guys shooting those low numbers than there used to be. I remember ten years ago in Atlanta, they were shooting 20-under-par and they're still shooting 20-under-par. Only now, there's more guys doing it. Andy Bean shot 23-under one year

[1979] and then the next score was like 15-under. Now, if somebody shoots 23-under, there's going to be a 22, some 21s and 20s and 19s."

Another popular theory about the Tour is that it suffers from a lack of rivalries. Walter Hagen and Gene Sarazen; Hogan had Nelson and Snead; Palmer, Nicklaus, Lee Trevino and Gary Player had each other; Nicklaus later had Johnny Miller and Watson. The question today is: Who has whom? The answer is everyone has everyone else.

It's not Fred Couples vs. Paul Azinger, or Curtis Strange vs. Greg Norman. It's those players against every other card-carrying Tour member. In the '30s, '40s, '50s and '60s when golf was developing its lore in this country, prize money was nearly non-existent and players had to win to keep the bill collectors at bay. Back then, rivalries were cultivated and players grew to hero status because those men weren't only battling to win a golf tournament, they were fighting to keep food on the table. Today, professional golfers don't have to win to live comfortably. Every player yearns to win, but the need to isn't as great. Bobby Wadkins has been playing eighteen years and has never finished first in a Tour event, yet he has won more than $2 million. Snead won 81 times on the Tour, played nearly five decades and earned $620,126! That total would have placed him 14th on last season's money list, just ahead of the $615,765 that 28-year-old Billy Andrade won.

But money isn't the only reason for this alleged paucity of rivalries.

"I think so many people are looking to say, 'Okay, Fred Couples and Paul Azinger are gonna battle it out.' But you're not going to see those two names on the leaderboard at the same time very often. Again, it's because there are too many good players. Anyone can win. And another reason is there's so many more tournaments. Back then, the big name guys were together so many times. Now, there's a tournament every week of the year. You're not going to get Couples and Azinger or whoever together as often because they don't play in every tournament."

Perhaps the biggest reason why people think rivalries have died is because today's players are like one big fraternity. Most are friendly with each other and that amiability is often misinterpreted.

"People see us hanging around and palling around and they ask, 'Doesn't that hurt your game because you guys are all such good friends?' Well, no, it helps our game. I'll go out and play with John Cook and I look forward to that, that's gonna be fun. It's better than going out with a bunch of guys who don't want to talk and it's miserable out there. It's hard to play for four hours and not talk. I don't know how Nick Faldo does it. I'd shoot myself before I lived my life like him.

"The whole reason I play golf is because it's fun and it's a great way to make a living and I enjoy the competition, not because I'm so intent on shooting a great score that day that I feel like if I have fun, that's not the way to play good. If I'm miserable, I play bad, it always goes together."

But while the players generally get along, there isn't one man on Tour who doesn't want to beat the pants off everyone else, no matter who it is.

"If you're duking it out with a friend or two and trying to win a tournament, you're not standing there and saying under your breath, 'Duck hook it into the water,' or 'Hit it out of bounds so I can win,'" says Mark Calcavecchia. "You're just playing your own game and trying to play the golf course and if one of your friends wins then after it's all over, you're happy for him. But if I lose, I'm pissed. I want to win."

Says Davis: "Mike Hulbert and I are great friends, but at Kapalua last year, it got pretty quiet. There wasn't too much 'Nice shot,' or 'Chip it in.' There wasn't much friendliness about golf, and I was terribly disappointed that he beat me. But we might have talked about what we were going to do for dinner while we were walking. That's always been the way golf has been; it's no different now than it ever was. I know that when I went out with my dad, that's one thing that I enjoyed seeing was that everyone was friendly to each other and enjoying themselves. You can go back and ask Nicklaus and guys from his era, and Sam Snead and his era, it's always been that way.

"The same thing happened with me and Ian Baker-Finch at the Heritage last year. I was so happy that I was winning the golf tournament going down 18 after he hits the ball in the bunker, but I felt so bad for him because he bogeyed the last two holes and didn't win. It's hard to explain. I'm sorry he didn't win, but I'm glad I did.

"It's hard to pull against people out here because everybody's friends for the most part. That was the most enjoyable round of golf that I've played in a long time and you can go ask Ian about how he felt and he'll say the same thing, even though I won and he lost. The next week we were still friends and there was no love lost.

"He came up to me afterwards and said that he was so impressed that I had a triple bogey on that one hole and came back and won. He liked the fact that my putting routine had stayed the same on the last few holes and I told him what I had learned from my sports psychologist, Bob Rotella. After that, he started working with Bob. Now here's a guy who made everything that week until the last two holes of the tournament, he putted better than I did, but he wanted to work with Bob Rotella because my routine stayed the same on the 71st hole and 72nd hole and his didn't. He talks to Bob about it and then he goes on and wins the British Open. It wasn't like he walked off the course and said, 'Damn it, Davis beat me, I'm mad, I'm going to go beat balls.' He came right back and asked me, 'How did you feel about this and that, and who are you working with and what are you doing on your routine?' and he went and tried to improve himself. And he improved an already great game a little bit more.

"If we were trying so hard to beat each other and we didn't talk all the way around and he was upset when he lost, he would have never learned what he learned, he wouldn't have talked to Bob and he might not have won the British Open. That's a big part of it. Going out and playing to win, but still being nice about it.

"That's the greatest thing about the Tour is you can walk in the locker room and there can be twenty people in there and you can go sit down with any of them and eat lunch and have fun. Or you can go in a restaurant knowing there's probably a bunch of Tour players in there and you can probably go find someone to sit and have dinner with without any problems. People always say, 'Oh, it must be hard to be away from your friends and be gone all the time,' but when I go home, I miss my friends because they're all out on the Tour. I'd say half of my really, really close friends, or even 75 percent of them, are Tour players and I'm sure it will always be like that.

"Of course it's a different sport. In the NBA, your team plays my team, we go at it for forty-eight minutes and then we leave. It's a clash of teams fighting it out. But out here, we play with one or two guys for four or five hours and the next day you get one or two other guys. It's the gentleman's game or whatever they call it.

"I don't think you can go out and play golf and be clashing against somebody. You've got to ask them to do things on the golf course while you're playing, like moving their coin over or asking if you can get a drop or replace a ball and stuff like that and if you don't get along, it's going to be hard to do. You almost can't play without talking to your partners and it's also boring if you're out there playing in a twosome or threesome on Sunday and the only person you're talking to is your caddie. You want to enjoy who you're playing with. It's nice to look at the pairings and say, 'Oh, I'm playing with Fred Couples. This is going to be fun,' or 'I'm playing with Tom Watson. He's a nice guy; this will be a fun day.' It's hard to draw a bad pairing out here. You almost always enjoy who you're playing with and if you don't know 'em, like with Daly, odds are you're going to enjoy playing with him. It's a big family almost. We're staying basically in the same hotels, we're all at the course, all the kids are going to be in the nursery together. My little girl will meet another little girl and she'll say, 'Mommy, I want to play with so-and-so,' and you say, 'Who's that?' and we have to go over and find out whose kid that is. We've made friends just from kids playing together. And for the younger guys who aren't married and don't have kids, it's like a big fraternity of young guys doing whatever they want to do, whether it's going out to dinner, going to the bars, going to the movies, baseball games or whatever."

It is 10:30 and Davis feels well rested after a surprisingly long night of sleep. Normally, he and Robin get up when Lexie awakes and that's usually very early, but this morning, she stayed down until almost 9:30. In the players' lounge, he sits down with Tom

Purtzer and Billy Ray Brown and eats breakfast while carrying on playful conversation about a variety of subjects, one being John Daly's habit of rushing around on the range.

Davis takes his time at breakfast, unlike yesterday, and when he finishes, he says good-bye to Robin and Lexie, walks outside and meets Mark in front of the locker room. Then the two brothers walk down the hill to the range.

The first thing Davis does when he gets to the practice area is reach into a pocket in his golf bag and take out a bottle of Advil. He was fine when he got to the course, but now, a headache has developed. He pops two painkillers into his mouth and washes them down with water. To his right, Daly is hitting wedge shots while balancing a cigarette between his lips. Davis pulls out another tool of the trade, sunscreen, and he applies the lotion to his face and neck as he watches Daly swing.

It is now 11:15, a little more than a half hour before game-time, so Davis leisurely gets loosened up, first arching his back, then twisting it from side to side. As he stretches, his former caddie, Mike Harmon, walks over and says hello and the two speak briefly about the course. Davis asks Harmon what he has planned after L.A. and Harmon tells him that he's taking a couple of weeks off, so Davis invites Harmon, who also lives in Georgia, to stop by his house in Sea Island next week and Harmon tells him maybe he will.

Feeling comfortable and confident about his swing, Davis only spends about 15 minutes on the range before walking back up the hill to the putting green. A look of discomfort settles over his face because his headache is really bothering him. Mark hands him his putter, tells him that it's 11:30 and this surprises Davis because he thought it was a little later than that. Now, he has almost twenty minutes to kill before he tees off.

The sky is slightly overcast, but the sun is still shining through the haze, which isn't helping Davis's head. It is already about 80 degrees and it's going to peak near 86 by mid-afternoon. Coupled with a larger Friday afternoon gallery, Davis knows this has the makings of a struggle. Already, fans are in a rambunctious mood on the clubhouse terrace that overlooks the first tee and the marshals can be heard telling the crowd to be quiet as each threesome attempts to tee off.

Davis strokes a few long putts back and forth on the green, then begins rolling 5- and 10-footers. He looks calm, even bored, as a very slight breeze ruffles his olive green pants and white shirt.

Daly, dressed in a turquoise shirt and white pants, appears on the green and the fans gathered around the outskirts of the surface give him encouragement. He spots Davis, walks over and says hello, then goes about his business. John Cook arrives a few minutes later, dressed in tan pants and a white shirt.

After brief hellos, there is no conversation between Davis, Daly and Cook. All are in their own little worlds as they mentally prepare themselves for the day ahead. At 11:45, a marshal announces that the three are due on the tee, and on command, the caddies hoist the bags over their shoulders and begin walking to the tee, golfers in tow.

The same pre-round routine takes place with the players and caddies getting organized in front of the tent, and then one by one, the players are introduced to the crowd. Right away, it's obvious that the crowd is more vocal than yesterday's gathering. As Cook prepares to tee off, he has to back away when the noise distracts him and he shoots an icy glare over his shoulder. He repeats his routine and is able to complete it, but he pushes his drive into the first cut of rough on the right side. As he walks back over to hand his club to his caddie, Andy Martinez, he says to Davis, "Assholes," referring to the loudmouths on the terrace.

Davis grins, then takes his place between the tee markers. After he is introduced, he greets the applause with a wave, then directs his attention to the green expanse in front of him. His head is still throbbing, but he manages to put the pain out of his mind and unloads a terrific drive that nearly reaches the end of the fairway more than 300 yards away before coming to a stop in the first cut of rough on the left side.

Almost as if Cook and Davis were the undercard, the crowd really gets noisy as Daly steps up. The fans overlook the fact that he is going to hit 1-iron again on this hole and give him a rousing ovation. The marshals signal for quiet and just as it becomes silent, a rebel on the terrace yells, "Pump it up, John," and that draws laughter from the rest of the crowd, but no reaction from Daly. He does the same thing as yesterday here, pulling his drive into the left rough.

As the three players stroll down the fairway, the scoreboard shows Tom Sieckmann in sole possession of first at 8-under while Sandy Lyle is 7-under and Keith Clearwater 6-under.

From 238 yards out, Cook elects to use his 4-wood and this shot also stays to the right and he misses the green. With 232 yards left, Daly hits 2-iron and he manages to catch the front left edge of the green, but is still seventy feet from the hole. Davis, with a mere 192, only needs a 6-iron and he strikes it perfectly. The ball hits to the left of the pin and stops quickly just eight feet from the cup and the crowd at the green cheers approvingly.

Moments later, they whoop it up again as Cook dazzles them with a brilliant chip to one foot and he taps in for birdie to go to 5-under. Daly rolls his eagle putt to within three feet of the hole and decides to mark.

While Cook and Daly were playing, Davis had been studying his putt and now, he crouches down and looks at it again with Mark peering over his right shoulder. Davis knows it will break right and it will be fast, he knows he has to be careful with this putt. But he isn't. It gets away from him going down the hill and runs almost four feet by the hole.

"It didn't have a chance to go in because it was going too fast, I just powered it right through the break," he says. An excellent eagle opportunity is wasted and now, the birdie attempt is no gimme. He looks carefully at the line, settles over the ball and knocks it dead center to get to 5-under. Daly completes the hat trick for the group by making his birdie to get down to 4-under.

The tee at No. 2 has been moved a little bit today, back to where it normally is, so Davis doesn't have to choose between driver and 3-wood. There's no doubt that driver is the club, and besides, based on what happened to yesterday's pulled 3-wood, he prefers to keep that club in the bag here. He hits a little fade out into the middle of the fairway, the same shot Cook played just before him. Daly uses his 1-iron and pulls it into the rough.

Daly hits 4-iron from 209 and he leaves it short of the green. Then Cook hits a perfect 4-iron from 184 and is pin-high to the left with a 10-footer for birdie. From 178 yards uphill with a little wind in his face, Davis uses his 5-iron and tries to fade the shot because the pin is cut only four yards from the right edge and eighteen back on a green that is thirty-three yards deep. However, he cuts it too much and he winds up on the hill to the right of the green. "Not where you want to be," he says.

After Daly hits a poor chip that scoots past the hole by thirteen feet, Davis takes out his L-wedge and while Daly is marking, he tests how the club will cut through the grass on the hill. He takes four swings, then walks down to the hole and checks to see if there are any impediments that need to be laundered away. Satisfied that the area is clean, he strides back to his ball, stares at the section of fringe that he wants to land the ball in, opens the face of the club so he will get more loft, then swings through and picks the ball out of the deep grass. It plops into the fringe, releases down to the pin and stops eighteen inches away. Cook says, "Wow." Davis replies with a smile, "New L-wedge," and Cook smiles back and says, "That'll do it."

"With all new clubs, the grooves are sharper obviously when you first get them so you can plan for the ball to stop quickly like that," Davis says. "When you're hitting a wedge or a 9-iron to a green with a new set, you figure it's going to back up a little so you plan on it."

After Davis taps in for par, Daly saves his par by making his slippery downhill putt, then Cook leaves his birdie attempt on the lip and he too taps in for par.

Davis explains how he played the flop shot.

"On a sidehill, you're swinging down the hill, so no matter how open you get the face, the ball's going to come out low. People are always trying to hit it high and they kind of pop it straight up. You have to plan on it coming out low and spinning rather than high and lobbing. Even if you have a 60-degree loft and you open it up to 70 degrees effective loft, when you hit it you take a 25-degree hill into account and now you're back to, like a 9-iron. And if you're uphill, it's the same thing, but the other way, you have to plan on it going up."

At the 441-yard third, Cook drives into the middle, Davis rips a good drive to the left side of the fairway and Daly's struggles continue as he pulls his tee shot twenty-five yards off the fairway into the left rough. "I'm hittin' it like shit and I'm gettin' tired of it," Daly grumbles after banging his clubhead into the ground.

When he gets to his ball, it looks like a gathering at a grave site as a crowd of people surround the Maxfli. Daly's not dead, though, because the ball is not in a bad lie. He waits as Cook rails a 6-iron onto the green, fifteen feet to the left of the hole and Davis hits a solid 7-iron from 164 yards that checks up seven feet below the cup. Daly's caddie, Greg Rita, gives him a yardage of 155, so Daly elects to use 8-iron. As he swings through, the mourners start dancing as Daly's ball soars toward the green. However, silence falls when he comes up short and catches the upslope of the front bunker and the ball buries itself in the sand.

Daly has to slam his club deep into the sand to get at the ball, and he is successful because it comes out and clears the lip of the trap, hits just in front of the pin and then rolls six feet past, which is a pretty damn good effort considering his lie. He manages a small grin as he steps out of the bunker.

Cook two-putts for his par, then Davis strokes his birdie putt into the middle of the cup to get to six-under.

"It broke a little right, just outside the hole, one of those ones where you had to carry a little speed into the hole because the easier it was, the more it would break," he says. "I hit it hard and kicked it right in there."

Daly then makes his second straight superb save of par, swishing his six-footer.

On the tee at No. 4, Davis and Mark talk about finishing while they wait for the group of Ben Crenshaw, David Peoples and Billy Ray Brown to clear the green. Two birdies in three holes has helped, but full credit must go to Advil because Davis' headache is under control.

Once play resumes, Davis has to take a few extra practice swings to compensate for the ten-minute inactive period. The hole is playing 234 yards with a slight breeze in his face so Davis hits his 1-iron. The ball flies out low, underneath the wind and skips off the back edge of the green and comes to rest 10 feet behind the fringe. Like yesterday, Cook comes up short, this time using a 3-wood. And Daly hits another lousy drive, pulling a 2-iron way left, down the hill and across the cart path.

All three players have again missed this hard-to-hit fourth green, but also like yesterday, they each rely on outstanding short games to escape trouble.

First, Daly hits a delicate chip that bumps onto the green and trickles down within seven feet of the cup. Cook then chips from the fringe and his ball gets to within two feet. Then Davis outdoes both of them by using his L-wedge to chip in from about forty feet for his third birdie of the day.

The crowd cheers raucously and as Daly's caddie, Greg Rita, pulls the ball out and tosses it to Davis, Davis just smiles and waves to the fans.

"I wanted to land it just on the green and let it land real soft and roll down to the hole," he explains. "I hit it and I said, 'Oh gosh, it's gonna be short.' As soon as you hit it, you know where it's going to end up. But then it hits on the collar of the fringe—which it does all the time for some reason—so now it's going too fast and I'm thinking it's five feet by. I'm going, 'Whoa, whoa, whoa,' but it hit the pin and went in. It was a good break, bad break thing. I was looking at having to make a testy putt for par, to making birdie. I was pretty happy."

For the third hole in a row, Daly makes a terrific one-putt par, then Cook finishes his work in the required three strokes.

At seven-under, Davis has pulled to within one shot of Tom Sieckmann and is tied with Fred Couples and Sandy Lyle for second place. His head feels fine, his game is in gear, and because Daly hasn't even used driver yet, the crowd has not gotten overbearing. So far, it has been a pleasant stroll around Riviera. Of course, now he has to play the 419-yard fifth.

"I'm thinking I've got this side wired and now all I have to do is keep it in the fairway, so that's what I'm thinking on five," Davis says. "I'm not gonna hit driver because I hit it too far yesterday, but I wanted to hit the same shot, low down the left side and cut it back to the middle. So I take 3-wood, but once again, I hit a low pull, it runs down over the hill and now I have no shot. So now it's back to work."

Yesterday, his ball stayed on the sidehill. Today, it has slid down to the bottom and the birch tree is right in front of him so he can't aim at the flagstick.

"I tried to duck hook it around the tree with an 8-iron, but I caught a little bit of a flyer and they don't tend to curve very much because you get the grass on the clubface and the ball shoots out and there's no sidespin, it goes straight. So it didn't draw hardly at all." His shot sails over the back right side of the green and ends up 60 feet from the hole in the deep rough.

Davis explains how to bend the ball around a tree or another obstruction.

"It comes from a lot of practice, first of all," he says. "You can't just go out and do it, you have to practice it. To hook it, what you do is aim to the right and swing down the starting line with the clubface closing as you hit the ball. As far as strengthening the grip, different guys do different things. Azinger can't get his grip any stronger so he couldn't do it, but some guys like José-Marie Olazabal with a real weak grip, he'd have to strengthen it so he can turn it over. Some guys play it back in their stance and try to roll their hands over, some guys just naturally flip their hands over and put hook spin on it."

Using his pitching wedge, Davis lofts a good chip that squirts to the right because he had to dig down to get the ball and that put some cut spin on it. Still, he is left with a 6-footer uphill, "which, after that drive and second shot I hit, isn't bad. I had an easy putt, but I didn't even give it a chance. I put a weak stroke on it and missed it. That was disappointing because anytime you get a putt at it for par after all that mess, it feels good to knock one in and you get to the next hole and you feel like you can make anything."

Daly's streak of missed fairways and greens continues, but his streak of one-putt pars ends as he misses from thirteen feet and his bogey drops him to 3-under. Davis is back to 6-under after his bogey while Cook 2-putts for par to remain at 5-under. On the leaderboard, Sieckmann, Lyle and Keith Clearwater all share the top spot at 8-under.

Davis is still 2-under through five, though, and his confidence certainly hasn't been shaken. The pin at No. 6 is cut on the left side of the green, thirteen yards back and five from the left edge. Davis watches as Cook hits a 6-iron into the left bunker, leaving himself a tremendously difficult task to get up-and-down. Davis' yardage is 163 with a slight breath of wind in his face so he opts for the 7-iron. Surprisingly, he hits it twenty-five feet past the hole and he too has a tough chore to get down in par. Daly finally hits one straight, an 8-iron that stops six feet behind the pin.

Cook gets into the bunker and finds his ball stuck in the upslope. The hole is just twenty-five feet away, and on the other side is the bunker in the middle of the green. Cook has to attack the shot, but he must be concerned with blading it across and into the other sand trap. He takes his time, the crowd hushed all around the green. He pulls his wedge back, then slashes it into the sand and the ball floats out gently, hits five feet in front of the pin and rolls five feet past. It is a great shot.

Davis has a downhill 25-footer breaking about two feet to the left. He needs to feed it into the hill so the ball will run down there, but he misses his target and runs off below the hole and stops six feet short.

"Another weak putt and now I'm still downhill with a putt that'll break about a foot so I'm thinking, 'Oh great, nice going, you were going great and now you're sitting here with a six-footer for par.'"

Here, Davis goes to school. Daly is putting on virtually the same line for birdie so Davis watches him miss over the right edge. He lines himself up, picks his target, rolls the ball right at it and he finds the cup for a nice par.

"I played it half in and half out," Davis says. "If it breaks, the ball will go in and if it doesn't break, it still has a chance. This one didn't break, but I hit a solid putt and it fell in.

"I always watch to see how the ball rolls around the hole. Even if a guy is putting from the other side of the hole, his ball might come up to the hole and miss, keep going and then break and it'll show you where the slope is on your side. Even if it comes up and breaks two feet and goes in, then you have to think that yours is going to break a pretty good bit coming from the other side. So I always watch, unless I look at my putt and know exactly what it's going to do.

"If I look at it and say, 'Yeah, that's just outside the hole, I know that thing is going to break two inches to the right,' then I'm not going to even watch him because he might hit a pull or catch it unsolid and his will break even more, say three inches, but still go in. Then I play a three-inch break, catch mine solid and my ball goes right through the break. So if I think I know what it's going to do, I'll just go ahead and putt and not even pay attention to his."

Davis has one thought on his mind at the 410-yard seventh: "Get the right club in my hand. I should have hit 1-iron off the fifth tee, and something was wrong at six. Just get the right club in your hand, you're swinging so good."

The right club is a 3-wood and he couldn't have walked out to the fairway and dropped it any better. His tee shot stops on the flat portion of the hump in the middle of the fairway.

With 152 yards left, Davis is stuck between an 8- and a 9-iron so Mark makes up his mind for him.

"I asked Mark if he liked 8 or 9 and he said, "Use 8 because if you hit 8, that hill [on the green] is going to stop it.' That's what happened. I hit it past the hole, but it spun back and I end up with a two-footer for birdie. If you've got a backstop, you ought to use it, because if you hit a perfect shot, it'll stop right by the hole. If you hit it a little too far like I did, it'll come back down the hill a little bit. That was kind of lucky, but I've had just as many land by the hole and suck back fifteen feet. If you asked an outside observer what shots were lucky, he'd say I was lucky for chipping in at No. 4. But this one was a lucky shot."

Cook and Daly make pars and Davis's birdie gets him to seven-under and into a tie for third place with Couples and Clearwater, one shot behind Sieckmann and Lyle.

The 368-yard eighth is mere target practice for Davis and Cook. Each hits a 1-iron into the middle of the fairway. Cook sticks a 9-iron approach from 134 yards to three feet and Davis follows with a 119-yard pitching wedge to two feet. Each makes birdie.

Daly isn't as fortunate. He pulls a 1-iron into the left rough, pulls a sand wedge left of the green, then duffs his chip, leaving himself a 15-footer for par from the fringe. He misses that and taps in for bogey to fall to two-under.

Daly's frustration is beginning to show. He watches Davis and Cook hit perfect drives at the 421-yard ninth, then grabs his driver out of the bag and treats the fans—who despite his troubles today are still 100 percent behind him—to an absolutely mammoth drive that carries past the spectator crossing in the fairway that is supposed to be unreachable. He is twenty-four yards past Davis, who had hit his tee shot very well.

The pin is tucked on the back level of the odd ninth green, five yards from the left edge. It is a hard green to judge because it sits sideways and is shaped like a football and the ridge that runs through the middle divides it into two small parts. Cook hits a 7-iron from 154 yards to the back edge and Davis follows with a 9-iron from 140 that hits near the back, then spins back down to within six feet of the hole. Daly hits a sand wedge from 116 that checks up twelve feet underneath the hole.

Cook rolls his putt three feet past and marks, Daly misses his birdie attempt and taps in for par and then Davis gets ready to stroke his putt. Cook had been on the same line, but he provides Davis with no help.

"I thought I would learn off Cook's, but he hit it too hard to the right, so it was like I'm not even going to pay attention to that one. It didn't matter, though. Mark's reading the greens real good here. He had some trouble at the AT&T and at Torrey Pines because the water was affecting it, but he's doing a lot better here."

Davis and Mark read the putt as right edge and they are right. The birdie is Davis's third in a row, sixth of the day, and it gives him sole possession of first place at 9-under. Cook misses his 3-footer and settles for a bogey that drops him to 6-under.

On the 10th tee, Davis is aware that he is in the lead. There are scoreboards everywhere on the course and even the players who claim they try never to look at a scoreboard, find it difficult not to. But just because he has the lead, he is not going to change his gameplan. It's still much too early in the week to be concerned with leading the tournament. So as he squints to see the green at No. 10, he notes that the pin is up and in a position where he can take a crack at driving the green. Forget about playing safe, he wants to keep trying to make things happen.

With that strategy in mind, Davis must wait until Crenshaw, Brown and Peoples clear the green. He drinks a cup of water, then walks over to the cooler, pulls out an apple and takes a refreshing bite. The temperature has climbed into the mid-80s and the humidity is higher than it has been all week. He is feeling a little uncomfortable, but the water and apple replenish his energy.

There is an even larger gallery following the group now. Because they are back near the clubhouse, more people are milling around and knowing that Davis has surged into the lead, curious fans have wandered over and will walk with him to see why he's playing so well. He also seems to have won over a few fans. Earlier in the day, and all of Thursday, everything Daly did drew a roar. With Davis having made six birdies already, some fair-weather fans have switched allegiances and are rooting for Davis.

After a five-minute wait, Davis swings a little too fast with his driver and pulls the ball into almost the same position he was in yesterday. He tries to locate the ball, but he can't tell exactly where it is. He knows that it probably isn't in trouble, but the hole is cut just five yards from the left edge so his chip might be a difficult one. He pulls his tee out of the ground, comes over to where Mark is standing with the bag and just shrugs his shoulders, saying nothing.

Cook pushes a driver into the right rough, a place you really don't want to be. Then Daly electrifies the crowd with his second awesome drive in a row, reaching the front edge of the green.

When Davis locates his ball, he grins and says to the encircled crowd, "I have to carry the water," and laughter erupts. His ball is about twelve feet behind a brick water fountain that stands about four feet high. Actually, getting over the water fountain is the least of his problems. His ball is nestled down in the rough, and an overhanging limb from a palm tree will force him to play a bump and run chip, rather than a lob shot. Because the pin is cut close to the near edge, getting a bump and run shot close is going to be difficult.

"I was more concerned with the limb rather than just getting up there and hitting the shot," Davis says after stubbing his chip and leaving it in the rough, six feet shy of the green and twenty-one feet from the hole.

Cook is in the same predicament because he had flown a sand wedge over the left side of the green and, like Davis, is lying two with a tricky uphill chip. Davis is away and, using a 9-iron, he lightly punches his ball out of the rough and into the slope. It hits with a little backspin, but climbs over the ridge before running out of gas three feet short. He slaps his clubhead to the ground, upset that he hasn't got a tap-in for par.

Cook wishes he could do as well. With a slightly steeper angle of approach, Cook uses his sand wedge with the intention of lofting his ball further up the ridge. However, he catches it fat, it gets halfway up and then rolls back down toward him and he watches in dismay as the ball comes to rest in the fringe, barely ten feet from where he had originally been. Cook is frustrated. He is coming off a 3-putt bogey and now he has an uphill 15-footer for par.

While Cook quietly burns with anger, Daly finally gets to attempt his eagle putt. He leaves it three feet short and the crowd groans. Cook composes himself and gives his par putt a good roll, but it misses wide to the right and he taps in for bogey. Daly makes his birdie to get to 3-under, and Davis follows suit by sinking his three-foot par-saver.

"You make sure you concentrate on that one because if you miss it, then you make bogey like Cook did on a hole you're expecting to birdie," Davis says. "After leaving the first chip short, it was nice to get it up and down and get out of there. That's two days in a row that I've had to get up and down on a pretty easy hole all because I didn't hit a good drive."

The tee shot at No. 9 seems to have pumped Daly up and at the 566-yard 11th, he uncorks another big drive and even though it goes into the left rough, the gallery gets into an uproar. They are still murmuring when Davis is ready to hit, so he takes a little extra time going through his routine. When silence is finally achieved, he prepares himself to swing. He hits it solidly, but the ball wiggles into the first cut of rough on the right. Cook places his drive into the right-center of the fairway.

Davis finds his ball sitting up in a nice lie. The pin is just eight yards from the front edge on a green that is thirty yards deep, and knowing that his swing is really in sync today, he decides to try and jump on a 3-wood with the hope of catching the front of the green. He almost pulls the shot off, but doesn't quite get enough of it and his ball fades to the right and gets caught in the rough, ten yards short of the green.

Daly had already lined a 1-iron to within forty yards and now Cook decides to lay up with a 4-iron and, like Daly, hits the fairway. Cook pitches to twelve feet behind the hole, then Daly stiffs one to six feet. But this is Davis' show today. He uses his L-wedge and almost holes his shot, leaning back and dropping his club in disbelief as the ball rolls six inches past the right edge. He walks up smiling and taps in his seventh birdie in 11 holes, bringing him to 10-under, then watches from the side of the green as first Cook, then Daly, match his birdie.

A stretch of five straight holes that usually play into the wind starts at the par-4, 415-yard 12th. With the huge eucalyptus trees bordering the right side of the fairway, the drive must be positioned in the middle. An errant drive that forces a player to scramble is dangerous because the barranca runs across the fairway about fifty yards short of the green; any ball that ends up in there is probably better off in Death Valley. The grass and scrub is shin high and extricating a ball from there is painfully difficult, in some cases impossible, so players have to take an unplayable lie, tack on a penalty stroke to their score, go back to the fairway and drop and play their next shot from there. The right side of the green is protected by a sand trap and on the left, a huge sycamore that one longtime member says "has caught more rubber than any LA freeway gutter" stands menacingly. Two good shots are needed here.

And Davis produces them. He hits a perfect drive down the middle and then a solid pitching wedge 15 feet behind the hole. His putt is a little downhill, but it doesn't matter today. Almost effortlessly, he rolls it dead center for yet another birdie to get to 11-under. Daly 2-putts from twenty feet and Cook, now back on track after his stumble in the middle, makes a seven-footer for birdie to get back to 6-under.

"I really felt good over that one," Davis says. "I knew I was flowing good then. That's a great feeling when you feel like you almost didn't even try and you still pour it right in there. You know you're not grinding to make it, it's almost nonchalant, real simple. When you're grinding, you're not going to make many anyway, so you're better off freeing it up. That gave me five birdies in the last six holes, so that's a helluva stretch at Riviera."

The course record at Riviera is 9-under 62 shared by Fred Couples (1990) and Larry Mize (1985). Davis is already seven-under for the day and just when he starts thinking about this, his brother provides some amusing relief.

After driving into the left-corner portion of the fairway at No. 13, Davis' rhythm gets slowed down because Cook has pulled his tee shot into the trees on the left and Daly's drive is shorter than usual because he caught a tree limb on the left side. While he waits for Cook to map out his shot, Davis checks his yardage and the wind conditions. After Cook pushes a 4-iron into the bunker that guards the right front of the green and Daly hits a 7-iron onto the green, eighteen feet to the right of the pin, Davis notices that the wind doesn't seem to be blowing as hard as it had been moments before. He turns to ask Mark what he thinks, but Mark isn't paying attention.

"I'm telling him that I saw a flag up on the hill and it was blowing in, but it wasn't blowing that hard, and he was over looking at some girls in the gallery and that kind of loosened me up," Davis explains. "He's good about not getting too intense. He's real relaxed, good or bad, and that's good for me."

Davis elects to hit a 9-iron from 139 and it winds up ten feet past the hole, another excellent birdie opportunity.

Cook finds his ball stuck on the upslope of the bunker. He can't control it out of there and winds up in the back fringe, staring at a 25-footer for par. He chooses to pitch and he stubs it, leaving himself a 6-footer for bogey. The Tour's leading money winner is having a tough day.

Daly hits an excellent putt that hangs on the lip and refuses to drop. He smiles, walks slowly to the ball and the fans start blowing in a mock effort to create a breeze so the ball will fall into the cup. It doesn't work and he has to nudge it in with his putter. Davis then puts a weak stroke on his birdie attempt and has to tap in for par. Cook saves bogey, but drops to 5-under.

The 14th is playing 179 yards and Davis considers hitting 6-iron, then goes with his 7-iron, but comes off it a little and he mutters, "Oh, lovely shot," as the ball climbs unusually high and fails to get back to the pin, falling sixty feet short of the flag. It is a difficult putt, but Davis gets the ball to within a foot and walks away with a hard-earned par. Daly and Cook also 2-putt for par.

Davis is talking to his ball on the tee at 15 as well. Yesterday on this demanding 447-yard dogleg right, he was able to drive over the corner of the dogleg. Today, he wants to aim down the left side and fade it back to the middle, but as soon as he swings through with his driver, he says, "Bite, bite." The ball, as usual, doesn't listen and it caroms into the left rough.

When he gets to his ball, he sees it is in a bad lie.

"You want it to sit up, but when it doesn't, it's not like you got a bad break, you just didn't get a good one. It's typical when you miss a fairway, you're going to pay for it."

With 166 to the hole, he tries to chop it out with a 7-iron, but he swings too hard trying to knock the grass out of the way and "as usual, when you swing hard in the rough, the club gets caught up and it goes left." Here, he catches a break because his ball hits the tree on the left side of the green and drops straight down, leaving him a reasonably clear shot at the pin. Had it not hit the branches, it would have flown way over the green.

Daly and Cook each arrive in regulation from the left rough and they wait as Davis calculates how he wants to play his third shot. The cup is cut five yards from the left edge and his ball is another twelve yards off the green. He chooses his L-wedge and tries to chip the ball to the fringe and let it trickle to the hole, but he doesn't hit it hard enough. It lands in the rough and barely manages to skip to the fringe.

Bogey is in the making and he knows it, so his main concern is to stop the bleeding, get this putt close, take the bogey and get out of here. He has a downhill 17-footer and he says, "You want to try to make it, but you don't want to blow it by. You don't want to take a double and ruin your day."

He reads the putt as straight, but it breaks to the right, rolls three feet by and the look on his face clearly reveals that he's pissed because he has done what he didn't want to do—leave himself a missable putt. He marks his ball, watches Cook make a four-footer to save par, then studies his bogey-saver and steps up and calmly rolls it in. He has slipped to 10-under and any thoughts of breaking the course record have evaporated. Daly completes his par, and the threesome walks to the 16th tee.

The par-3 16th drops downhill, and getting the yardage is tricky because the prevailing wind that blows against the players often catches shots and dumps them in the front bunker. That bunker has a high lip and hides part of the green so it gives players the illusion that the green is smaller than it really is. It's a matter of picking the right club and stroking it confidently.

Today, the hole is playing 165 yards and there isn't any wind. Daly is up first and he hits a hard 8-iron that ends up ten feet below the hole.

"When I saw that, I knew I could hit an easy seven and it would be perfect," Davis says. "A lot of time on par-3s, a guy will get up and hit and you don't even need a yardage, you see a guy, you know how he plays, you see him hit and you know what you have to do. I hit the easy seven pretty good." He ends up fifteen feet behind the hole. Cook pulls a 6-iron twenty feet left of the pin.

Cook rolls his birdie attempt a foot past and cleans that up for par. Davis squats down and squints at the hole while Mark stands behind him, squinting as well. This putt isn't going to break much, and Davis is boiling over in determination to make up for the bogey at 15. He puts a good stroke on the ball and when it gets halfway to the hole, he knows it's going in and it does. The fans cheer as he retrieves the Titleist and waves in acknowledgment.

"Anytime it's inside the hole, you feel like all you have to do is hit it solid and it shouldn't get out," Davis says. "When it's going to break a lot, a lot of things can happen like a bad bounce that throws it off line and makes it break more. Everyone always says the hardest putt is a straight putt, but I don't know how that can be. The hardest putt is the one that's breaking big time. I hit a good putt and I felt again like it was another good stroke and I knew it was in as soon as I hit it. That was a good birdie to make coming off a bogey."

His ninth birdie of the day gets him back to 11-under, giving him a three-stroke lead over Tom Sieckmann and Sandy Lyle, who have both finished their rounds and are at 8-under 134. Sieckmann has posted a 68 today and Lyle a 67. Fred Couples is also done and after a 67, he's at 7-under 135, currently four shots behind Davis.

Once again, Davis is shocked by Daly's length off the tee after Long John blasts one at the 17th.

"I hit a pretty good drive right in the middle, but Daly just crushed one," Davis says. "He was thirty yards past me. I went to Mark and said, 'I killed it and that'll be thirty or forty yards from him,' and Mark said, 'If you're lucky.' When he killed that, I just told myself to hit my normal drive, don't try to kill it, he's probably gonna knock it on the green in two and you're not."

Cook followed with a perfect tee ball into the middle, then he pushes a 4-wood into the right rough fifty-five yards short of the green.

The hole is cut five yards from the left edge, twenty back on

145

a green that is forty yards deep. Davis is out far enough in the fairway where if he had to, he could try to reach the green, but considering the way he is playing, he decides it's smarter to get close, then chip and putt for his birdie. He aims for the right side of the bunker that juts out from the left side of the fairway, hoping to get his ball in front of the green where he'll have a good portion of the putting surface to work with when he hits his chip. However, he swings a little fast, catches the ball solid and pulls it a bit. The shot clears the trap easily, bounds through the rough on the left side and almost gets to the green, a mere ten yards away.

Daly can't take advantage of his big drive as he pushes a 1-iron into the right rough short of the green.

Davis watches Cook hit a sand wedge to ten feet, then sees Daly hit the same club to eight feet. When they finish marking, he surveys the terrain in his path. Rather than loft a wedge up there, he elects to play a 9-iron bump and run shot because the pin is just above the ridge that runs through the middle of the green and he wants to get his ball rolling up rather than bouncing. However, he hits it a little too hard and he skips it ten feet past, leaving himself a slick downhill putt.

"That was a mistake," he says. "You'd rather be ten feet below than even four feet above. But then again, you have to get it over the ridge or it'll roll all the way back down and then you'll have a thirty-footer."

His putt breaks right-to-left about two inches, but he misses it and settles for a rather disappointing par, as do Cook and Daly.

As Davis walks to the 18th tee, Robin comes over with Lexie in her arms and she tells Davis she's taking off before the traffic starts. She's been out on Tour long enough to know that her husband's day is far from over now. Because he's leading, he'll have to go to the press room, plus do other one-on-one interviews, so rather than wait around, she's going to leave and let him catch a ride back to the hotel with one of the other players. She gives him a kiss and then he bends down, kisses Lexie and tells her that he'll see her in a little while.

Daly still has honors and his errant drive with a 1-iron winds up in the trees on the right, reminding Davis that the round isn't complete and it isn't time to lose his concentration.

"I just wanted to hit a solid drive. That's the whole key to the hole," Davis says. "Daly blasted it right into the trees and that'll start you thinking about what's over there, so I just gathered my concentration and hit it right where I was aiming and really killed it. It seems like whenever I'm just trying to hit a smooth one in the fairway, that's when I hit my longest ones."

How big was his drive? He has just 159 yards left to the hole and because he's a little pumped up, he decides to pull 8-iron out of his bag as he waits for his partners to play. He had never hit anything less than 6-iron here in the past. After Daly pitches back to the fairway, he hits a 7-iron to the back of the green, leaving himself a 40-footer for par. Cook then puts his second shot twenty-two feet to the left of the hole.

Now it is Davis's turn and the large crowd that has given the grassy amphitheater surrounding the green the look of a stadium starts hooting and hollering and pleading with him to stick one in tight. He obliges. His ball flies right at the pin, hits two feet to the left of it and rolls eight feet behind the hole. The crowd had roared when the ball landed, then continued to cheer raucously when it finally came to a halt.

Robin sees the shot and decides to wait until Davis finishes the hole before she bolts.

Davis and Mark walk up the fairway, the fans cheering all the way, but they're not hearing the noise because they are wrapped up in conversation.

"That's what people don't understand," Davis explains. "We're not grinding the whole time we're out there playing. We were coming up 18 and I was telling Mark that it's going to take me a long time before I'm ready to go so I told him to take the bag up to the locker room and catch a ride with someone because there was no reason for him to wait around. Then he tells me what we're going to do tonight. We're making plans for after the round. It wasn't a whole lot of talking about making the putt or how we're playing.

"It's different than people expect. They think you're out there all pumped up and thinking about the putt, but when you get done playing, you still have to take care of stuff, get back to the hotel, arrange dinner and all that. At the end of the round, that's what you're thinking about."

When he reaches the green, the cheering gets even louder and with a smile, he waves to the fans.

Daly nearly makes his long par attempt, leaving it a foot short and the fans groan loudly when the ball stops. He walks up, waving to the cheering crowd, and taps in for bogey to finish off an indifferent round of 70.

Cook's birdie attempt breaks at the last instant below the hole, and he too strides up and bumps in for his par to complete an equally up-and-down round of 70.

Davis and Mark are a bit indecisive on what this putt is going to do. Davis knows that the softer he hits it, the more it will break. The question is, how soft should he hit it?

"You always tend to play more break than you need when it's downhill because it always seems to dive off," Davis explains. "On this one, I didn't. I hit it just soft enough to take the break. At first, it looked like it wasn't going to, but at the last second it dove right into the hole."

Another huge roar from the gallery and after he takes the ball out of the cup, Davis holds the ball in one hand, his putter in the other, and raises both arms in the air in triumph.

An 8-under-par round of 63, one shot off the course record and a four-shot lead after two rounds. It has been quite a day.

Daly and Cook both walk over and shake his hand and he thanks them for their kind words. He then hugs Mark and the fans continue to applaud him.

As he walks toward the scorer's tent, he stops Daly's caddie, Greg Rita, and reminds him about the shafts in Daly's clubs.

"I told Greg, 'You have to get him out of those clubs. They're holding him back, the shafts aren't stiff enough,' and he said, 'Yeah, you're right.' I told Greg I'd already told John, but to make sure that he does it. Greg is working hard for the guy and I think he appreciated that I said something. He knows I wouldn't say anything if I didn't feel strongly about it. If John hadn't agreed with me on the course, I wouldn't have said a thing, but he said it before I even said anything, so that's when I jumped in.

"I figured it out yesterday why he was hitting it all over the place and I just wanted to tell him every time he hit a bad one. Greg's doing a great job working with John and helping him. It's easy for a guy to get upset and not push his club people to get him the right things, so if your caddie is bugging you about it, you'll go ahead and get it done. I want Greg to tell him, 'Look, it's not you, it's the clubs. Let's get rid of them.' If I knew John better, I'd tell him to go get his Pings back because he played better with them."

After talking to Rita, Davis accepts congratulations from the officials working in the tent, then carefully attests his score to make sure everything is in order. When that is done, he sees that Robin hasn't left so he tells one of the marshals to let her inside the ropes so they can talk. They decide that Robin will drive Mark back to his hotel so he doesn't have to scramble for a ride, and Davis will find his own way back. He kisses her goodbye again, shakes Mark's hand, then composes himself for the media blitz that is about to begin.

Just outside the ropes, two TV reporters, electronically attached to cameramen, are impatiently waiting to interview him. When he ducks under the ropes, they pounce on him and he spends three minutes blandly discussing his round. Davis knows the media. He understands that the print journalists need more in-depth conversation and he knows that TV reporters just want simple, easy-to-edit, sound-bite material. So that's what he gives these two vidiots. They thank him and walk away, seeking their next victim, leaving Davis to fight off the horde of autograph hounds. Luckily, he isn't besieged for very long because a Tour media relations staffer has a cart ready to whisk him away so he won't have to walk through the large crowd. He hops on and away they go to the cart barn located next to the first fairway which, during L.A. Open week, serves as the press center.

The barn is divided into three areas by temporary walls. As you enter, the front section is the interview room. In the back, there is a platform for television cameras and in the front, also on a platform, there are two upholstered lounge chairs, one for the golfer and one for the Tour PR man, separated by a coffee table that contains a microphone for the player to hold while he discusses his round, and a decorative bouquet of flowers. There are also flower displays on each side of the platform. In between the two platforms are folding chairs for the reporters to sit on.

The middle portion of the press center is three times the size of the interview area. This is the main working area where the reporters write their stories. There are ten rows of long, narrow, maroon cloth–covered tables set up, with portable computers, briefcases and telephones scattered about. Stapled onto the front wall are off-white cardboard score sheets with every player in the field listed and his hole-by-hole totals neatly scripted in. In the front left corner is a scoreboard, with up-to-the-minute standings that show how many shots under or over par the leaders are and what hole they are on. In the back, the media officials from the Tour—this week Marty Caffey and Lee Patterson are on hand—and the L.A. Open press room staff—Bob Levey and Jan Fambro—are seated at a table that is littered with press releases, messages, statistics books and other reporter-friendly information. To the left of where Caffey and Patterson sit, a fiberglass radio booth has been constructed so that when the various broadcasters go on the air, they are shielded from the noise elsewhere in the room. There are also two large color televisions, a table containing five credit-card phones, and six IBM computer monitors that are linked directly to tournament scoring control and enable the reporters to obtain information on any player instantly.

The back section of the press center is the dining area. A caterer has set up tables and chairs and along the temporary wall is a buffet spread complete with lunch meats and cheeses, breads, fruit, beverages and desserts.

Davis is escorted into the interview area and takes a seat in the chair to the reporters' left.

"It was real close to perfect," he says of his round. "I made 10 birdies and when you're playing that good you figure you shouldn't make any bogeys, but I hit two bad drives [at Nos. 5 and 15] and they cost me two shots. Those were my only mistakes. I felt like I was hitting it real good going into the tournament, and I played pretty well yesterday, and then today, I was real patient and played a solid round. One of the keys to the whole day was every time that I did something that wasn't perfect, I did something good coming right back. After the bogeys at 5 and 15, I birdied 6 and 16.

It gives you a lot of confidence knowing that if a U.S. Open or a PGA comes here, you can shoot real low scores if you're patient and hit it well.

"This was as good as I've played on this hard of a course since Firestone last year. I've played some real good rounds and shot some low scores, but it's all relative. Of course, the course was probably playing two shots easier than it normally would so you have to take that into consideration. I wouldn't say I putted great, but I made a lot of putts that you're supposed to make. I just hit it so well that I couldn't help but shoot what I did."

A reporter asks Davis if he feels comfortable with a four-shot lead.

"You know the scoring is going well if you're 12-under after two days, so you have to keep playing well because someone else can come out and shoot 63. You have to go out and play and try to birdie every hole, that's how I got here. I've birdied almost half of the holes [17 of the first 36] I've played the first two days, so there's no reason to do anything else. Sometimes people might say that'll get you in trouble, but it can get you in a lot of good places if that's all you're thinking about is making birdies. It gets you thinking about the same thing on every hole, playing the best way you can to make birdie."

Another reporter asks if he was consciously trying to avoid getting into a driving contest with Daly.

"I'm not in his category as far as length, nobody is," Davis answers. "I'm not concerned with how far my drives go, I just want to win golf tournaments. I'm paying more attention to hitting fairways than how far the ball goes."

He is then asked what it was like with the huge gallery following him around because of Daly's presence.

"It's amazing how many people come out to watch," Davis begins. "I was pretty prepared to just go out and pay attention and concentrate and not let the fans get to me. I knew if I started playing bad, it was going to be hard, especially if I got frustrated. I knew today was going to be a lot worse than yesterday, yesterday was just a warm-up for today. The rest of the week is going to seem like cake after today. They were getting fired up, but it wasn't that bad. If John was hittin' it good, blastin' it down there every time with his driver, it would have been a lot worse."

When the general session is over, he talks briefly on air to a radio reporter, then spends about fifteen minutes talking to Jaime Diaz of the *New York Times* and Gary Van Sickle of *Golf World* about a variety of subjects, mainly the *Golf Digest* article that examines the state of the Tour.

Finally, a tournament volunteer gives him a cart ride back up the hill to the locker room and after he gathers his belongings, he goes to the transportation department to arrange getting a ride home.

Daly is sitting at his locker, as usual, smoking a cigarette. Play is concluded for the day and he stands at six-under 138, tied for 17th place, eight shots behind Davis. As far as he's concerned, he's lucky to still be playing this weekend even though he has made the cut by four shots.

"It was probably the worst I've hit the golf ball in months. It was gross," he says with a look of disgust on his face. "I'm usually a good 1-iron player, but Davis is right, my shafts are a little weak and I have to work on that right now."

Despite his erratic play, the fans remained entrenched behind him and for that, he is thankful. He has a peculiar relationship with the fans. It seems as if the mob gets too unruly and at times they tamper with his concentration. But at the same time, he draws inspiration from them. He loves all the support and it sure beats playing in front of nobody, which was the case before he won the PGA.

"They don't bother me, are you kidding, I love it," he says. "They don't drive me crazy. I feel like I drive them crazy when I play like shit, like today. When I'm playing great, they're all up and when I'm playing bad, they're kind of down. The great thing about it is I had my head down all day and I figured those people were going to leave me. But when I got my head down, they never gave up on me, even though I was so damn embarrassed. I mean I play golf for them.

"It's hard to keep my head up when I'm hitting 2-irons thirty yards left and 8-irons thirty yards left. I feel good about myself that I'm hanging in there, but it's so damn frustrating that I'm not hitting any fairways or greens. I love all the support when I'm playing good, but it's hard to hit the shots that I've hit the last two days and feel proud of myself. I feel like when I play bad, I don't let myself down, I let the fans down. That's how much I care about them and I want to play for them."

As it turns out, Davis probably could have walked out to Sunset and hitched a ride and gotten back to the hotel quicker than relying on the transportation department. A female volunteer in her mid-40s needs to take one of the courtesy cars home with her tonight so she will have a way to get back to Riviera tomorrow morning, and she offers to drop Davis off at the Guest Quarters. She is given the keys to car No. 88 and she and Davis go to the lot where the car is supposed to be parked. She checks the cars on the left side, Davis the right side, but car 88 is nowhere to be found.

Davis notices two cars in an adjacent lot, so they walk up to those, and again, neither is car 88. Davis knows car 88 has to be here, and he finally realizes what's going on. Obviously, she must not have seen the number when she checked the cars in the first lot. He takes the keys and tells her to go back to transportation to make sure they gave her the right set of keys and he says he'll check the cars again. Sure enough, car 88 is the second one in line on the left side. She missed it. So he loads it up and pulls around to pick her up.

"Where did you find it," she asks, and he replies politely, "Well, it was up there on your side."

Davis stays in the driver's seat and the volunteer gets in on the passenger side. As he starts zipping through the traffic on Sunset, she asks him, "Do you like driving fast?" and Davis says "Yeah." She then informs him that she teaches driver-education courses and he says, "Then you're probably not going to like my driving."

When he gets back to the hotel, she slides over into his seat, wishes him well, then drives away. Slowly.

Davis goes up to his suite, opens the door, and is greeted by Robin who is wearing a "Where have you been?" look on her face. After some general conversation about the day and some fun-time with Lexie, they go to pick up Mark and head to an Italian restaurant for dinner.

Like last night, there is no talk about golf. The hottest topic is how many pieces of pizza Lexie will eat.

"There's not a whole lot of golf talk when you're playing good or bad," Davis says. "That's what people don't understand, we're not out here playing golf all the time, thinking about golf every second of the day. We're living our lives. Golf is our job during the day and when it's over, most everyone wants to get away from it. Even when my teacher is here and we're working on golf, we go to dinner and we don't talk about golf. We might talk indirectly about it like, 'How's Freddie doing?' or who's playing what tournaments, but we don't discuss rounds or the swing."

After the meal, it's straight back to the hotel, and Davis reads Lexie one of the books she has brought along. Robin joins them on the bed and by the time he finishes reading, both are asleep.

Davis isn't tired so he stays up and watches *Cheers*, does some reading, and eventually, he too closes his eyes for the evening.

6 Saturday

It is a problem that is not intrinsic to professional golf, but one that is societal in its scope. It is the act of stereotyping.

See a blond woman and you think she's dumb; see a white man in his early forties with long hair and you connect him with Woodstock; see a black man driving a Cadillac in a run-down neighborhood and you assume he's a drug dealer and/or a pimp; the guy who cuts you off on the highway is automatically an asshole.

We don't associate pretty blonds with masters degrees; we don't consider that perhaps the forty-something white man is just overdue for a trim; we don't allow that maybe the black man in the Cadillac is a suburbanite who made a wrong turn; perhaps the guy on the highway was just daydreaming and lost his concentration for a second.

Stereotyping occurs every day in our lives. Ask any caddie on the PGA Tour.

"The groundwork was laid long ago and it's just a matter of getting over that," says veteran Mike Harmon, a clean-cut forty-two-year-old white man and former banker who smashes people's perceptions of what a caddie should look or act like.

"A lot of it was racial with a lot of the caddies back then [in the '60s and '70s] being black," says another veteran looper, Mike Carrick, who taught school before becoming a full-time caddie. "But just as much as race, caddies had a bad name—possibly justifiably so—as being drunks, reprobates, dishonest bums, you name it. There wasn't much money to be made back then so it didn't attract a very high-class individual, so maybe a lot of those views were valid. But not anymore."

Still, caddies face a never-ending battle for respect and

dignity. Perhaps that is because the role of a caddie has not changed through the years and remains very much the same as that of the medieval serf. His sole purpose is to serve the master, in this case, the player.

The caddie carries the heavy golf bag from car to locker room to driving range to putting green to first tee to 18th green. He cleans the clubs, picks up and replaces divots, rakes the sand traps, takes the flagstick out of the hole and puts it back. If the player wants to play a practice round at 6:30 A.M., it is the caddie's job to be there. If the player wants to hit balls on the range for two hours, the caddie stands dutifully next to the bag drying off the practice balls, doing more club washing, or, if he knows enough about his player's swing, helping him figure out a certain problem. If the player wants to work on his putting for an hour, the caddie retrieves the balls and tosses them back. The caddie performs just about any task asked of him. He's a mother, a father, a spouse, a maid, a cheerleader, a psychologist, a therapist, a masseuse. He even babysits on occasion. Have we left anything out? Most assuredly.

"The caddie is a subservient role, it's the role of a servant," admits Andy Martinez, John Cook's caddie.

Says Jim Mackay, who is carrying for Scott Simpson: "You have to care about nothing else but your pro and making him more comfortable and happy so he can go out there and play to the best of his ability. You do whatever it takes."

Caddies know the job description before they apply and they can live with that reality. What they can't swallow is the hackneyed stereotyping of their profession. It's one thing to work like a serf, but to be treated like one is an entirely different matter.

"After a couple of years with the caddie association, we started bragging that we'd worked our way up to second-class citizens," says Carrick, who, along with former bag-toter Joe "Gypsy" Grillo, formed the Professional Tour Caddies Association back in 1981 in an effort to fight the discrimination and degradation that caddies faced at nearly every stop on the PGA Tour. "The association had to work to overcome that stereotype about caddies and we had to upgrade the image of the caddies.

"The worst-case scenarios were a few tournaments where

you had to wait in a holding area on Monday and Tuesday until your player arrived. You weren't allowed to enter the grounds. When your player showed up, then you were escorted onto the course to meet him. You caddied and once he was finished playing, you were escorted off the grounds. We had parking problems, we had nowhere to gather while we were waiting to play, we had nowhere to eat, we couldn't even watch the rest of a tournament if we missed the cut.

"We had talked about the problems for a long time. Whenever the caddies would get together, we'd bitch about the treatment and say we've got to do something about it, but we never did. Finally at the TPC [at Sawgrass] in '81, myself and Gypsy decided to call a meeting and see what the interest was. We put up notices and we had about seventy to eighty guys show up. We figured if nobody showed, we'd forget about it, but obviously there was an interest.

"The conditions had been getting better little by little each year, but once we organized it was amazing how fast the changes came and within the last few years, it's even gone beyond that. At the start, we brought to the players, the Tour and the sponsors the problems that we had. A lot of times they were problems that they didn't realize existed. Like parking. We had to park with the public, take shuttle buses in and try to make your tee time. The Tour and the sponsors were concerned that they couldn't fit all of our cars, but once we communicated to them that we didn't have a lot of cars because guys usually drove together, then it was much easier to find a place reasonably close to the clubhouse area.

"Our point was that we are a part of the tournament, we're there every week, and if you're taking care of the player, part of that is taking care of the caddie because if we're late or we arrive hassled, that affects the job we do and that in turn affects the player. We weren't attempting to be like the player or be on the same level as them, but I feel as if we're on the next level below them. I realize the problem with the sponsors, he puts up a lot of money and he wants a good parking spot, but with them, they don't have a time schedule. If he's coming out to watch, if he's a little late, it's not affecting his job, his livelihood."

The association also pushed for, and was granted, a place to park its recreational vehicle, which serves as a hangout for the caddies. Gypsy is paid by the association to drive the motor home around the country and provide a food, folks and fun atmosphere. The standard fare is coffee and donuts in the morning, sandwiches in the afternoon and entertaining conversation and friendship all day long.

"I think the best thing that's ever happened to caddies in general is the association and being able to have our home on wheels," says Harmon. "You're not a player and you don't have the privileges of a player. You're allowed inside the ropes to work with the player, but that's it. You have to always keep that in the back of your mind, that you're just the caddie and there are situations where you're not granted the things that they are given. It's not hard for me to accept. Especially now that we have the RV. It's a place where we can go when the weather is bad or we can grab a cup of coffee before an early morning tee time, or get a bite to eat while our player is in the clubhouse eating or making phone calls or whatever."

The association also instituted a photo identification system so that when a caddie arrives at a tournament site, he has an ID card to prove who he is so he can enter the grounds.

"It used to be when a caddie would get to a tournament, he would have no form of ID," Carrick says. "The Tour didn't provide anything, so you'd get to the gate and the guard would ask for your badge. Well, we'd try to tell them that we had to get inside to register so we could get it and the guards would say, 'You can't get in without a badge.' A lot of time you'd be fighting before the week even started. So we got a picture ID card and the various tournaments put it on their security list. Most of the tournaments now don't use caddie badges, they use our card.

"The tournament sponsors have been the best as far as helping us out. They realized that what we were doing was helping them as much as us. Now we have the motor home, which gives the guys a place to go so they're not hanging around the clubhouse area. Also, if a sponsor has a problem with a caddie, they have somebody to come to who can take care of it."

Other items on the association's agenda included getting

sponsors to relinquish some guest badges for caddies to distribute to their friends and family who live near a tournament site. And a few years ago, caddies began wearing advertising on their visors like players, and were paid to do so. The first company that signed up was MCI, then Nabisco took over the contract, but since Nabisco has cut back drastically on golf sponsorship, the PGA Tour is now paying caddies to wear its logo. A percentage of that money goes directly into the association's bank account to help pay for the new motor home, which is currently being built and will be ready sometime in April.

The association has labored hard to improve working conditions for its members. But one thing that didn't have to be enhanced was the players' respect for the caddies. Caddies may not have been held in very high esteem by anyone else, but the players have always known the importance of the caddie to their well-being.

"We can't do our jobs without caddies," Davis says.

Because of the importance he places on caddies, Davis decided to replace Harmon with Mark last month.

"It was one of the hardest things I've ever had to do," Davis recalls. "Mike's a great caddie and a great friend. I was worried about whether our friendship would survive and it's going to be hard with him working for other people and us not spending a lot of time together. That was like breaking up with a girlfriend or losing touch with a family member. But I had to do what was best for me and unfortunately that wasn't what was best for Mike."

Davis opted to take Mark on Tour with him because Mark knows his golf swing as well as anybody. By working at every tournament, Mark can serve as a traveling teacher and point out flaws in Davis's game that Jack Lumpkin and Butch Harmon would see if they were on Tour with him.

"Mark wasn't really happy with what he was doing and I wasn't happy because my swing would be really good when my teachers were around and then it would get off when they weren't around," Davis explains. "I know he can do the caddying stuff, the green reading, getting the yardages, carrying the bag. What I was missing was someone that I could trust who knew my swing for a long time and that could keep an eye on me. I wanted somebody who grew up in the same atmosphere I did. If Butch Harmon caddied for me, I'd swing good every week. Of course that's not possible, so Mark's job is to learn more about my swing and help me to do the same things all the time.

"I'm trying to push myself to the next level and I feel like he can help me be more consistent week in and week out with my full swing. That's what I'm missing in my game, the consistency of fairways and greens hit. I can get it up and down with anybody, I can chip with anybody, I can almost putt with anybody on my good weeks, but there are guys out here who are hitting a lot more fairways and greens than me.

"The only thing I'll lose is the golf course experience that Mike had. Mark hadn't even been to Riviera until this week. With Mike, I could say, 'Doesn't this green slope a little?' or 'Doesn't this break funny?' or Mike would say, 'Remember, this green is always faster.' Mark will get that pretty soon. And I've been out here long enough where I can do that stuff on my own. It makes me a little more self-reliant, which I think is going to be good. It'll make me more aware of what I'm doing, rather than just showing up at the ball. I'm carrying my own yardage book again and that helps me. It gives you a better understanding of the golf courses. It's just like changing clubs, it's something that I'll have to get used to."

Mark is sitting on a bench in front of the players' locker room reading the *Los Angeles Times* sports section. Mark has read the *Times* a lot this week.

"One thing about this job," he says. "You do an awful lot of waiting."

The caddies have a saying that if they had just thirty minutes to live, they hope it's a Tour player's thirty minutes because that would mean they'd have an hour or an hour and a half left.

The waiting around doesn't bother Mark very much. He's laid-back and is never in a rush to get anywhere. Besides, this idea of caddying for Davis is a pretty good deal.

Mark followed his brother to the University of North Carolina, but after three undistinguished years—academically as well as athletically—he transferred to Valdosta (Georgia) State and earned a communications degree as well as renewed confidence in his golf game.

"I decided to play my last year there and I played well," Mark says. "When I got out of school, I wanted to play and I did for a year, but I didn't play well enough where I thought it was reasonable to keep trying to do that."

So he went back to Sea Island early last year and took a job as an instructor at the *Golf Digest* schools. He taught and helped direct the schools for the season and he was happy in those roles, but only because he was in the golf business. He needed something more. During the year, Davis had mentioned a couple of times in passing that Mark should come out on Tour and caddie, but Mark never thought he was serious because Davis and Harmon worked so well together.

"It really started more as an offhand comment, then I began thinking about it and when I told him I was serious about it, he started giving it some thought and we both felt like it would be a good idea for lots of reasons," Mark says.

"One, with the amount of money these players are making now, I'll be earning a lot more than I was when I was working five to six days a week teaching high handicappers.

"Two, being out here, being able to be around the best players in the world, watching their golf swings, listening to the things that they talk about, the way they talk about equipment or what's important to them, it's as good an experience as I could possibly have. By no means am I finished as a teacher. I was secure in my ability to help them get better, but I was not secure enough with low handicappers and professionals, being able to notice the subtleties that make a difference at this level. There isn't a better place to learn that than out here.

"And for Davis, as successful as he was last year and as successful as he plans to be in the future, he thinks I can help him get to the next level. Instead of being a top 20 player, he wants to be one of the best in the world. Jack Lumpkin and Butch Harmon both told me what to look for in Davis' swing when he's hitting it bad and what things to tell him and what not to tell him. They can't be here all the time, so I will look at the films of his swing with Butch, and Butch will point out what his tendencies are. Instead of Davis going two or three weeks of playing bad before he can see Jack or Butch, I can be in contact with them and say, 'Look, his ball's doing this,' or 'I see him coming out of it,' or whatever. They know his swing well enough so they can say, 'Okay, this is what his tendency is, this is what he's probably doing. Tell him to do this and call me back.' Hopefully throughout the year, he won't have to have spells where he has to figure it out on his own.

"He has always been receptive to my comments and that started a long time ago. Whatever he was working on with Dad, I was always aware of and he was always aware of what I was working on. I'd watch him and see if he was doing what he was supposed to do and he'd watch me, so we've always done that. I give him suggestions, tell him what I see and then he takes whatever part of it he likes or thinks might be useful and he tries that."

Chico Fernandez is sitting on the same bench as Mark, the one across from the entrance to the players' locker room. Like Mark and the rest of the caddies, Chico can't go in there to change his clothes, wash his hands or just chat with his employer, Mike Reid. Caddies aren't allowed in the players' locker room. Chico doesn't care. There have been a lot of things he hasn't been able to do during his fifty-nine years and not being able to go into the locker room at Riviera is the least of the inconveniences he has had to endure.

Born in Cuba, Chico has seen hell and lived to tell about it.

"Fidel, he is sick in the head," the diminutive Cuban says of Fidel Castro, the ruthless dictator of his native country. "Cuba is bad right now. For the last thirty years, he has completely destroyed that country. Before him, it was hard times, but compared to now, it was perfect. You ate three meals a day, a lot of rice and beans, and we made it all right. If I live to be ninety years old, I can sit on the front porch of my house and say many thanks."

Chico is one of the lucky ones. He got out of Cuba, came to America, pursued a dream, and has lived the kind of life he wishes everyone can live. A happy one.

"I got no complaints," he says. "I got no money, I'm just making my ends meet, but I've had a great life. I played ten years of pro baseball, I went to Knoxville and raised a family and now I'm doing something that I love to do."

Like so many Cuban boys, Chico started playing baseball around the time he learned to walk. When he first slipped a beat-up "little rinky-dink" glove on his hand, it did not occur to him that baseball could someday be his ticket out of Cuba. Only when an American scout from the Washington Senators named Joe Cambria spotted Chico playing on the well-manicured sandlots and offered him the opportunity to play in Sherman, Texas—a town with an independent Class D minor league team—did he realize that he could escape Castro's stranglehold for six months a year.

"Everybody in Cuba plays baseball," Chico says. "I stuck with the game and I grew up and developed into a pretty decent ballplayer. When I was seventeen or eighteen, I was playing amateur baseball, which is real good baseball, very strong. Some of the scouts from this country would go down there every year and I was one of the ones that they approached. My dream was to come to America and play baseball, that's every Cuban player's dream. I signed my first contract in 1951. I was so excited, I didn't sleep the next five days."

For five years, Chico played summer ball in the United States, then had to return to Cuba where he played in the winter. He was only allowed a six-month visa to play in America and when that expired he had to go home. This was before the Cuban missile crisis and the Cold War, a time when the U.S. and Cuba still had a peaceable relationship. Chico realized that going back to Cuba each fall was meaningless, so he investigated the possibility of leaving for good to live in the U.S.

"I fell in love with this country. I saw the freedom and the opportunities that are here," he says.

In 1956, he went back to Cuba to play winter ball and he told his mother that the following spring, he was going to report to the American embassy and try to fix his papers so that he could relocate to the U.S. permanently. Castro allowed him to leave, the

U.S. accepted him, and Chico began a new life for himself that summer in America.

He wound up playing minor league ball for ten years. After an excellent season playing shortstop and second base at Sherman, the Cubs purchased him and he wallowed in the low minors for three years with them. He later played in the Orioles' organization and finished his career in the Tigers' system, never advancing past Double-A. Near the end of his baseball career, he played in Knoxville with future Tiger greats Mickey Lolich and Dick McAuliffe.

"I played for almost ten years in the minor leagues and I loved it," he says. "If I had to do it all over again, I'd do it because I just love the game. I never got to the big leagues. Sometimes I just didn't get the right break, but that's okay."

He may not have gotten the breaks in baseball, but he sure caught one when he was transferred to Knoxville. There, he met his wife Charlotte, "a little hillbilly from Tennessee," as he playfully describes her.

He got married, had a little girl, and began the task of providing for a family. He worked in a department store for a while, then, "I got me a big job—well, I call it a big job—at a factory making Plexiglas and I worked there for twenty-five years."

With baseball out of his system, Chico found a new athletic endeavor to pass the few spare hours he had to himself. He took up golf, became enamored with the game, and then recognized an opportunity to get out of the factory and get back outdoors.

"There was a pro tournament in Knoxville and they needed some caddies so I applied and got myself a job and it got in my blood and I just loved it," he explains. "I caddied a couple of times in Knoxville and then I took three weeks of vacation one year and told my wife I was going to Florida, which is where they [the Tour] are early in the year, and lucky enough I got together with a player, Artie McNichols. He was a rookie and he never accomplished anything, but he was my first player so I remember him real well."

He worked part-time on the Tour, caddying for whoever would hire him. He used to have to beg his foreman for time off so he could get out and caddie. "The foreman used to hide from me because he knew I was coming to ask for time off." Finally, he quit

164

his job at the factory six years ago and made the career change that will carry him into retirement.

"I want to do it until I'm about sixty-two. I want to do it as long as I feel I can help some of these boys and right now, I do. I'm not telling you that I'm better at this job than anyone else, but I've been doing it for eighteen years and I feel like I can do this job. Not that I'm getting rich, because I'm not, but it's paying my bills. And I love it."

Which is more than Chico's brother Louis can say.

Chico's mother, four brothers, Raul, Roberto, Nino and Frank, and his sister, Bertie Castelleros, have joined him in America over the years, but Louis remains trapped in Cuba. Castro would not let him come to America because he had sons who had to serve in the Cuban army. He is still in Cuba to this day, and since Chico left his homeland for good in 1956, he has seen Louis just once—in the summer of '91—when Castro allowed him to come to the U.S. for a short visit.

"He was here for forty days and he said it was like a dream come true," Chico says. "He said we don't realize how lucky we are. I took him to a supermarket and he asked me, 'You mean you can buy anything you want here?' and the hair on my arms just stuck right up. He said that was the first time in thirty years he had been to a supermarket where you could pick out anything you wanted. They stand in line for a piece of bread like they do in Russia. They give you enough to eat for two weeks, twice a month, and you have to make it stretch. It's tough. Sometimes we take things for granted here and we complain, but you don't hear me complain much, no way José.

"I get up every morning and I feel the same way. I know right this minute that people back home are going hungry about four or five days a week. It's rough over there. If things don't go your way, hey, take it easy, time out, I think about my brother back home and the hard times and that makes me thankful."

Mike Harmon thinks back to the time when he decided to pursue caddying as a full-time job and he remembers a longtime looper telling him, "They're all running from something, whether it's good or bad."

165

Harmon was running from the world of suits and ties. He had majored in finance at the University of Florida and upon graduation, worked as a commercial loan officer at Bankers Trust. Later he worked as a loan specialist for a small business, but Harmon admits, "It got boring."

He had grown up in Augusta, Georgia, home to a little tournament known as The Masters, so he was familiar with the world of golf.

"When I was in junior high school and high school, I used to work out there in the gallery holding the crosswalk ropes," Harmon says, smiling as he thinks back on those spine-tingling days watching the golfing greats roam the green cathedral of Augusta National. "Occasionally a ticket would pop up, or we also used to sneak in there through a hole in the fence off Berkman Road. We'd sneak in and run down to the 16th hole and we'd sit there because that's where all the Pinkertons were. And if anyone wanted something to drink or something to eat, they would send one person in with a badge, and then you wouldn't come back and you didn't worry at the end of the day when it was time to leave and you got caught because you'd been in there all day."

Back then, Harmon thought that being a caddie would probably be a neat job to have, but it wasn't until 1981, when he visited with Mike Carrick for a couple of days at the Heritage Classic in Hilton Head, South Carolina, that he seriously considered working on the PGA Tour.

Carrick, who was working for Tom Kite (he still does today), was introduced to Harmon at the Atlanta Classic in 1978 through a mutual female friend. The two men had stayed in touch through letters and an occasional visit before Carrick invited Harmon to Hilton Head.

"I inquired about caddie life and Mike could see that I was interesting in caddying," Harmon says. "He said, 'Why don't you just come out and caddie?' At that time, I wasn't ready to do it, I was just curious about it, but that kind of put a bug in my ear and I wondered if maybe I'd want to do that. He told me it was going to be tough and I was going to have some hard times. The money was getting better and caddies were making more and if I got a good player, worked hard and treated it like a job, he said I'd be all right.

166

It got to the point where I was single, wasn't tied down, banking was boring and I needed a change. I said, 'If I never do it, I'll always wonder what if,' so I took a chance and it worked out."

Harmon had always been interested in golf, though he only played recreationally. The opportunity to learn more about the game by watching and working with the best players in the world is what drew him to caddying.

"I saw a professional golfer and a professional caddie working together as a team and that right there told me that that was something I'd like to do," he said. "I knew I'd like to work alongside a professional golfer, learn all about it and be a caddie who could be helpful to a player. That intrigued me. I knew it would be a challenge and I wanted to see if I could do it. I had carried a bag when I was a kid so I knew I could do that. I wanted to see if I could caddie in situations that might be stressful, where a player might depend on me and my knowledge of the game."

Carrick was the only person Harmon knew on Tour. Unlike Mark Love, Harmon didn't have a job when he joined the caddie ranks. He had to do what most rookie caddies do—stalk the players' parking lot asking for a job.

"I went in cold turkey," Harmon says. "I went to Memphis, Tennessee, and stood in the parking lot and asked everyone that came by if they needed a caddie. I actually lied about my first job. I told the guy that I had worked for a couple of years, so he said, 'Okay.' I went to the parking lot and just told myself that I was going to get a job and I did it.

"I was prepared for the rejection. But I also knew that if someone gave me a chance and let me get my foot in the door that I could take it from there."

Harmon worked for Davis for two and a half years and won twice with him. Previously, he'd worked with Mark Wiebe for two and a half years and won once with him; he caddied for Bill Glasson when he won the Kemper Open in 1985; and he has also worked for other high-profile players such as Curtis Strange, Corey Pavin, Peter Jacobsen and Tom Purtzer. Now, he is toting for Ben Crenshaw.

"The turnover here is just unbelievable," he says. "Players

and caddies, for whatever reason, split up. It happens to everybody."

Like most caddies when they first come out on Tour, Harmon bounced around from player to player and usually, those players weren't very good. All the top guys had steady caddies. So to augment his scant income, Harmon worked for CBS on weekends if his man didn't make the cut.

"I worked as a spotter to earn a few extra dollars to get me to the next tournament," he said. "I've come a long way. I used to have to ask everybody for a job, but I don't have to do that now. There are players who inquire about me, when I might be available to work for them on an off week. The players know who the good caddies are because they talk in the locker room or on the range. They know who's available and who's not and who can go under the heat and who can't. I don't pursue it anymore.

"It used to be if there were forty-two tournaments, I was working forty-two weeks. But now I don't need to and basically I don't want to, I need the time off. Just like players can get burned out, so can caddies. If you're out four or five weeks in a row, you need some time off to get refreshed."

The hard part for caddies is the travel. Players can afford to fly around the country, but the caddies generally can't. When Harmon worked for Davis, Davis would occasionally pay for his plane fare, but most of the time, Harmon drove to each tournament site.

"I still enjoy driving and seeing the country," Harmon says. "It's a grind, but I don't look at it that way. Normally you'll have somebody driving with you and you share the duties. And I don't drive through the night anymore. We've lost a few caddies out here in car accidents who have tried to make it from Sunday afternoon to Monday morning, ten, twelve hours away. I won't kill myself to get from one place to another. Sometimes it's a little tough, but most of the time you've got Monday off so you use that time to recuperate.

"There are a lot of caddies out here living paycheck to paycheck like I used to and if I was driving eighteen to twenty hours from stop to stop, then it would be a grind. I used to hitch rides and drive through the night just to get a free ride to a place.

I took a lot of chances when I first got out here, but I didn't have any money and I was working week to week and I had to do those things. Like I said, I've come a long way."

Andy Martinez' story rings a bell. He started caddying because he loved the game and he thought it would be a nice job to help him make ends meet until he could find real work. Twenty-three years later, Martinez is still lugging a bag around the plush fairways of the PGA Tour.

"I feel blessed that I have the opportunity to make a living doing something that I enjoy," he says. "Not too many people have jobs that they love and look forward to coming to work."

The forty-two-year-old Mexican grew up in San Pedro, California, about thirty-five miles from Riviera, and caddied for Grier Jones in the 1969 Los Angeles Open. One year later, he began working for Johnny Miller.

"And shortly thereafter, John started to play some phenomenal golf and it became a career for me. I never thought that I would be out here this long.

"John Miller is one of the greatest talents in the game and we blended very well together. We had a lot of things in common. We're both very spiritually motivated, our relationship with God is important to both of us. We both grew up in California, we both had older brothers who died in the ocean; my brother Pete died in 1962 surfing and John's brother was fishing off the rocks in San Francisco and a big wave came and took him in."

Martinez and Miller formed one of the finest tandems in golf. They were the essence of the player-caddie relationship.

"It got to the point during rounds where I knew what he was thinking and he knew what I was thinking without even talking. We could read each other's minds," Martinez says. "When the golfer and caddie are that much in concert, then you don't make too many mistakes. It doesn't get much better. We had really good communication, we were a good team. He asked me a lot of things and that made it a lot of fun for me, it made me want to work harder and make sure I had all the information. I really cared for John Miller."

Today, there is no one Martinez cares for more than Jesus Christ.

"Jesus Christ is what keeps me out here, he's my motivating factor in life," he says. "I believe I do missionary work out here. I try to preach about the gospel and tell people about Jesus Christ. I mean without Jesus Christ, life is pretty unsatisfactory. It may seem at times that you have things pretty much under control, but sooner or later, you're going to get to the point in your life where things are going to get very difficult and you're not going to know where to turn. Everybody gets to that point, I know I did a few years ago with my marriage breaking up and getting fired on the Tour in '87. Everything came at one time and when that happens, there's only one way to look. Fortunately for me, I found truth, but it wasn't easy.

"Being a caddie is like being a servant and with my new way of thinking, it fits in even better and makes the job so much easier. Jesus Christ is the one I emulate and Jesus Christ came to earth as a servant. He came here to serve God the father and he served his fellow man. Now that I'm keyed in to Jesus Christ, it makes it a lot easier to realize how important service is."

Since he and Miller split up in 1982, Martinez has worked for Bobby Clampett, Bob Gilder, Gary Hallberg, Hal Sutton, Gilder again and now John Cook for almost three years. He is one of the best caddies in the business and he will always have work so he stays on the circuit.

"Caddies can make a lot of money out here," he says. "A lot of people envy us for our job. We're outdoors, we're with the best players in the world and there are other fringe benefits. Things have gotten a lot better for caddies. In the old days, there were a few things that irritated me, things that were pretty absurd like not being able to go on the golf course without your player and being herded into a holding area until your player arrived. They never gave us any consideration and we were thought of more or less as a necessary evil. Some of those things have changed, though. I love this life."

Joe LaCava's plan was to go out to the West Coast at the start of the 1987 Tour season, watch his cousin, Ken Green, play in a few tournaments, then come home to Connecticut and put his business degree from Western Connecticut State to use.

"I just wanted to hang out, go out there for vacation and have a good time," says LaCava. "Ken's sister was caddying for him, but then that ended at the end of 1986. I called him at Christmas time to make sure everything was all set for me to come out with him and he asked me, 'Why don't you just caddie for me?' I said, 'Sure, I'd love to caddie.' After my second week he asked me to do it full-time. I had no commitments, so I said, 'Sure.'"

The business world could wait.

"You can struggle out here, but I think if a person doesn't have any commitments, such as a girlfriend or a wife and family, or a business, it's not a bad life-style. If you get a good player and you do a good job, it can be financially rewarding as well as emotionally satisfying. If you want to keep your job, you better do a good job and be on the ball. There's a million guys who would love to have this job."

That's probably an understatement when you talk about the job LaCava has now.

He worked for Green through 1989 and then Green's brother, Bill, was out of work and needed a job so Ken told LaCava he had to let Bill caddie for him. LaCava understood that, so he pursued another player, a guy named Fred Couples.

"Early that year, Fred and his caddie had parted ways, so at the end of '89, I talked to Fred and asked him if he'd give me a shot," LaCava says. "He called me at Christmas time and said, 'I'm going to play four or five on the West Coast. Come out and we'll give it a try.' The timing was right."

Today, LaCava has the primo caddie job, carrying for the hottest player in the world.

"With a guy like Fred, I'd caddie forever," LaCava says. "This is the greatest job in the world working for Fred Couples. C'mon, what could be better? I love it, but it's easy to love it when you have a great player."

LaCava is a preppy twenty-eight-year-old with a receding hairline. On the road, he hears all kinds of stories of caddies enjoying the night-life, but most of it, he says, is just that. Stories.

"I think caddies get a bad rap," he says. "Guys who are out

here are mostly clean-cut guys and they look at caddying as a professional job and they take it seriously. To be honest with you, I don't even listen to the stories. I do my job and I don't do a lot. This is my typical day. I'm here all day working, then I go back to wherever I'm staying and relax and read the paper. Then I try to get a nice dinner, come back and watch TV. In the winter months, I watch college basketball and hockey almost every night. Sometimes I'll go to a bar and try to find one of my New York teams on cable."

As is the case with most caddies who have worked for the same player for a long time, no one on Tour knows Couples better than LaCava. And LaCava gets emotional when people get on Couples for his alleged lack of desire.

"People get the impression that he's so laid-back that he doesn't care, but that isn't so. He does care," LaCava says, the pitch of his voice rising. "He gets as mad as anybody else when he hits a bad shot, he just tries not to let it bother him because he has to hit the next shot. He knows who he is and what he's done. He gets a bad rap."

The third round is well underway by the time Davis gets down to the range. The practice area is nearly barren and only his playing partners, Tom Sieckmann and Scotland's Sandy Lyle, and one of the men who will be in the group ahead of him, Fred Couples, are still lingering.

"I woke up a little early this morning because I was anxious to get started," Davis says. "I'm excited about how I'm playing and I was ready to get going when I got up. That's usually the hardest thing, you're always so ready to go, you don't want it to take so long. It only takes four hours out of every twenty-four hours to play so being patient and waiting for the round to start can be difficult.

"And you're more anxious when you're in the lead. You always want to play and get started, but when you're leading, you want to get going so you can get the results quicker."

As Davis starts to loosen up, Lyle completes his business on the range and he and his wife/caddie, Jolande, walk over to where

Davis and Couples are chatting. Lyle is wearing a peculiar color combination of yellowish, olive green pants and a lime green shirt. Couples takes a look and with a smile says, "That's interesting."

Couples is wearing a blue- and green-striped Ashworth shirt and Lyle jokingly asks him, "Do you have underwear to match that shirt?" Couples comes back with, "Nice shoes." Lyle's shoes are also unique because they have green stripes on the sides that make them look like baseball cleats.

Jolande turns to Davis and announces in her English accent, "We're playing with the man who made 10 birdies yesterday. God, what did you have for breakfast?" Davis says with a smile, "Wheaties."

The Lyles say goodbye and begin making their way up to the putting green, followed closely behind by Couples who is teeing off in a few minutes. Davis is left alone on the range with Sieckmann, and the two competitors launch iron shots into a sky that is slightly overcast.

Within ten minutes, Sieckmann finishes and walks away. Five minutes later, Davis is hiking up the hill to the putting green. Ten minutes after Davis strokes his first putt, he, Sieckmann and Lyle are called to the tee.

The crowd around the first tee is large, larger than yesterday's group even though Daly is long gone, having teed off more than an hour earlier. Davis has a four-shot lead but appears to be a little nervous as he steps between the tee markers, pushes his peg into the ground and balances his ball on top of it.

He backs up and stares at the fairway below as the announcer introduces him to the gallery. They applaud loudly and he waves in appreciation, then returns his attention to the landing area. He picks out a target, addresses the ball, winds up and slings an absolutely perfect drive down the middle. The fans roar admiringly.

Sieckmann looks nervous too and his tee shot reflects that as it fades into the trees on the right. Lyle also pushes his tee ball into the right rough.

The threesome walks down the hill and on to their positions in silence, mainly because Sieckmann and Lyle have tough shots ahead of them and need to start thinking about what they have to do.

Sieckmann cannot get to the green from where he is, so he uses his 7-iron to hit a low fade into the fairway that comes up 60 yards short of the green, an excellent recovery which will give him a good chance to get up and down for birdie.

Lyle is sixty yards ahead of Sieckmann, but he can't take a shot at the pin because it's tucked just six paces from the right edge of the green and a tree thirty yards in front of his ball is blocking his path. From 215 yards, he tries to fade a 3-iron to the middle of the green, but he hits it a little thin and dumps the shot into the huge front bunker.

Davis is still a little tense as he and Mark discuss the approach. They deduce that he has 206 yards to the hole with a slight breeze coming from behind. He has been hitting the ball solid and his adrenaline is flowing a little faster, so he takes his 5-iron out. He takes his time, makes sure his alignment is correct, settles and swings. He knows it's good as soon as the club slaps his back on his follow-through. The ball lands just in front of the pin and skips seven feet past. Another great shot, another great roar from the crowd and his nervousness is quelled.

As he and Mark walk to the green, he is smiling and telling his brother about last night's episode of *Cheers* and both of them laugh as he chronicles the exploits of Norm and Cliff and the gang.

Sieckmann hits a pitching wedge to the back edge, thirteen feet from the hole, then Lyle hits a masterful bunker shot to five feet.

After Sieckmann misses his birdie attempt and taps in for par, Davis lines up his eagle try and spends little time doing so.

"I had a perfect putt, right to left from seven feet, I hit it and I looked up and I couldn't believe when it missed," Davis says. "That was kind of disappointing because that would have been the perfect start, make eagle, get to 14-under and you're cruising."

At least he gets to 13-under with the easy birdie, which keeps him four shots ahead of Lyle because Lyle makes his birdie putt moments later to get to 9-under.

At the 459-yard second, Davis chooses to hit 3-wood because the wind is at his back, and unlike Thursday's 3-wood, he hits this one down the middle and clear of any trouble. Lyle pulls a 2-iron into the left rough and Sieckmann hits a 3-wood into the fairway.

Lyle's ball is sitting in a clump of thick grass 211 yards from the hole. The wind is at his back and Lyle is a strong man, but 5-iron obviously isn't enough club here and he comes up thirty yards short of the green in the first cut of rough on the right. From 195, Sieckmann stiffs a 5-iron to two feet. Davis uses 6-iron from 182 and it fades into the right fringe, eighteen feet from the hole.

"The wind kind of stopped and it was real calm, but Mark said I could get the 6-iron in there," Davis says. "I hit it hard rather than trying to hit an easy one like yesterday and I hit it pretty good, but it drifted a little and got in the fringe pin high."

After watching Lyle chip to six feet, Davis nearly holes a 9-iron pitch and settles for a par. Lyle saves par with a solid putt and Sieckmann rolls in his short birdie putt to get to 9-under.

Sieckmann is playing very well this week, but no one in the gallery is paying much attention to him. His score isn't nearly as interesting to the fans as his offensive-looking putter. It looks like a miniature catamaran and some fans have been overheard calling it a weed eater, a hang glider and the Hyatt hotels symbol. The face of the club is larger than most standard putters and there is a t-shaped extension off the back of the face. The design, by Dave Pelz, is a spinoff from Pelz's three-ball putter that was banned for competition by the USGA.

"It's wild looking," Davis says. "Basically, what's behind the putter face doesn't matter. I guess all that stuff on the back is supposed to be for alignment. It sounds pretty solid when he hits it, but I couldn't putt with that for anything because it wouldn't look right. I need something that looks right. Whatever works, I guess."

"It's for balance and alignment," Sieckmann says. "The theory is that at the moment of inertia, when the weight is that far back, you get less twisting in the clubface on off-center hits. Occasionally I hear comments, but my wife gets the brunt of most of that stuff out there in the gallery. When you're playing, you don't hear much. I've used it so long, it's just a putter to me."

It's a putter that hasn't been working too well this season. In five starts prior to Los Angeles, Sieckmann has missed two cuts and his best finish was a tie for 20th at Pebble Beach. He currently ranks 66th in the Tour putting statistics and what makes that stat even worse is that he ranks just 80th in greens hit in regulation.

Sieckmann is like so many other Tour players who have enough talent to be out here, but need to take that next step and start challenging consistently for tournament titles.

"I enjoy playing," Sieckmann says. "Golf is a great challenge—it's such a difficult game, it's so complex and there's always something to work on. I've always wanted to do this and you get discouraged at times, but it's still what I want to do.

"People don't understand this life. It's a tough life. Most players make the majority of their money in four to six weeks out of the year so there's a lot of struggling going on in between, a lot of negative things happening. It's sure not all peaches and cream out here, especially with all the traveling. People see you win a lot of money in one week, but what about those other weeks when we miss the cut and don't make a dime? It's got its drawbacks."

Sieckmann grew up in Nebraska playing basketball, but loving golf. "You had to either play football, basketball or baseball to be taken seriously as an athlete when I was growing up. Golf was considered a sissy sport," he once told *Golf* magazine. In his senior year at Miller High, he sank a twenty-five-foot jump shot at the buzzer to win the conference championship.

The University of Nebraska liked that and it offered him a basketball scholarship. He attended the Lincoln campus for a year, but realized that even though he was six-foot-five, he was better suited to the "sissy" sport and he transferred to Oklahoma State, which had a powerful golf program.

Sieckmann enjoyed enough success in college to consider giving a pro golf career a try. For a long time, he wondered if he had made the right choice. He turned professional in 1977 and began by playing the Tours overseas. And he played well, winning seven times, three of those victories coming in 1981 when he captured the Brazilian, Phillipine and Thailand Opens. Tired of traveling the world, he mercifully survived the Q-School in 1984, finishing runner-up, and was able to return to North America.

176

"I played around the world because I needed to elevate my game a little bit before I played the [American] Tour," Sieckmann says. "I played the European Tour, South Africa, the Far East, South America. It was tough at times because very rarely did you get a good practice facility, but I learned a lot about myself and the rest of the world."

Unfortunately, coming home wasn't as pleasant as it should have been. He earned just $30,052 in 1985 and had to go back to Q-School. He won medalist honors this time, and in '86, he managed to hold on to his card, albeit barely, when he held down the 125th and final exempt spot on the money list. It was back to Q-School when he finished 146th on the money list in '87, and again, he regained his privileges.

It looked like the same old story in '88. He had missed the cut in 13 of his first 16 starts, including a pitiful stretch of 12 straight. A 19th-place finish at the Western Open snapped the streak and he went to the Anheuser-Busch Classic in Kingsmill, Virginia, with renewed confidence.

He had hoped to make the cut again and continue the rehabilitation of his game. Instead, he stayed close to the top of the leaderboard with rounds of 69–66 the first two days to trail Peter Jacobsen by three, then fired another 66 to tie for the lead with Jacobsen and Kenny Knox.

On Sunday, Mark Wiebe got hot, shot 68, and entered the clubhouse as the leader at 14-under. Jacobsen and Knox faltered, so it was left for Sieckmann to challenge Wiebe. A birdie at the 17th pulled him even, and on the second playoff hole, a routine two-putt par bettered Wiebe's bogey and Sieckmann was finally a winner in the U.S.

It has been almost four years and Sieckmann has not re-peated that feat. He slipped to 128th on the money list in '89, but kept his card because as a tournament winner, he had a two-year exemption on Tour. In '90, he played poorly and finished 110th, but that was good enough to retain his privileges, and then last year, he broke through by earning $278,598 to place 54th, thanks mainly to three top 10 finishes.

"One of my problems has always been that I don't play well enough to get into contention like the great players," Sieckmann says. "Nicklaus is known for his wins, but he finished second more than anybody else, he was always there, and that's the key. It's a game of probabilities and if you do enough things right over a long enough period of time, things happen your way.

"Occasionally you'll have some bad luck, but you get it the other way around too, you get some bad shots that turn out good. You have to play well over a long period of time."

Davis crushes his drive at the 441-yard third and has just 114 yards left for his second shot. He hits a smooth pitching wedge to six feet pin high. Mark tells him the putt isn't going to break much, that it is inside the hole, but Davis thinks it'll break more so he overrules, plays it an inch out to the left and cooly rolls it in for another birdie, dropping him to 14-under and establishing a five-shot lead.

"I'm thinking these guys are gonna make birdies. Couples is up there and you know he's gonna make a lot of birdies, so I just told myself that I have to be patient and make as many birdies as I can today."

Couples, Rocco Mediate and Bob Estes are just walking to the green at the par-3 fourth when Davis and his group arrive at the tee, so there will be about a ten-minute wait.

Sieckmann asks Davis if he has read the *Golf Digest* article yet and Davis says that he has.

Sieckmann was interviewed for the story and he was a little pissed because he claims 99 percent of what he said about the Tour and the way commissioner Deane Beman is operating it was positive, but the magazine chose to quote him on the one percent that was negative.

"We all got a copy of an early issue in our lockers so we'd be prepared when it did come out for all the questions we're going to get about it," Davis explains. "It's about Deane's control of the Tour. Tom said that he said one thing bad about Deane and that's what they used, but that's typical. You say one thing negative and that's all they remember. If you say a bunch of boring stuff and one thing that's exciting, that's what they're going to use, so you have to be careful.

"As far as the media, I think it's important to get to know the guys and know what questions they're going to ask and how to take care of them and help them out. If you help them out, talk to them and be friendly, it's a lot easier in the long run. The same thing with the TV guys. If you know them by name, that can work to your advantage. They're more comfortable around you and you're more comfortable with them when they're running all over the fairways."

Sieckmann walks over to the cooler and gets a cup of water, leaving Lyle to ask Davis, "Did you see where that shot hit?" referring to his approach back at No. 3, which hit the ground and didn't advance any further. Davis replies, "It looked like it hit and bounced straight up or even backwards," and Lyle says, "I didn't think a golf ball could do that."

The pin at No. 4 is stationed in the middle of the green, but on a slight slope, so an already difficult hole now becomes a tricky one as well. Davis pulls out his 3-iron because he had been long with his 1-iron the first two days. He hits what he thinks is a perfect high fade that lands about ten feet short of the hole, but it releases hard and runs to the back fringe.

Lyle turns to Davis and says, "I don't know what you're supposed to do because that's as good as you can hit it."

Sieckmann misses the green to the right with a 2-iron, and Lyle doesn't hit his 4-iron very well, missing to the left.

All Davis wants to do is get this one close because he knows the cup is cut in a precarious position. From forty feet, he leaves himself an uphill 3-footer for par and after watching Lyle chip to seven feet and save par and Sieckmann chip to five feet and miss, Davis happily makes his par.

"It was not one that you're trying to make, you get it close and if it goes in, fine," Davis says. "On the second putt, I wanted to make sure that I took my time. I didn't want to get careless, so I made sure I went through my routine. That gave me a lot of confidence, getting through 2 and 4, which are the hard holes, and making birdie at one and three."

After placing a perfect 1-iron into the middle of the fifth fairway, Davis turns to Mark and asks, "Why haven't we been hitting 1-iron here all week?" After two days in a row of pulled 3-woods down the embankment on the left, Davis will be approaching the fifth green from a new vantage point.

Sieckmann will also be getting a different view of No. 5. He pulled his 2-iron tee shot into the left rough and while his ball didn't roll down the hill, it is far enough left so that the ominous birch, which had caused so much trouble for Davis the first two rounds, must be dealt with.

Sieckmann finds his ball sitting up in a decent lie, 190 yards from the green, so he decides to try and get the ball up quickly over the birch with a 6-iron rather than try to hook it around the tree. The plan goes awry when he hits the tree. His ball shoots across the fairway at a 90-degree angle and lodges into the rough close to the out-of-bounds stakes on the right, providing another unenviable perspective. Sieckmann has no idea where the ball landed, but Lyle, who is waiting to play his approach from the middle of the fairway, sees it. After Lyle hits a 7-iron to within fifteen feet and Davis hits a marvelous 7-iron to within three feet, Lyle walks into the rough and shows Sieckmann where his ball is.

Sieckmann and his caddie, Rich Jordan, size up the situation while Lyle and Davis wait in the fairway. Sieckmann looks calm and seemingly unperturbed by this chain of events as he paces from his ball back to the nearest sprinkler head to get a precise yardage. When he returns, he pulls out his pitching wedge, takes four practice swings and then hits a pretty good shot to within thirty feet of the hole.

When he gets to the green, he is still away. Again, he looks tranquil, even though he's staring at a probable bogey. His composure pays off as he slam dunks the putt into the back of the cup to save par. While the crowd reacts with a stunned cheer, Sieckmann pumps his fist and waves to them as he walks to retrieve his ball. He also breathes a sigh of relief; had he missed the cup, the ball would have ended up off the green because it was really moving. Lyle jokingly walks up to the cup and peers inside to see if the rim has been bent and the fans let out a collective chuckle.

Lyle brings another roar when he makes his birdie attempt to get to 10-under. Davis completes the succession of one-putts by sinking his short birdie, which enables him to maintain his five-shot advantage over Lyle.

Lyle is now alone in second place. The thirty-four-year-old Scot remembers a time not too long ago when second place wouldn't have been good enough. It was back in 1988, the year he won The Masters and stood atop the world of golf, slugging it out with Greg Norman, Curtis Strange and Seve Ballesteros for global supremacy.

Back then, Lyle was one of the best. An awesome striker of the ball off the tee, a crisp iron player and deftly keen on the greens, Lyle split his time on the American and European Tours and beat up competitors on both sides of the pond.

In '88, within a three-month period, he followed victories in Phoenix and Greensboro with a superb triumph at The Masters. Before '88, he had won the British Open at Royal St. George's in '85, Greensboro in '86, The Players Championship in '87, piled up 27 international victories—including 14 on the European Tour— and played for the European Ryder Cup team five times.

And then, something went wrong. Suddenly in '89, the ball wasn't going as far, wasn't going as straight and the putts were lipping out instead of dying into the hole. He got into contention a few times early in the season, tying for second at the Hope and here at Riviera and he tied for third at Pebble Beach. But at the Nestle Invitational, he walked off the course in disgust, then missed the cut in seven of his next eight starts, including Augusta, where he failed miserably in his green jacket defense. In Europe, his best finishes were an eighth place in the European Open and a fourth at the Volvo Masters. He was so disillusioned with his game, he told Ryder Cup captain Tony Jacklin to not even consider picking him for the team. At year's end, there were no victories and no sign of a pulse.

It was worse in 1990. Lyle could not resuscitate himself and was clinically dead much of the season. He rarely got close to the top of a leaderboard. He played more often in Europe than in

America and although the competition is not nearly as strong in his native land, it was far more than Lyle could handle. He was a nonfactor and plummeted out of the top 50 in the Order of Merit, the European Tour's money list.

Lyle sought help from swing guru David Leadbetter, the man who Nick Faldo credits with making him a consistent winner. Leadbetter noticed that Lyle was moving his head behind the ball and his hips were going the other way. This threw his balance out of whack and caused him to hit behind the ball, which sapped much of his length.

Lyle had taught himself how to play as a youngster and while his swing was thought to be unorthodox, it was effective. Until his collapse. For much of '91, he had to retrain himself, implementing Leadbetter's methods. His losing ways continued as he struggled to tailor his new swing, but he finally broke through and won the BMW International Open in Munich in October.

The victory provided Lyle a desperately needed shot of confidence and while he isn't ready to proclaim himself as the Lyle of old, he is at least heading in that direction. The color has returned to his cheeks and the blood is flowing once again.

"I'm still trying to adjust to getting back to winning tournaments," Lyle says. "I won last year, but to be back in the thick of things again is really quite new to me at the moment. The nerve ends are a little tingly, but I'm certainly enjoying this. It's nice to be able to shoot under par again and the swing seems to be holding up at the moment, so I'm very pleased with it.

"It's been an uphill climb, a very steep climb. I think I'm coming back better equipped because I'm swinging better, hitting the ball further and stronger and I'm more consistent. Who knows what can happen."

Lyle began playing the game as a young boy in England under the watchful eye of his father, Alex, who was a club pro. By the time he was thirteen, Sandy was playing to a 3-handicap and began playing the European amateur circuit. He quit school at 15 and played golf all spring, summer and fall, then did manual labor in the off-season.

His practice habits were legendary.

"My bedroom overlooked the 18th green [of his father's club] and the driving range was just on the other side of the 18th green so it was very nice to be so close to the golf course and have the freedom to play whenever I wanted," he says.

When he was nineteen, he turned professional and at twenty, he shot a 61 and won the Nigerian Open. Over the next decade, he became one of the most dominant European players.

He had dreamed of winning the British Open and that fantasy was fulfilled when he won at Royal St. George's, becoming the first "home" winner since Englishman Tony Jacklin won in 1969.

The Masters, however, was the tournament that everyone thought would propel him to superstardom.

"I think now that I've won The Masters and had a year to think about it," he said back in early 1989, "it was a very important win for me. To be the first Scottish player to ever win The Masters has really made people realize that maybe I'm a better player than everyone thought I was. It's had a lot of coverage in Europe and I've gotten a lot of miles out of it."

Figuratively as well as literally. Part of Lyle's problem, he says, was the worldwide travel and demands on his time that came with winning the green jacket.

"Obviously you're a popular player when you win The Masters and you've got to make hay when the sun shines," he says. "You're invited to different things and you have to compete in those money tournaments. There's a lot of traveling, the schedule is very hectic and there's not a lot of free time. It's like John Daly after winning the PGA. His life has been changed dramatically in the last six or seven months and the same thing happened to me.

"You get tired of competing and you get a bit stale. It can happen to any sportsman in any sort of career—if they do too much of it, it can get stale. You feel great at the time, but your concentration doesn't last as long and you don't put as much fight into it. It was the hardest couple of years of my life."

Jolande has been a big help to him, at first emotionally and now professionally since she began carrying his bag earlier this year.

"Jolande has been good for my swing balance because she used to be a ballet teacher," Lyle says. "I use a little bit of the ballet sequences in my swing and I've been very successful with it."

And as far as her work as a caddie, Lyle says: "This is the sixth or seventh time and it's working very well. Actually she's quite a good caddie. But I can't argue with her, the penalties are too severe."

The birdie at five really has Davis stoked with confidence. He is at 15-under, he has a five-shot lead on Lyle and Doug Martin, and the always dangerous Fred Couples is seven behind.

"Now I'm feeling good, I just have to keep hitting it like I'm hitting it and I'm gonna make a ton of birdies," he says.

The sixth is playing 168 yards with the cup five yards from the left edge and twenty back on a green that is twenty-seven deep.

"I'd hit it past the hole yesterday and the pin was farther back today, so again I didn't even need a yardage. I knew it was a 7-iron because that's where I hit it yesterday."

He hits it there again today and is left with a 6-footer for birdie. However, the putt is a tricky one because it goes downhill before coming back uphill and he strikes it too solidly and the ball hits the back of the cup and bounces out. The crowd groans and Davis stares disbelievingly at the hole.

"It wasn't a long enough putt to slow down going back up the hill and it hit right in the corner," Davis explains. "Sandy said, 'That should have gone in,' and I said, 'Well, it was going pretty hard,' and he said, 'Well, look at Tom's on the last hole.' He had a good point. If you hit a perfect putt and you get absolutely hosed, that's one thing. But when you hit it too hard, oh well. I was disappointed, but I didn't feel like I had gotten a bad break."

Sieckmann had hit a 7-iron to ten feet and made birdie to get to 9-under while Lyle settled for par after missing a testy downhill 7-footer.

As the group walks to the seventh tee, a loud cheer rises from the seventh green where Couples has just made a 12-foot birdie putt to get to 9-under.

Davis tries to fade a 3-wood into the middle, but it stays straight and runs through the fairway on the left side. Lyle misses into the left rough with a 2-iron and Sieckmann pulls a 3-wood way left into the rough.

The three players get to their positions and Sieckmann has to play traffic cop because his ball has scattered the gallery. As he is directing people on where they're going to have to stand, a tremendous roar explodes from up ahead and echoes all around Riviera. Davis knows immediately what has happened.

"I said to Mark, 'Freddie canned it for two,'" Davis says. "You can tell the difference between Freddie holing one and Rocco holing one." Couples had pitched in from eighty-six yards with a sand wedge for eagle-2 at No. 8 to get to 11-under. The move that Davis knew Couples would make sooner or later has begun.

Sieckmann finally gets the crowd settled and hits a crisp 8-iron over a tree in front of him and onto the green, 12 feet above the hole. Davis then hits his first poor iron shot of the day, but it is poor only by his high standards. He pulls a 9-iron slightly and has to be content with an 18-footer for birdie. Lyle hits a 9-iron nine feet above the hole.

Davis misses his putt and makes a two-footer to save par, Sieckmann sinks his downhill slider for birdie to get to 10-under and Lyle 2-putts from the same line as Sieckmann.

At the 368-yard eighth, Davis hits a perfect 1-iron off the tee for the third day in a row; lobs a pitching wedge from 124 yards to within seven feet; rolls the putt in and for the third day in a row, he marks a three on his scorecard. Threes are wild here as Sieckmann makes a three as well, his third birdie in a row to get to 11-under.

Davis is now 16-under, four-under for the day, and as he walks to the ninth tee, a fan yells, "Another 63 today, Davis," and he says, "I hope so." As he gets to the tee, he starts thinking he might need another 63 because he sees the fans whooping it up around the green. Couples is on fire. This time it's a 12-footer for birdie to get to 12-under, and now, the man who has been the best player in the world during the last eight months has it going here at Riviera, a course that he won on two years ago. Couples has shot a front side 30 and Davis knows he is the man to watch.

"I wasn't really concerned," Davis says. "I knew what he was doing up there because he's a good friend and I'm interested in what he's doing. I was paying attention, but I always pay attention if a friend of mine is in front of me playing."

Davis hasn't hit a driver since the third hole and this thought crosses his mind as he stands over his tee ball. He gets out of his rhythm, tries to kill one and catches it on the heel of the clubface, hitting a weak cut that fortunately goes straight.

"When you try to hit it hard that's when you miss it," Davis says. "But that was a good miss, or whiff, because it went straight, only it was forty yards shorter than where I'd usually be."

He has to use a different sprinkler head than normal to get his yardage, then he checks that with George Lucas's book. As it turns out, he still has only an 8-iron left and that's good because the pin is five yards from the front and five from the right edge, down in the very small front portion of the green where accuracy is a must.

"I tried to cut it in with the wind, but it didn't move, it stayed right were I aimed and it came out ten feet left of the hole," Davis says. "I was telling it to cut, but that was still a pretty good shot because at the bottom of that green, there's no room. If you're on the green and the pin's down there, you're close."

After making a nice stroke back on the eighth, Davis puts a lousy one on his birdie attempt here and leaves it a foot short.

"The last one felt so nice and smooth so I just kind of got up there and said nice and smooth and didn't even get it there. That was a weak putt."

He taps in for par, watches Sieckmann do the same to snap his birdie streak, then sees Lyle roll in a 3½-footer for birdie to get him even with Sieckmann at 11-under.

Davis strides to No. 10 with a four-shot lead over Couples and a five-shot margin on Sieckmann and Lyle. He is 4-under for the day and feeling like he can go at least 4-under on the back. But this goal is not dominating his thoughts right now. What he wants to do is make birdie at 10. He has tried to drive the green two days in a row, missed left and had to scramble to make par. It's an easy hole that he has made difficult.

Couples, Mediate and Estes are still on the green, but Lyle decides he's going to lay up with a 3-iron and he places his shot in the left-center portion of the fairway. Sieckmann also lays up and he hits a 2-iron into the first cut of rough on the right. Now Davis has to make a decision. The pin is nineteen back and four from the right edge, so it is tucked near the bunker. If he hits a driver to the front edge of the green, which is 290 yards away, he'll have almost a sixty-foot uphill putt. If he lays up, he figures he'll pitch it up tight and make birdie because he's hitting his wedges so well. The temptation to try and get an eagle putt wins out, and Davis pulls his driver out of the bag.

"Sooner or later you're going to knock it up there and make eagle," he says, "but I hit the exact same shot as yesterday and the day before. I don't know why I hook it on that hole, maybe because I'm trying to keep from blowing it way right where you have no shot."

This time, he has pulled it across the cart path, past the water fountain which came into play yesterday and although he has more green to work with on his pitch, he is in a tougher predicament.

"I had a lot harder shot than yesterday because it went farther and I had to go around the tree rather than just under it," he explains. "The tree was between me and the flag, but I learned from yesterday. I just figured out what I was going to do, didn't worry about a yardage, got up and slapped it and it was a great shot."

His ball stops thirteen feet below the hole.

"It's amazing when you don't try, you just look at it and hit it, how much better you do, rather than thinking about everything that can go right or wrong. Just let your instincts take over. That was a perfect shot."

He thinks he has hit the perfect putt, too, but just like back on No. 6, his ball goes virtually into the hole and pops back out. "I wish you could study it and figure out what makes balls miss," he says with a grin. "That was going down and it just U-turned right out."

Sieckmann and Lyle had both hit wedges in tight, and after Davis' miss, each makes their birdie to get to 12-under and tie Couples for second, four behind Davis.

At the par-5 11th, all three players hit outstanding wedge shots. After a hooked drive and layup, Sieckmann strikes a pitching wedge from 111 yards to five feet. Davis, after a pushed drive and a pulled 3-wood, nearly holes an L-wedge from 30 yards with the ball stopping a foot to the right. "Another one where I just got up, looked at the hole and hit it stiff." Lyle had hit driver and 3-wood and came up just short of the green. He uses his sand wedge to bump the ball to within four feet.

And one after another, they all swish their birdie putts.

"Now I'm 17-under and I'm cruising along," Davis says, "but it's no time to relax because the guys I'm playing with birdied and they're 13 and Freddie's up there and you know he's gonna make some birdies coming in."

So he gets to the 415-yard 12th, watches Sieckmann and Lyle tee off, then steps up planning to carbon copy the drive that Lyle has just hit, a fade around the dogleg that will set up a wedge approach.

As his ball soars through the warm air, it appears destined to end up side by side with Lyle's. However it strays just a fraction to the right, catches a limb on one of the huge eucalyptus trees and falls straight down, costing him about one hundred yards of distance.

It is just past one o'clock on the West Coast and CBS is now on the air, so for the first time, the cameramen are roaming the fairways. Davis is good friends with David Finch, one of CBS' best cameramen, and when he gets to his ball, Finch has just finished running back from where Lyle's ball is to get into position behind Davis for his shot.

"Sorry I'm making you guys run so far," Davis says with a smile to Finch and the guy who is dragging the cables.

Davis' ball is sitting in an area that has been trampled down by the gallery so he has a nice, tight lie. That's the good news. The bad news is the limbs of the trees out in front of him about one hundred yards are hanging in his flight path so he is going to have to play a fade under and around those branches. Mark tells him the yardage is 205 to the hole and he checks to make sure it's correct. Satisfied that it is, he pulls his 4-iron out.

"I could probably get 5-iron there, but the wind was blowing in and there were big limbs up above that I had to keep it under, so I wanted to hit a nice normal 4-iron to the left side of the green, let it cut in there and if it gets to the bunker or it's short, no big deal, I can get it up and down," he explains.

He can't get it up and down from where his ball winds up, though. He overcuts the shot, it hits one of those hanging limbs and shoots down into the ball-swallowing barranca.

Davis has no idea where his ball has gone. He knows he's not on the green, but he is under the impression that he is in a decent position. Sieckmann and Lyle both hit their approaches on the green and only when Davis sees Lyle walking down in the barranca does he know that he's in trouble.

"It looked like it fell down okay on the other side of the barranca so I'm going down the fairway and then I see Sandy go into the ditch, and I said, 'Oh man, now I'm in trouble.'"

Oh man is right.

His options are simple. Either pick it up, declare it unplayable, take a penalty stroke and walk back to the fairway to hit his fourth shot; or try to whack it out of the knee-high grass and brush.

"I had a pretty bad lie, but I felt like I could get it out if I could get down to the ball," he says. "It was high grass, but it was kind of in a clear area. I had one big bush of grass behind the ball and I thought if I got through that, the ball would come out. You're more concerned about the grass in front because if the ball hits that, it takes all the speed off it and you stay in there. So I felt if I got through to the ball, it would come out good."

He doesn't, and it doesn't.

He takes a big swing with his sand wedge, hits the middle of the ball rather than underneath it, and it nosedives into the front bank, still buried in the hazard, only twenty yards closer to the hole. He takes a swipe at the high grass with his club in aggravation, curses himself, then trudges through the weeds in search of his abused ball.

He finds it, composes himself, then takes another swing, his fourth on the par-4, and manages to extricate the ball, but he comes up short of the green.

"That lie looked better, but it was probably worse because it was in that kikuyu grass that's grown off the fairway and it's real matted and thick. I could have gotten it on the green, but if you slow down at all into the ball, it's just going to stop it and that's what I did. I didn't swing through and dumped it in front of the green."

All this time, Sieckmann and Lyle are at the green, waiting for Davis to join them. Davis looks at his ball, which is seven yards shy of the putting surface, thirteen yards away from the hole, and notices it is cut, probably from his first hack in the barranca. He calls Lyle over and asks him if he can replace the ball and Lyle agrees.

Fresh ball and a fresh start is his thought.

"I said to Mark, 'All right, I'm gonna chip this one in,'" he says. "All I'm thinking about is chipping it in for five and getting out of there."

But he doesn't catch it solid with his sand wedge and the shot checks up and feebly stops seven feet short of the flag.

"It had spin on it and it just stopped dead, so now I've got that left. I'm trying not to get upset. I have that putt for double bogey and I'm trying to get my composure to hit the putt. Maybe I should have gotten mad and gotten it over with. But I went through my routine, had a little too much tension built up, didn't hit it solid and that goes by a foot and a half. I said to Sandy and Tom, 'All right, guys, I'll finish,' and I plowed that one into the hole, so that made me feel better to smash one in there when you're pissed off."

The triple bogey has sliced him back to 14-under. Couples had birdied No. 12 moments earlier so he is at 13-under, as are Sieckmann and Lyle. Fifteen minutes ago, he was running away with the tournament. Now he has come crawling back to the field, bloodied and bruised by the mean-spirited 12th hole.

Still, as he stands on the side of the green counting the strokes to make sure he has the mess correct on his scorecard, he somehow manages a smile.

"I told Mark I still haven't made a double this year," he says, "I have two triples, one here and one in Phoenix. Then I said, 'Let's go get some more birdies,' and he said, 'Just keep playing like you're playing.'

"Looking back, if we had had three or four guys out there and we sat down and said, 'Okay, here are the options and if you studied every option, yeah, maybe I would have taken an unplayable, then hit a wedge on the green and tried to make a putt for bogey. But that's not my style, I don't usually do that. When I've got a clear shot like I thought I had, I'm usually going to take it no matter what the situation. I made a decision, went ahead and played it. I don't feel bad about it. I made two bad swings, a bad chip and a bad putt. If I look at it that way, I was lucky to make seven. Every shot was bad, it was just one of those things. I was upset, but I said, 'Hey, you've got a long way to go. You're playing good, just get back on track.'"

Sieckmann hits 3-wood and Lyle 2-iron perfectly into the middle at the 422-yard 13th. Davis takes his 3-wood and literally talks himself into hitting a draw around the corner. Coming off the disaster at 12, his confidence is a little shaky and he questions whether he can turn the ball the way he wants. He convinces himself that he can, and he does.

Couples has missed the green and by the time Davis is ready to hit his 8-iron from 160 yards, Couples has settled for a bogey to slip back to 12-under. However, Rocco Mediate made birdie and now he's at 13-under. Davis hits a solid shot to within 12 feet and appears to have regained his composure.

However, he misses the putt for birdie and walks away feeling like he has thrown another shot away.

"That could have been the turnaround right there," he says. "I hit a nice solid putt, but it bounced a lot and it got left of the hole. It didn't look like it had a chance, but I wouldn't try to hit it any better. It only missed by an inch. Making that would have been the difference, that would have gotten me going again, would have been better for my confidence." Lyle and Sieckmann remain at 13-under with two-putt pars.

Robin and Lexie walk with him to No. 14, and Robin asks "What happened back there?" He replies, "Well, a lot of bad shots and a couple of bad breaks, but that was a long time ago." She looks at him quizically, then she realizes that she shouldn't have brought it up. She rubs him gently on the back and tells him she'll see him later and she walks toward the 14th green.

On the way, she hears the cheering when Couples makes a 15-footer for birdie to get back to 13-under.

"I saw Freddie can it, so now I know he's at 13 and there's a whole bunch of guys at 13," Davis says. "I said to Mark, 'Well, now we've got us a tournament here.' You tend to change your focus because now I'm mixed up in a battle with a bunch of guys. I just tried to forget about it and started playing to stay in the lead."

Sieckmann and Lyle each hit 6-irons and Davis chooses the same club. He has 174 yards, downhill and into the wind, so he tries to fade the shot, but it stays straight and comes down 30 feet to the left of the cup.

At the green, trying to generate some positive thoughts, he says to Mark, 'Ya know, I haven't made a 30-footer this week.'"

He still hasn't. He runs it past the hole by two feet, finishes that off, then watches his partners two-putt for par. He stays at 14-under, Sieckmann and Lyle remain at 13-under to tie Couples, while Mediate has dropped back to 12-under after a bogey at 14 earlier.

At the 447-yard 15th, Lyle hits a flameout to the right that hits a tree limb and bounces out over the bunker and into the rough, leaving him a difficult, yet clear shot to the green.

Davis watches this and says, "Why couldn't that happen to me? I get that bounce at 12 and I'm down there in the right rough and I'm wedging it on the green and making par or birdie. That's typical the way breaks run."

___

192

Davis pushes his drive around the corner, but it doesn't get out to the fairway and sticks in the first cut of rough out past the bunker on the right. Sieckmann pulls his drive into the left rough.

When he gets to his ball, he finds it sitting in front of a lumpy clump of grass. He measures the distance to the hole at 157 yards, sees that the wind is blowing into his face, and now he has to decide on a 7- or 8-iron.

"With the grass behind the ball, I know I have to hit it really perfect to get it down there to the green, but I didn't want to hit 7-iron and take a chance of getting it way by the hole and back into that swale."

So he hits the 8-iron and the clump of grass slows the club down, he doesn't catch it cleanly and he comes up 30 feet short of the green. Just as he taps his divot back into place, Riviera is rocked by another roar that can only be for Couples. Davis looks up, squints at the 16th green and sees a ball sitting about a foot from the hole. Couples's tee shot on the par-3 almost went in, so now the tap-in birdie will get him to 14-under and tie him for the lead with Davis.

Sieckmann has mis-hit a 7-iron into the front bunker and Lyle's luck runs out when he pulls an 8-iron way left, about sixty feet from the hole. Sieckmann finds his ball up against the lip of the trap and he swings mightily and barely gets it out. He then chips to within a foot, walks up and marks his ball rather than finish because Davis is still off the green.

Davis' chip is not difficult, but he makes it look like it was. Again, he doesn't clip the ball squarely and he leaves it six feet short of the hole.

"I didn't quite catch it, but it should have run down there a lot better," he says. "Some greens are fast and some aren't. I thought I had to be careful to keep it from going too far back and it surprised me that it was that short. Obviously, this green wasn't fast.

"I got over the putt and I'm thinking, 'Well, I can make this. I haven't made one in a few holes, I'm due.' I hit a good putt, but it wiggled to the right. I had it inside right edge to break left and instead it went right. You just say to yourself, 'How in the world is all this happening? I'm hitting pretty decent shots and I'm making bogey.'"

For the first time since the eighth hole on Friday, Davis is no longer leading the tournament. At 14-under, Couples now has a one-shot advantage over Davis and Lyle and a two-stroke margin on Sieckmann and Mediate. Davis is not happy. After six holes today, he was seven shots ahead of Couples. Now he trails. But this is where Davis' work with Dr. Bob Rotella has paid off. He doesn't take a negative attitude to the tee at 16. Instead, he's thinking, "Okay, I made birdie on this hole yesterday after making bogey [at 15]. You've got three holes left today, all day tomorrow, just forget about everything and try to get some birdie putts."

His yardage is 171, the hole plays downhill, and the wind is in his face, so he chooses a 7-iron. And then, more bad luck intervenes.

"I got up over it, I'm thinking this is a good 7-iron shot, and the wind just lays down and I'm in the middle of my swing and I just quit on it because I'm thinking I'm gonna hit it too far now because there's no wind. I was trying to cut it and now it cuts even more and it goes in the trap. That made me mad, but I said to Mark, 'As long as I don't have a buried lie I'm all right.'"

His ball is not buried, but the lip of the bunker is five feet high and the shot is only about forty feet long, so he has to get it up quick, then get it down just as fast.

"Basically, it was an easy bunker shot, one that I've hit so many times, except that I just made triple bogey, par, par, bogey, and I'm not feeling too good about the way things are going and this is an important shot. So I just said the only way to get it close is to try to hole it. So I just jumped down in there and hit it and I almost holed it. It was about six inches from the hole and as I'm walking up there, Sandy said to me, 'That was a touch of class.'

"That's my way of hitting bunker shots, just get in there and hit 'em. I'm always real confident in the bunkers. I've used the L-wedge forever, ever since college, and I'm real comfortable in the sand. So when I get in a bunker, I'm trying to hole it, and if not, I feel like I can at least get a tap-in. Bunker shots are so much feel and touch instead of mechanics. Seve Ballesteros told me one time on bunker shots, he just tries to get in and hit the shot as quick as he can and not think about it because he feels like if he gets in there and just makes a practice swing and hits his shot, just from hitting so many bunker shots, he'll take the right amount of sand, he'll land it in the right place, he'll have it all figured out. So the quicker you get in there and make a practice swing and just hit it like a normal shot, you can get it really close.

"Plus I know my bunker shots don't usually roll more than fifteen feet so I know where to land it. Now, if you get one that's going downhill or you get a buried lie, you have to get cute with it and hit it real soft or with some spin on it. But that one was pretty basic."

Lyle hit a poor 7-iron 40 feet left of the hole and comes away with a two-putt par while Sieckmann had stuck a 7-iron to within three feet and he rolls that home to get back to 13-under and into a tie with Davis and Lyle, one shot behind Couples.

"Last year, I made a decision on the last day to go ahead and try and kill one and get it way down there and try to knock it on the green in two," Davis says in reference to the long par-5 17th. "So today, I figured this is the time to turn the day around. 'Let's bust one out there and if you go in the rough, just lay it up and it's no big deal.' So I tried to kill it. Every once in a while I'll try to goose it a little extra."

He swings a little too hard, though, and pulls the shot into the left rough. Fortunately, he has a good lie and surmises that he can still rip a 3-wood and get very close to the green.

While he is thinking about what to do, there is a groan up at the green. Couples has missed a one-foot tap-in birdie that would have gotten him to 15-under and he has to be content with a par. "You never know what Freddie's gonna do," Davis says with a chuckle. "That's Freddie. He'll miss one of those every couple of weeks. It's just like me with my driver. About once a week, I'll hit a drive that just goes off the charts."

Sieckmann has put his drive on the right side of the fairway and he hits a perfect 5-wood to the middle, ninety-six yards short of the green. Lyle has pulled a driver into the left rough and like

Davis, elects to hit a 3-wood. He hits it hard, but pushes it into the right rough, seventy-seven yards from the green.

Davis sees what Lyle has done, but pays no attention. He has his plan and he's going to stick to it.

"I thought I could hit a flyer and get it over the trap," Davis says. "But I hit it on the heel so it never really climbed, it was kind of a bullet. If it had been to the right, it would have run past the trap, but it went left and went into the bunker. For some reason, when you're hitting a ball up a hill, it's easier to pull. I don't know why."

Two quick swings have landed him in trouble and now a birdie is going to be tough to attain.

"I had a sidehill lie in the trap and it's sixty-five yards to the hole, which is a long way out of a bunker. That's a scary shot trying to catch it clean and not hitting the sand first. So I figured the best way to play it was with a super long blast to get it on top."

Rather than use his L-wedge, he takes his sand wedge and takes a big swing and smashes the club into the beach. The sand sprays out in front of him and the ball comes out lower than he had hoped. The pin is twenty-seven yards back on a green that is forty deep, and the ridge that runs through the putting surface is about twenty yards back. The ball hits the ridge, taking the steam off the shot and it just sort of dies there, twenty-five feet below the cup.

The putt is uphill and will break about two feet to the right. He has to be careful because once he gets it over the hill, the cup is cut on a flat portion and the ball will smoke right by. He takes that into account and winds up leaving it two feet short.

He marks his ball, cleans away a piece of debris, then watches Lyle lip out for birdie from seven feet. Sieckmann has hit a pitching wedge to five feet and when he makes his second straight birdie, he pulls himself into a tie for the lead with Couples at 14-under. Davis then cleans up his par to remain tied with Lyle at 13-under.

He birdied the brutal 18th yesterday, and again Davis has forgotten about the previous hole already as he carries a positive thought to the 448-yard finishing hole. Sieckmann's share of the lead is in danger as he pushes his drive way right, into the trees just as John Daly had done yesterday. Lyle then hits an awesomely long drive into the right side of the fairway, leaving him just 171 yards to the hole. Davis compliments Lyle, then steps up and betters him by six yards, also on the right side of the fairway.

"I just like that driving hole, it sets up good for me because I'm a long-hitting fader," Davis says.

The big scoreboard shows that Couples has finished with a par at 18 to cap off a brilliant round of 7-under 64. His score of 14-under will put him in the last group tomorrow.

Sieckmann punches into the fairway with a 7-iron and will have to get up and down for par from eighty-two yards to remain tied with Couples.

The wind is blowing into the players' faces. Lyle chooses an 8-iron, but that proves to be one club short as his ball hits in front of the green and stops shy of the surface, leaving him a 45-foot chip. Davis had considered hitting 9-iron, but sees what happened to Lyle's shot; he selects his 8-iron. He tries to fade it to make sure he stays away from the hill on the left and he does so, but it cuts too much and winds up pin high in the fringe, thirty-five feet to the right of the flag.

Sieckmann hits a pitching wedge thirty feet behind the hole, and after his ball settles, he joins Davis and Lyle for the walk to the green and the fans stand and cheer the entire group. Davis waves in acknowledgment, but his thoughts are on his chip. The air has cooled down considerably and the wind has picked up. Supposedly, a storm is on its way to southern California and the forecasters are saying it could hit tomorrow. After what happened last week in San Diego, Davis starts thinking that the round could be washed out and if he doesn't make birdie and get even with Couples, he might lose the tournament.

"People were saying, 'Chip it in,' and I was thinking the same thing," he says. "I saw Freddie at 14 and I said to myself, 'Yeah, I have to chip this in just in case something happens like last week and if we don't get to play, at least I'll be tied with him.'"

Lyle bumps his ball up to two feet and marks, and then Davis prepares to hit his shot with his 8-iron. As he gets over the ball, a little boy directly behind him is musing to himself, but it is loud enough to distract Davis. Davis turns around and politely puts his forefinger to his mouth and with a smile, tells the youngster to please be quiet.

"I looked at him and told him to shoosh and that calmed me down, it was kind of funny," he says. "And then I hit a great chip and I thought it was in. It broke an inch too much."

He taps that in for par, sees Sieckmann two-putt for bogey and Lyle complete his par, and after shaking hands with his fellow competitors, they walk into the scorer's tent. Couples is in the lead alone at 14-under and Davis, Sieckmann and Lyle are all at 13. Davis and Sieckmann will play in the final threesome with Couples.

Couples is still in the tent and he says to Davis, "I'll see ya tomorrow." Davis then asks him, "Are you going to the hockey game tonight?" referring to tonight's National Hockey League game at the Forum between the Los Angeles Kings and Montreal Canadiens. "Yeah, I think we're going." Couples then pats Davis on the back and walks away.

Davis sits down and begins checking his card when Glenn Tait, one of the tournament officials, tells him there could be a problem.

"Glenn said, 'Check your scorecard carefully, but don't sign it until we talk to you about something,'" Davis explains. Apparently, a fan had called in and questioned whether Davis had grounded his club in the hazard at No. 12 when he swiped at the tall grass after his first shot from the barranca failed to make it out. That would necessitate a two-stroke penalty.

"Did you hit a shot from the barranca that didn't get out of the barranca on 12?" Tait asks Davis. He replies, "Yeah," and then Tait asks, "Did you hit the ground after the shot?" and Davis says, "No, I don't know how I could have because I couldn't hit the ground when I hit the ball, I just took a swipe at the grass with one hand." Tait says, "All right, we're going to check it on tape and see what it looks like."

This will take a few minutes because CBS is still live on the air and they don't have a tape machine available to use.

Tait then turns to Sieckmann, who was keeping Davis' card, and asks him if he thought Davis hit the ground and Sieckmann says, "No, he just swished at the grass, I didn't see any dirt fly up."

Davis chimes in defensively, "I swung as hard as I could at the ball and I couldn't hit the ground."

Davis looks irritated, but he's not worried because he is confident that he did not commit a violation of the sometimes goofy rules of golf. At this point, another Tour official, George Boutell, comes into the tent and Sieckmann asks him if he is needed any longer and Boutell tells him no. A third official, Mark Russell, who had gone up to look at the tape once CBS went off the air, then calls the tent and tells Boutell that there was inconclusive evidence that Davis hit the ground. So now, it is Davis' word that the officials will rely on.

"If it had even been close, they would have taken me to the truck and had me look at it," Davis says. "I knew it was a phone-in because if an official or a player had seen it, they would have taken me to the truck immediately to look at it. If I had thought I had hit the grass, I would have said something at the time, I would have told Tom or Sandy that I hit the ground."

Davis reiterates that he didn't hit the ground, so Boutell tells him to go ahead and sign his card. He does, satisfied that justice has been correctly served, but then he gets a brief scare when Russell questions something else on the tape.

Davis turns around and says excitedly, "Well now I've signed my card, guys!" Davis is worried because if he signs his card without deducting a two-stroke penalty, then he has signed for an incorrect score and has to be disqualified from the tournament. Boutell tells him not to worry because they instructed him to sign, so he's safe.

A few seconds later, the whole matter is dismissed, Davis' round goes into the books as a 70, and he will start tomorrow in the final group, one shot behind Couples.

It is not a pleasant way to conclude a frustrating day on the course and Davis is visibly unnerved. As he says goodbye to the officials and accepts their apologies for the disturbance, he is confronted with L.A. Open media assistants who request his presence in the press room.

"Look," Davis begins, "you've got a lot of guys at 13-under. I'm going to go hit some balls." The assistants don't take the hint that he doesn't want to meet the press. One of them says that he'll bring a golf cart down to the range and transport him over to the media center when he's finished hitting balls. Davis shakes his head and says, "Look, if I play well tomorrow, I'll come in. I just want to go hit some balls and take it easy."

Neither of the Tour media representatives, Marty Caffey or Lee Patterson, are present so Davis knows that it isn't imperative that he shows up. He also knows that the writers who really need him, like the beat writers from the local papers, will eventually come to the range and talk to him and he'll take some time then.

He spends the next few minutes talking to Robin about this evening's hockey game and tells her to take the car and he'll get a ride with Jeff Sluman later on when he's finished practicing. Then he and Mark trek down to the range and he signs autographs along the way.

At the range, his nerves begin to reconnect and as he starts to hit crisp iron shots, he starts to unwind and relax.

"I went to hit balls more for just a release than to practice and it felt good to hit a few and not have any pressure or to have to talk to anybody," he explains. "I got out some frustration and I just wanted to get something positive going for the next day and I did because I hit 'em pretty good.

"I was a little upset, not about the one hole, but that I let the whole back nine get away from me after getting to 17-under. I could see making a couple bogeys, but I should have balanced them out with a few birdies. I wasn't too happy playing 4-over for the last seven holes.

"You look back and it wasn't all that bad, except for No. 12. I played aggressive. I could have fallen apart after the triple. I'm disappointed to be at 13-under, but Mark said when we got done, 'You're still in good position, we'll get 'em tomorrow.'"

He does know, however, that he is going to have to play much better to beat Couples, especially now that he's spotting him a one-shot lead.

"I'm not really upset about losing the lead. Freddie played really good," he ways. "After what happened, I should have lost a lot of my lead, but I shouldn't have let him get in front of me. I knew Freddie was going to be the one who could run out and catch me. I wasn't really worried about anyone else."

Keith Clearwater is standing next to Davis on the range, hitting the ball extremely well, and Davis turns around and says, "Man, it sounds like you're really puring it." Clearwater nods and returns the compliment to Davis, then asks what happened at 12 and Davis gives him a brief explanation.

Davis notices that the range balls are really beat up and he tells Clearwater, "These things aren't going anywhere." Davis then rifles one with his driver that almost clears the 50-foot-high screen 250 yards away. "That didn't look like it went too short," says Clearwater, who can't get his driver anywhere near the top of the screen.

Rocco Mediate then ambles up and says to Davis, "Man, I couldn't believe your chip on 18 didn't go in. I was standing right there and I couldn't believe it." Davis just shrugs.

After a few more swings, he packs up and heads to the putting green, spends about five minutes aimlessly stroking long putts, then decides to call it a day.

He goes over to the fitness trailer and sits in a chair outside while he waits for Sluman to finish his workout. When he does, Sluman retrieves his car, his girlfriend Linda and his father George, and the group drives back to the Guest Quarters.

Sluman and Linda are also going to go to the Kings game, so they discuss their plans and after a shower and a change of clothes, Davis, Robin, Lexie, Sluman and Linda pile back into the car and drive to the Forum in Inglewood.

Davis is not overly excited to go because he had heard that Wayne Gretzky is nursing a knee injury and might not play. However, as soon as he walks in, the first player he notices skating is Gretzky and now he's glad he's there.

Davis' crew, as well as a few other players and their families and the fitness trailer therapists, Mike Ploski and Paul Hospenthal, are all sitting in the same section. The tickets have been provided by Kings owner Bruce McNall and they are in his private section, so Davis is pleased with the view. Waitresses come around and take orders for food and drinks, and hot dogs and pizza are the choice of fare in the first period.

The game is a good one, but watching Lexie enjoying herself gives Davis the most pleasure. Lexie has said she wants to learn how to ice skate and when she sees the Kings and Canadiens whipping around the ice, she becomes even more intrigued. She asks plenty of questions and Davis spends time explaining to her that the guys in the white shirts are trying to get the puck into the red guys' goal and vice versa. She is listening intently until the Kings mascot wanders up into their section, picks her up and playfully entertains her. For the rest of the night, she spies on him and whenever she sees him pop up in another area of the arena, she informs everyone exactly where he is.

Another highlight for her is watching the Zamboni resurface the ice between periods. She also gets a kick when Davis buys her a Gretzky t-shirt and a puck during the second intermission. But the capper is when all of the adults give her the prizes from their boxes of Cracker Jacks.

The original plan was to leave midway through the third period, but the game is tied at 3–3 and everyone decides to stay until the end. With 3:32 left, Gretzky sets up Tomas Sandstrom for the winning goal and then Gretzky wraps it up with an empty netter in the final seconds.

After the game, Sluman can't figure out exactly where the freeway entrance is and Davis and Sluman remark that this always happens when they leave the Forum.

Within an hour, Robin and Lexie are asleep and Davis takes some time to pack his bags so that Robin will have an easier time getting things together in the morning. They are checking out tomorrow and moving to a hotel closer to the airport tomorrow night because they have an 8 A.M. flight Monday.

Davis is expecting to play well tomorrow. He knows he has played well all week and despite an off day, he is still in the last group and that's where every player in the field wants to be on Sunday. He is a little nervous, but does not lie awake very long thinking about what will transpire tomorrow.

7 Sunday

It is 9:15 in the morning, one hour and ten minutes before he, Fred Couples and Tom Sieckmann are scheduled to begin the final lap in the quest for the $180,000 first prize. Davis is stuck in traffic on Sunset Boulevard and is growing impatient. There is hardly anyone driving east on Sunset, so Davis puts his flashers on, wheels into the oncoming lane and maneuvers his white Maxima up to Capri Drive and the entrance to Riviera. Luckily, policeman are not on duty, just volunteers directing spectators to the various parking lots around the club. Davis identifies himself when he gets to the gate and he is waved through by one of the volunteers. Only when he turns left onto Capri and the clubhouse comes into view does he realize he has forgotten something back at the hotel. His clubs.

"Damnit. I was gonna come in, get some breakfast, take my time . . ." he says in an annoyed tone that trails off as he spins the Maxima around and gets back on Sunset driving in the barren eastbound lane.

Sieckmann has been at the club since 8:15. He talked to his teacher, David Leadbetter, yesterday after he finished playing and Leadbetter noticed a flaw in his swing. Sieckmann is here early this morning so he can get on the range and work on the problem.

"I think I got off on my takeaway," Sieckmann explains as he sits in front of his locker lacing up his golf shoes. "David watched the telecast and he thought I got a little steep on the backswing so I worked on it last night and I'm going to do a little more this morning. David doesn't let you get away with much. He's really helped me with fundamentals. It hasn't been any one thing, it's just been a steady improvement. But being a golfer, it's natural to always feel like you should be doing better. I am improving and I guess that's the important part."

Sieckmann shot 66 yesterday even though it didn't feel like a 66.

"I didn't drive the ball very well, so I was pleased with the score. I'm going to have to drive it better today. That's what it's all about out here. You don't play well every day so one of the keys to success is being able to salvage some decent rounds when you do play poorly."

Which is what Davis failed to do after his triple bogey at No. 12 yesterday. Even though that wreck prevented a romp and brought a number of players back into contention, including himself, Sieckmann says he couldn't help but feel bad watching Davis hack it around in the barranca.

"I felt terrible for Davis," Sieckmann says. "He was playing so well through 11 holes. I thought he was going to run away, I thought we were all playing for second. He was in another world, playing at a different level. Emotionally, that has to be tough. It's sad to see something like that happen."

But because it did, Sieckmann has a chance to win today and he has that in mind as he walks out of the locker room en route to the range.

By the time Sieckmann gets there, it is close to 9:30 and Couples has finished breakfast and is on his way down to the practice area. As he walks, with his caddie Joe LaCava at his side, the fans let him know who they're rooting for today. "Go get 'em, Freddie," one man says. Another urges him to "light it up, Freddie." Others smile and say, "Good luck." And then when Couples is halfway down the hill, a guy standing up at the top yells down: "Don't choke!"

"Fuck you!" Couples spews back, looking over his shoulder.

"Way to tell 'em, Freddie," another fan bellows and Couples says, "I'll tell 'em."

When he strides onto the range, the incident is nearly absent from his mind. He slips back into his typically carefree state and starts doing what he does third-best in this world—behind playing golf and lounging on his couch with the remote control searching for sporting events to watch—and that's talking about sports.

Today's primary topic is hockey, a Couples favorite. He is leading the Los Angeles Open by one shot and in less than an hour will be hitting his drive on the first hole, but he couldn't be more relaxed if he was sleeping. All he has on his mind is the Kings-Canadiens game, which he attended the night before at the Forum.

"How about that pass by Coffey on the first goal," Couples says to Brian Claar's caddie as he positions a ball on the grass in front of him. "Unbelievable, it was just a perfect pass." Just as he completes the sentence, he swings his 9-iron and launches a shot high into the air.

Down the range a bit, another caddie is talking about baseball and he says, "This is the Red Sox year." Sieckmann hears this and says, "If I had a buck for every time I heard that . . ."

Claar's contribution to the sports-page review is a wisecrack about Prairie View, the Division I school in Texas that was winless in football and thus far is winless in basketball this season. Claar says, "Man, you can't accuse them of cheating. If they ever go on NCAA probation, you know they've got some bad coaches."

W ithin thirty minutes, Davis has returned to the hotel, collected his clubs, loaded them in the trunk and is nearly back to Riviera. Now, the traffic on Sunset has thickened and is stop and go from San Vicente to Capri. This is not good. On blink the flashers and over the yellow dividing line Davis goes again, trying to make up time. When he gets to Capri, the volunteer again waves him through and by the time he parks in the players' lot, it is 9:50. This is not the way to get ready to play the final round of a golf tournament, especially when you're just one stroke off the lead and have an excellent chance of winning.

To his credit, the hectic beginning has not frenzied Davis. He has maintained his composure, he is calm and the silly gaffe does not prey on his mind. He's here and while he won't have much time to get ready, by forgetting his clubs, he has taken his mind off the day ahead. He is turning a negative into a positive, implementing one of the most important lessons he has learned from sports psychologist Dr. Bob Rotella. Golf, just like life, will make you cry, scream, rant and rave, but only if you let it. Rotella stresses that a player must seek the good in everything he does on the golf course. His influence has greatly enhanced Davis' approach to the game, so much so that it has changed him off the course as well.

"I could have very easily just gone berserk," Davis says about forgetting his clubs. "I could have said, 'Oh no, now what am I going to do?' But since I started working with Bob, now, I tend to stay pretty calm and relaxed and try not to worry about anything. On the golf course, I kind of look like I don't care and I'm not paying a lot of attention or I'm not having any fun. It's not that at all. I'm so into concentrating and I'm trying to be calm and relaxed and trying not to get flustered.

"Bob says you have to think positively. I've learned to try to do that, but it's hard. You have to turn every little thing either into a positive or you have to make it a challenge and that's making it a positive. If I hit a bad shot, like Chip Beck always says, it's an opportunity to show off my abilities. That's how you have to look at it, you can't think of everything as a bad break or an impossible shot.

"So this morning, I was saying, 'All right, this will get me to where I have to do the things to get myself ready. No time to screw around, just do what I have to do and then go play. It's no big deal. I'll stretch, go to the locker room and get my shoes, hit a few balls and be ready to play and it'll keep me from thinking about winning or what I have to shoot. This will get me mentally focused on what I'm doing.'"

Bob Rotella grew up in Rutland, Vermont, loving all sports and playing them avidly. His next door neighbor, Bob Gauthier, was the caddie master at Rutland Country Club, a good golfer in his own right, and an excellent basketball player.

"He was my hero," Rotella says.

Through Gauthier, Rotella got a job in his early teen years as a caddie and he occasionally carried for the great Bobby Locke, the little South African master putter who had married a woman from Rutland and played regularly at the club. Golf really did not captivate Rotella, though. Caddies were allowed to play on Monday mornings, but that was the only time he would play the game. He was more interested in baseball in the summer, football in the fall and basketball in the winter.

Rotella excelled at all those sports in high school and went on to play them in college at the University of Connecticut. Upon completion of his undergraduate studies, he spent some time coaching lacrosse and basketball while he was working on his doctorate. What intrigued Rotella wasn't the strategical coaching of the games, but the mental side of athletics and finding a way to make an athlete become successful at playing the games. He came to realize that performance enhancement was every bit as important as calling the right play at the right time. From those roots, sports psychology has blossomed into a lucrative and highly satisfying profession for him.

"Whenever people ask me if I'm in love with sports psychology, I've always said, 'No, I'm not in love with it. I've always been in love with athletic performance and getting athletes to play to the best of their ability,'" Rotella says. "I look at myself as a coach of people's attitudes and minds. When I coached sports, I slowly learned that that was the most important thing we did. Pretty much everyone knew X's and O's because I would go to coaching clinics and that's all everyone would talk about, but behind closed doors, everyone talked about communication skills and inspiring people and getting them to believe in themselves and keeping their composure and getting them to concentrate.

"I'd find that everyone credited every win they had as a coach to having their heads in the right place or being ready to play or being confident. And when they lost, it was the opposite of that. So I started getting more and more interested in that part of coaching, which eventually led me to studying sports psychology in grad school and then doing it as a career. The love affair has always been getting athletes to perform to the best of their ability."

In 1976, Rotella went to the University of Virginia and set up a doctoral program in sports psychology and performance enhancement.

"You go through history and people have written about it, but it was fairly new in terms of really being applied and having people get into it," Rotella says of his vocation. "What I had going is that I played three sports in high school and college and had coached and I think I was able to take sports psychology theory and put it into practice and put it into a language that athletes and coaches could understand and be receptive to."

Rotella has worked with athletes in all different sports, but because golf is perceived to be such a mental game, he is perhaps best known for his work with pro golfers. However, Rotella debunks the theory that golf is the most cerebral of our games.

"I don't believe that, that's a misunderstanding of how important the mental aspect is in every other sport," he says. "Every sport I've ever been involved in, I've never seen one where the mental aspect wasn't unbelievably important. The fact that golf is an individual sport and you're out there alone, I suppose you can say something about that, but really, in every sport, it's absolutely essential."

And because golf is an individual game, the ability to think and focus is what usually separates the great players from everyone else.

"I have no idea how much of the game is physical and how much is mental, but I know at the very least, it's half and half," Rotella says. "The issue to me is, once you get to the professional level, everyone is a pretty good ball-striker so you're not going to beat everyone else out there just by having a better swing. At some point it's going to come down to mental.

"If we had a guy who had great talent and a great swing and a guy who had great talent and a terrible swing, maybe the physical things would be very crucial. But at the pro level, everyone already has pretty good mechanics. It's after everyone has those basic skills and everyone is pretty talented that the game becomes a mental challenge."

Back in 1987, Davis knew he had the physical talent to compete on the Tour. He also knew that something was missing, something was holding him back. He talked to his father and together they decided that Davis should work with Rotella.

"I felt like I had a good short game mechanically, but I wasn't using it," Davis begins. "I had heard from the teachers in the *Golf Digest* schools how much they liked Bob and how much they thought of what he was trying to teach. I had heard him speak and I liked his approach of sports psychology towards golf. It was more of what I could relate to than some of the other stuff I had heard. What he was saying was more target-oriented than visualization and it just seemed more athletic than mental to me.

"I could never figure out why my putting stroke looked good on film and felt right, but I wasn't getting a whole lot out of it. I didn't putt very well and I putted mechanically. I wasn't good at the touch of it. I wasn't athletic, I just did what most people did, work on the stroke so much so you feel like you have to make putts because the stroke is so good. So I went to Bob and he watched my routine and he had me work on hitting the ball to a small target rather than just trying to putt it into the hole. That's where we started. He wanted me to not think about holing my putt, he wanted me to think about hitting that small spot that I have picked out."

It has been five years since Davis first met with Rotella, but little has changed during their sessions. They still work probably 70 percent of the time on Davis' putting routine, then carry those discussions over into his chipping and overall approach to the game. And the sessions remain incredibly simple, almost to the point where the average player would wonder if Davis' elevator was going all the way to the top floor.

"It's real simple and it's the same stuff over and over and over," Davis admits. "In fact it's so simple that it's hard to do. All you're thinking about is reacting to that target rather than whether the ball went into the hole. You just want to hit it at that spot. Bob watches me putt and then he has me do a few basic things. He reminds me about picking out the target and making sure that I am committed to that target and that I am thinking about nothing else. Then he reminds me to make a practice stroke to it, then try to putt my ball to it. It's mostly just concentrating on your routine, how to keep concentrating on doing the things he wants you to do and keep on doing them.

"For example, I'll start a round and he'll tell me, 'Okay, on the first hole, try to do your routine and every hole after that, try to get better at it so that by the end of the day, you're doing it better than when you started.' It's very simple, but you always seem to have a tough time doing it. It's like your setup in your golf swing, it's easy to get it right, but it's the first thing that goes wrong because it's a feel and touch thing. The first thing you do when you start missing putts is you try harder and you start trying to make your putts and you get away from the routine that's been helping you.

"That's what happens to amateurs. Amateurs change their swing or their putting stroke every other hole. They say, 'Well, maybe if I try this,' or 'Maybe if I do something different I'll get better.' That's really the whole idea behind what Bob's doing. He is trying to get you to do the same thing over and over all day long and be consistent at it.

"Bob says, 'At the beginning of the year, how many strokes do you think you can save if you did your routine every single time all year long?' I'd say, 'Two shots a day,' and he says, 'Okay, that's all we're going to work on.' When you think about it in those terms, it really becomes obvious. I mean how many shots do you hit in a year that you weren't ready to hit or you weren't completely into mentally or you hadn't decided which was the right club? Probably tons. All the little things that are the things that seem to mess you up are the things in your routine. That's why I think you have to have somebody to remind you of how to do them. It's the same with teachers working with your full swing.

"You'll get in position to win enough times if you're a really, really good player. But you won't be super successful until you get completely comfortable in those situations and that's hard to do without being there mentally. Some guys learn by doing it enough times, but some guys are willing to try something like working with Bob and seeing if that will help them. For me, it helped a lot. There are guys out here who still say they don't need a teacher to help them with their swing, like John Daly. It just takes time for guys to accept [sports psychology]. People see that Fred Couples doesn't do it so they say, 'Why should I?' But, Fred Couples does it naturally and Jack Nicklaus does it naturally. They don't need anybody. It's guys who want to improve who need it.

"I have a plan and I try to stick to it every day. I'm trying to go out and birdie every hole. I've got a plan of how I can do that and if I do that, I'm going to play well and it gives me confidence because I know that every day, I'm not going to have to figure out something different to do to play well."

Rotella says that Davis has been a model student and he admits to feeling a sense of pride when he sees Davis playing well.

"I remember when his dad called me up and asked me what I thought and I told him, 'The thing I like best is that Davis isn't absolutely, totally in love with working harder than everyone else in the world.' His dad said, 'What?' and I said, 'What I like is that he's not in love with it. But, he shows me all the indications that he's willing to work absolutely as hard as he needs to to be as good as he can be. He doesn't work just for the sake of working. That shows me that he can really get interested in finding the most efficient way of being the best and he seems interested in finding the best way to have real quality practice and that's what you have to do to become a really good player.'

"A lot of guys will just go out and beat balls, but the question is, who can hit forty balls and be totally into every one? Davis has maintained it beautifully. As someone learns the power of the mind and the ability to focus their mind in the right place, I think they start finding out that if they start putting their mind in the right place, their ball goes good and that makes it easy to not feel like you have to hit balls all day.

"I feel very proud about Davis, but actually I still find myself having more thoughts about how happy his dad would have been. His dad and I were great friends. My last day with Davis Jr.—the week before he died, which I'll never forget because we ate an entire Pizza Hut Supreme pizza, which he washed down with ice cream—we probably spent three hours talking about Davis. I'm proud of Davis for doing the stuff he's doing. Davis doesn't make every putt he looks at, but what's impressive is he keeps doing the same thing on every putt whether they go in or not. It's one thing to know what someone has to do and to teach someone, it's another thing to have him do it and what's impressive to me is that Davis is doing it. The thing you get excited about or feel proud of is getting someone to keep doing it for a sustained time period.

"I know I have to find a way that works for everybody. There's a lot of people out there who say, 'All right, Rotella, I'll do that positive thinking stuff, but it better work.' Well with that attitude, don't even bother. If you only do it to get a result every time, you don't have a prayer. Just look at it as being honest. I can turn around and say, 'You just hit a bad shot, now be honest with yourself and realize that you're good enough that you can still make a birdie on this hole, or, if you make bogey, you're good enough that you'll make plenty of birdies if you keep your stuff together.' The bottom line is you have to go out and give yourself a chance and Davis is doing that.

"I spend hours just talking about every analogy that I can come up with to help him understand that putting is an athletic event or activity. You have to be an athlete, you have to feel and touch and in order to have feel and touch, you have to get your mind into the target. We talk about every sport under the sun. We talk about a basketball player looking and reacting, how much easier it is to shoot a jump shot when there's someone in your face than if the game's on the line and you have a wide open shot because they dropped back into a zone and leave you open, the urge is to take your time and get careful and make sure you make it. That's when you screw it up. You're taking the athleticism out of it and getting conscious. We talk about a shortstop running into the hole, picking up a grounder and just firing it over to first. I've showed him videotape of Larry Bird winning the three-point shooting contest, of him just looking and shooting and making a bunch in a row. Athletes in every sport do this, it's what separates them, the ability to just look and shoot when the game is on the line. Anybody can take their time and get careful.

"Another thing we talk about is him going out and watching people at his club. If they have three-foot putts and someone gives them the putt, watch how they just get up and hit it without trying or when they miss one, they rake it back the second time with so much less effort. It's a mind game."

Davis unpacks the car, then walks hurriedly to the fitness trailer and finds Mike Ploski and Paul Hospenthal closing down shop. Everyone else who uses the facilities has already done their pre-round exercises and stretching routines.

"Running a little late?" Ploski asks with a sly grin.

Davis explains his predicament and Ploski cuts him some slack and sets up a rubdown table while Hospenthal continues breaking down the truck.

While Ploski stretches Davis, he recalls the last time he had to do one of these last-minute jobs. Billy Ray Brown was so late before the final round of the Greater Hartford Open last year that the truck was almost completely packed up and hydraulically closed and he had to be stretched in the parking lot. He went on to win the tournament. Ploski spends about five minutes working the kinks out of Davis' body, then tells him he hopes the same thing happens to him today that happened to Brown last July. Davis says thanks, then hustles into the players' lounge to get a bowl of cereal and some orange juice.

He ingests breakfast, then rushes to the range, but before he hits any practice balls, he has to talk to Couples about the hockey game, which he thinks Couples skipped.

"You missed a good one last night," Davis says, shaking his head. He is surprised when Couples says, "No, I went."

"Where'd you sit?" Davis asks, and Couples explains that he sat down below, close to the ice.

"Wasn't Gretzky great?" Davis says of the Kings superstar who had a goal and three assists in Los Angeles' 5–3 victory.

Davis only has time to hit a few shots with his irons and one with his driver, which he mashes. He hands the driver to Mark and nods that he's ready to walk up the hill to the putting green.

Once there, he and Couples station themselves on the right side of the putting surface and after a few moments, they are joined by CBS commentator Gary McCord.

"Gary always likes to talk to guys before the round," Davis explains. "The TV guys like to know how you're feeling, how you're playing, what you're thinking about, things they can use on the air, and he didn't see us on the range so he got us on the green."

"Everyone tells me you're just playing great," McCord says

to Davis and Davis replies, "Yeah, I'm playing good, just a couple of bad holes."

McCord doesn't spend too much time working. Soon, the conversation turns to general chitchat. One of the subjects is the weather, which was supposed to get nasty today. Preparing for cold temperatures and rain, Davis wore dark corduroys with a navy blue shirt covered by a button-down blue-and-green checked sweater. The sweater is already off because after an overcast start, the sun is now shining brightly. Couples has on black pants, a green, blue, black and white striped shirt and the green sweater vest he had on at the range is now tucked away in his bag.

After a couple of minutes, McCord wishes them both luck and leaves them to their putting. A few minutes after that, Davis, Couples and Sieckmann are called to the tee.

"Let's go, Sieck," Couples says and Sieckmann replies, "Let's do it."

While they are exchanging pleasantries, Davis is dealing with a loudmouth fan. As he walks off the practice green, a thirtyish man yells down from the balcony, "Nice 12th hole yesterday." Davis looks up and in an uncharacteristic display of vulgarity mouths silently, "Go fuck yourself."

"I think he got the message," Davis says, "because he didn't say anything else."

That fan's comment indicates to Davis that this could be a long day. Just like the fans were rooting wholeheartedly for John Daly on Thursday and Friday, today, Couples will be "The Man."

Davis decides that he has to rise above that, not pay attention and just concentrate on every swing and block the partisan fans out of his thoughts.

Couples leads off on the first tee and shocks everyone by pulling his drive way left and apparently out of bounds. The excited crowd is murmuring when Davis is introduced.

"The people were still making a lot of noise when Freddie hit and I don't know if that bothered him or not, but when he hit it over there, that was kind of amazing," Davis says. "Most times you try to cut it back, but he just didn't get it going the right way. So I'm

214

standing up there thinking, 'Just get it down there in the fairway and pick up some strokes here real quick.'"

Davis plays his driver down the left side, but the wind does not move the ball back to the middle like he anticipated and he lands in the deep rough, but at least he's inbounds.

"I thought it was blowing right," he says to Mark as he hands him the club.

Sieckmann pulls his drive into the first cut of rough on the left, then Couples steps back up and hits what is now his third shot. He isn't positive that the first one is out of bounds, so this ball will be a provisional, but if the other one is out of play, this is the one he will use. And it isn't much better than the first as he blows it into the right rough.

"Now I'm thinking, 'Jeez, make birdie here and at least get one guy out of this bunch behind you,'" Davis says. "Him getting off to that kind of start is the last thing I expected."

Couples doesn't even bother walking to the ball on the left. He sends LaCava over and sure enough, the ball is on the sinister side of the out-of-bounds stake. A fan asks LaCava, "Do you want the ball?" and LaCava says, "You can keep that fuckin' thing."

LaCava trudges back across to the other side and hands Couples his 2-iron. He has trees on his right that are in his way and he must keep the ball under the limbs in order to get it anywhere near the green. He does this perfectly as his ball shoots out of the rough low, then gradually climbs into the air, carries the first part of the bunker and comes to rest in the fairway, sixty yards from the hole. The applause is boisterous and Couples waves thanks.

Sieckmann has 223 to the hole and he also uses his 2-iron, but he catches it thin and sends a weak fade into the right rough, forty yards short of the green.

Davis finds his ball in a terrible lie, nestled down in the thick rough. He has 219 to the hole, which is cut eight paces from the right edge, but aiming at the flag is out of the question.

"I tried to hit a flyer out of there and get it on the front left of the green for a two-putt," he says. "It was 201 to there, but it squirted out to the right and into the bunker which isn't a bad place to be."

After Couples hits a sand wedge to within eight feet of the

cup and Sieckmann pitches to within seven feet, Davis sizes up his sand shot.

The ball didn't get as far into the bunker as he thought so he is left with a 30-yarder off a precarious sidehill lie. In this instance, being in the sand isn't a very good break. He considers hitting his sand wedge, but because of the sidehill lie, he opts for the L-wedge to make sure he can get it over the lip of the trap. Sure enough, the ball comes out very low, just barely clears the lip, gets tangled in the rough in front of the green and dribbles onto the putting surface, stopping twenty-five feet short of the hole.

"The putt's uphill and I'm thinking, 'Get it up there, make it, it wouldn't be a pretty four, but it would be a four and Freddie's got to putt for six.'"

Davis settles for a two-shot swing as he and Couples both miss their putts, but while Davis taps in for par, Couples takes a fat seven to drop to 12-under, one shot behind Davis and two behind Sandy Lyle, who moments earlier opened his round with a birdie to get to 14-under. Sieckmann also 2-putts for par to remain at 13-under with Davis.

The wind is blowing right to left on the tee at No. 2 so Davis doesn't want to hit driver or 3-wood and run the risk of getting the ball up in the air and having the wind blow it into the rough. He hits 1-iron, doesn't catch it solid and sends a fade into the right portion of the fairway. Sieckmann pushes a 3-wood into the first cut of rough on the right and Couples takes out some aggression built up after his terrible start and blasts a 3-wood beyond the fairway and into the rough.

Davis has 195 to the hole and the wind has swung around and is at his back.

"I figured a good solid 6-iron because I was kind of pumped up and it was early in the round," he says.

He hits it too good, it lands behind the hole, doesn't check up and caroms all the way to the back of the green. The result doesn't bother him. He hit the shot pure and Mark reinforces that thought by telling him, "That's the smart thing to do today, take the club for the yardage and hit it because you're swinging so good."

216

Couples has a mere 140 yards left and he stiffs a 9-iron to three feet and that draws a loud roar from the gallery circled around the green.

Sieckmann had left a 5-iron just short of the green and after chipping his third shot up to four feet, Davis prepares to attempt his 45-footer. His ball is resting against the fringe, so he has to be careful about hitting it too hard. He hits it almost perfectly. His length is perfect, but his aim is one foot to the left. It's an easy tap-in and as he walks away from the hole, Couples says, "Nice putt, Davis."

Sieckmann saves his par, then Couples dunks his three-footer to get back to 13-under.

At the 441-yard third, Couples unleashes another savage drive, 328 yards down the right-center of the fairway and he turns and just grins a shy grin. His talent is enormous and he seems so unaware of it.

"Freddie just killed it down there," Davis says. "I was check-ing the wind and trying to figure out if that's why he was so far out there. The wind is blowing, and then it stops, so you have to check it on every shot today. It was helping here." Davis doesn't match Couples' bomb, but he hits a beauty down the middle.

The wind causes problems in his club selection for the approach. At 132 yards, it's either an easy 9-iron or a hard wedge. After a few moments, he asks for the wedge, settles over the ball, swings too hard and pulls the shot off the back edge into the short rough.

Couples hits a sand wedge from 113 yards, but doesn't hit a good shot. It checks up before the hole and spins back, leaving him twenty-two feet away, a poor effort from that distance.

Davis can't decide if he wants to putt or chip his third shot. He is twenty feet from the hole, but half of that is matted-down fringelike grass. He decides to chip it, but it bounces hard through the fringe, skips past the hole and stops eight feet past.

Couples rolls his birdie attempt to within a foot, walks to his ball, fishes a coin out of his pocket and tells Davis, "I'll wait," and Davis smiles and says, "Thanks, Jack."

"When he did that, I knew what he was doing," Davis says. "He was letting us finish before he putted because if he tapped in, everyone in the gallery would get up and take off. That's a Nicklaus move, saying I'll be nice and wait. It was the polite thing to do. The people are so wound up so he was taking us into consideration."

Davis makes his slider to save par, then walks over to where LaCava is standing.

"Man, these people are wild," he says to LaCava.

"Yeah I know," LaCava says. "What did you say to Freddie?"

"I said, 'Thanks, Jack.'"

LaCava just laughs.

Sieckmann experiences a nightmare on the green while Davis and LaCava are whispering to each other. After knocking a 50-foot birdie attempt three feet past the hole, Sieckmann lips out his par putt. He regroups, looks over the remaining two feet, then misses it. Finally, he manages to get his ball in the hole, but it goes on the scorecard as a four-putt and a double bogey. In the last two days, Sieckmann has putted seven times on this green and has played the hole in 3-over.

Couples taps his par putt in to remain tied with Davis at 13-under, one behind Lyle.

"Aw, get left," Davis tells his ball as it flies toward the fourth green. He had watched Couples hit an easy 3-iron fade to within 13 feet and decided that Fred had hit it too easy so he chose his 4-iron with the intention of swinging a little harder. The yardage is 231, but the wind is at his back, so this is the easiest this hole has played all week. Getting a 4-iron to hold isn't quite as difficult as stopping a 1-iron. The cup is cut 18 back and 10 from the left edge. He tries to start the shot on the left edge of the green and work it back, but instead, it starts straight at the hole and meanders to the right, hits into the side of the ridge on the green and stops 25 feet away. It's not what he was hoping for, but for the first time this week, he has a birdie putt on this green.

"On that hole, it's nice to have a putt that you can make," he says. "I was looking at the putt thinking, 'I can make this.'"

The power of Bob Rotella's positive thinking triumphs again. Davis strokes the putt a little too firmly, but it slaps against the back of the cup and falls in for birdie to lift him into a tie for the lead with Lyle at 14-under.

"It was downhill right-to-left and Mark really read it well," Davis says. "I thought it was going to break a little and he said, 'No, it's gonna break a little more than you think because of the ridge,' so I looked at it from a different angle and sure enough I saw the break."

As Couples is missing his birdie attempt and tapping in for par, Mark tells Davis, "About five feet from the hole, it just caught a little ridge and went right to the hole." Davis says, "Man, it was definitely gonna get there."

At the 419-yard fifth, Davis takes out 1-iron, feels the wind behind his back, changes to a 3-iron and smoothes one out into the fairway. Couples duplicates that position, also with a 3-iron.

From 163, Couples hits a hard 8-iron that gets past the hole by twenty feet.

"I could hear Fred and Joe talking and Fred was saying he had to hit 8-iron and he hit it solid so I said to Mark, 'I'm gonna hit an easy 8-iron,' but I caught it thin and when it hit the green, it just took off because it didn't have any backspin."

On the way to the green, the leaderboard shows that Davis is now alone in first because Lyle bogeyed the fifth. However, his lead is shortlived because he misses his 40-footer for birdie and before he can clean up his par, Couples makes his birdie attempt to get back to 14-under. The crowd is still making noise while Davis is putting, but he ignores them and rolls in his two-footer.

"What's this bozo doing back there," Couples says to LaCava, referring to a very amateurish photographer who has taken a position directly behind Couples on the sixth tee. Davis motions for the young man to move and he obliges.

"I like 8-iron," Couples says to LaCava and LaCava replies, "So do I." Davis doesn't. The hole is cut 7 yards on and 10 from the right edge and is 163 yards away. No way is 8-iron enough, Davis thinks. Especially, as it turns out, the way Couples hits his shot. He catches it thin and leaves it on a small mound just on the far side of the sand trap that looms in front of the green.

Seeing that, Davis knows it's an easy 7-iron and even though he doesn't get the ball to fade back to the hole the way he had hoped, it still finishes just twelve feet to the left.

Couples has a terrible lie and he tries to play a finesse pitch, but his club gets tangled in the rough and the ball just carries onto the green, stopping fifteen feet short of the hole and the crowd groans in disappointment.

"Fred's probably gonna make bogey so I'm thinking if I knock mine in, I can pick up two real quick," Davis says. Couples putts first, misses and settles for bogey to drop back to 13-under.

After studying his line with Mark, Davis goes through his routine and just as he's ready to stroke the ball, a jerk in the gallery mutters, "Miss it." It is just loud enough for Davis to hear, but at this point he can't stop because the putter has just been taken back. He is obviously distracted and the putt goes left of the hole and two feet by. Once it stops rolling, he turns around and stares in the direction of where the heckler is standing, although he isn't sure who it is.

"I at least wanted to let them know that they weren't going unnoticed and that I didn't like it," he explains, clearly perturbed by the incident. "That's really surprising that people would pull against you. I can understand people pulling for Freddie and not me, I have no problem with that. But it bothered me that they would actively and verbally pull against me."

There was a time, oh, for the first couple centuries, that golf was a gentleman's game, played by gentlemen and spectated in a gentlemanly manner. Today, it's hard to tell whether you're at Riviera Country Club or Dodger Stadium. And Los Angeles isn't the only place where crowds have gotten unruly. It is a disturbing trend that has mushroomed into a full-blown problem.

"Golf is getting more and more TV coverage, more and more sponsorship, more and more companies are using golfers and golf is just becoming so much more visible," Davis deadpans. "People

220

are getting accustomed to seeing our faces and they're identifying with a celebrity rather than for our golf games and liking Freddie because he's Freddie, not because of how he's playing.

"The fans are getting rowdier and rowdier. It's the same people who are going to football and baseball games. They think you're supposed to yell and scream, but that's not the way golf has been. Golf always had the most courteous fans of any sport, but that's all changing now. Even the last great hope, The Masters, with the most courteous crowds in golf, is getting pretty rowdy. People are realizing that they can yell and scream and be heard on TV if they're the first one that yells after a guy hits a shot. Then they can go back and watch the tape and listen to themselves and for some reason they think that's neat. We're gonna have to get used to it rather than hoping it changes because I don't think it'll ever change. It's just gonna get worse and worse, especially for Freddie. That's just part of being famous, you have to live your life differently. Freddie is gonna have to learn to play in a different atmosphere than me or a lot of other guys. He will have to get comfortable with it. And I have to get comfortable with playing with a guy like Freddie and handling it myself."

Jay Haas, who began the day six shots behind Couples, has birdied four of the first seven holes and has gotten to 12-under. Rocco Mediate is 1-under through six and is at 13-under along with Lyle and Couples. Davis, thanks to Couples' bogey, is back in sole possession of first at 14-under as he strides to the seventh tee with a pissed-off look on his face.

Anticipating bad weather, the Tour officials moved the tee at the 410-yard seventh up twenty yards to the forward tee box. Of course, the weather is fine, there is only a slight breeze blowing into the players' faces, so now they have a different type of tee shot than they're used to hitting here. Davis had hit 3-wood the first three days, but today, he chooses his 1-iron. He doesn't catch it solid and he misses the fairway to the right. He also has hit it fairly short and he is left with an uphill approach to a small green from 174 yards out.

From that distance, and with the pin stationed back left, this is one of the few holes where he will aim for the middle of the green, take a two-putt par and get out.

"It's a pretty dangerous shot if you miss the green back there," Davis explains. "So I didn't want to shoot for the pin."

He hits a sturdy 6-iron to the middle and leaves himself a safe, uneventful twenty-two feet for birdie. He will need to make that to maintain his hold on first because Mediate has just walked off the seventh green after making birdie to get to 14-under.

Couples had tried to blast a driver, but he pulled it left onto a cart path. After Davis and Sieckmann hit their approach shots, Tour official George Boutell tells Couples where he can drop and Couples follows instructions. Once the crowd is moved and settled, Couples studies the angle, decides to use his pitching wedge from 120 yards and hits a routine shot that winds up twenty-five feet below the hole. He and Davis both 2-putt for par and Davis and Mediate remain tied at 14-under.

After hitting a 1-iron into the fairway at the 368-yard eighth, Davis isn't sure what club to hit on his approach.

"I had 134 to the hole into the wind so I figured a 9-iron or wedge," Davis says. "I decided on the nine and Mark said, 'Yeah, if you hit wedge it'll hit the front slope and spin back too much.' So I thought a good solid nine would be perfect. Actually, I hit it a little long and it went past the hole and that gave me a downhill putt. I'm hitting the ball so solid that I'm never coming up short of the hole."

This is one time he would have liked to have been short. He has fifteen slippery feet to cover and as soon as he hits the putt, he knows it's going further than fifteen feet. It slides over the left side and runs four feet past. "Man, I thought I lobbed that one," he says to Mark as he walks past the hole to mark his ball. His attention is then diverted by the crowd.

"I heard the fans giving me shit again," he says. "They were saying stuff like, 'Oh, he's got a tester, he's got a tester.' They were happy that I didn't make it and that I still had some work left. So, I made myself concentrate and I said to myself, 'They're gonna be pullin' against you all day. Show 'em how good you can putt, knock this one in and don't let them faze you.' So I went through my routine real well and hit a good putt."

His par-saver matches Couples's one-foot tap-in and Davis remains tied atop the leaderboard with Mediate at 14-under followed by Couples at 13-under. Lyle is down to 12-under after a bogey at No. 7. Since his disaster at No. 3, Sieckmann has parred five in a row and remains at 11-under. Haas is also at 11-under after a bogey at No. 8 has slowed his charge.

The crowd has grown to problematic proportions because of the people who had been following their favorite players earlier in the day are now tagging along with the lead group. Getting from green to tee is becoming a struggle, especially here at the ninth where the path is longer than normal. There are now extra marshals patrolling, but still, the players have to fight their way through the throng.

"It's hard, people are yelling at you and trying to talk to you and get autographs, and you'd do it if you could, but we can't," Davis says.

After stepping into the sanctuary inside the ropes, Davis settles down, takes his time and rips a good drive down the right side of the fairway.

"You carried that one a little farther than you did yesterday," Sieckmann says with a smile, recalling Davis' mis-hit drive here during the third round. Davis replies, 'Yeah, that one had some roll on it.' Then he walks over to chat with LaCava, and LaCava asks him, 'What did you hit off the tee here yesterday?' Couples was playing in front of Davis yesterday and LaCava remembered being surprised that Davis was so far back in the fairway on the 421-yard hole.

"I thought you tried something different," LaCava says, "because you were way back. I was thinking maybe you had a different strategy or something." Davis says, "No, just hit it lousy."

Davis has 151 yards to the hole, uphill with a slight breeze behind him. He had been past the hole a couple of times when the pin was on top and it's on the top shelf again today, twenty-one back on a green that's thirty-two deep, and five from the left edge, so the plan is to hit a nice smooth 8-iron and try to get it below or even with the hole. He swings a little too easy, though, the ball hits into the ridge and sucks back down, leaving him an uphill 45-footer.

From 140 yards, Couples sends a 9-iron just off the back right edge and with a downhill 25-footer from the fringe, he isn't in much better shape than Davis.

"I said to myself that I definitely need a 2-putt here because Freddie could 3-putt from where he is," Davis says. "I wanted to make sure I got it up there, but I didn't hit it hard enough and left it four feet short."

Couples then puts the heat on by trickling his lag down to within a foot and he taps that in for par. Again, Davis can hear the partisan fans whispering as he lines up his par-saver.

"It was the same stuff, saying, 'He's got a tester,' or 'He's gotta make this.' It was starting to wear on me a little bit."

Regardless, he gets a positive read on the putt and calmly knocks it in and it is obvious that that one has made him feel good. He has left himself two tough par putts in a row and has made them both and because of that, he makes the turn tied for the lead with Mediate.

"I'm thinking, 'You've made two in a row, damn good. The crowd's not with you, so what. Let's go play a good back nine and prove to them that you're a player,'" Davis says. "I was feeling pretty good because no one was doing much, no one had gone out and shot 5-under on the front. I did notice that Jay Haas was coming up so that got me thinking about not getting wrapped up in playing just against Freddie or watching what the group in front of us was doing because there were guys out there like [Yoshinori] Kaneko and Haas going good, they don't have the crowd and the pressure, they're way out ahead, they can post something and feel good about it."

As Davis walks to the 10th tee, Robin and Lexie are nearby and Lexie says in a muffled voice, "Hi, Daddy," but he doesn't hear her. He has left the planet for a few moments, caught up in a daydream, and as he wanders around the tee owning honors, but not doing anything about it, Couples finally has to bring him back to this stratosphere by saying, 'You're up.'

"Sorry, I'm lost," Davis says, shaking his head as if he was trying to rattle his brains back into place.

He checks the pin sheet, looks down the fairway, then realizes that for the first time this week and for the first time in God knows how long, he's going to lay up off the tee on this short 312-yard hole rather than go for the green.

"With that pin [twenty-nine back, four from the right edge], the best thing was to lay it up and set up a wedge shot because there's no room to go," Davis explains. "Over the green or right is dead so lay it up and take the straight in shot."

He chooses 3-iron and hits it well, but he's not sure where it's going to end up. First he tells it to get up as he watches it soar toward the trap. Then when he sees it's going to clear that hazard, he tells it to get down because he doesn't want it to get too far down to the green where he'd have a tricky half-wedge shot. As he walks down the fairway, his feeling is one of relief because his ball is resting safely in the fairway.

Couples and Sieckmann also laid up and then both hit their approach shots past the hole, which gets Davis thinking that he better recheck the yardage. He concludes that the pin isn't really twenty-nine back from the angle that he has to come in on. He figures it's twenty-two yards of green to carry the trap, then three more to the hole, which gives him twenty-five yards of green. Add it all up and he surmises that he is eighty-eight yards away. It's a sand wedge distance, and as it turns out, it's almost a perfect sand wedge distance.

"I hit a nice one there," he admits. "I've worked hard on those shots and I've gotten a lot better at them. It had a chance to go in and I was thinking before I hit it that it was makeable. Then I said to myself, 'Pretty easy, wasn't it. Why didn't you just lay it up every day and hit that sand wedge in and get yourself a short putt rather than scrambling around every day trying to get two and end up making four.'"

Couples 2-putts for par, as does Sieckmann, and then Davis taps in from eighteen inches for birdie to move into sole possession of first at 15-under.

Hunger doesn't care that it's the last round of the Los Angeles Open and Davis is holding a one-shot lead. Hunger doesn't have a schedule, it has only a need to be quenched. And as he stands on the tee at the 566-yard 11th, the time has come for Davis to fill that need. His light, rapid breakfast this morning has finally caught up to him and now he's hungry. Playing in the last group of the day, he can only hope that there is some fruit left in the cooler next to the tee box.

He manages to forget his growling stomach as he surveys the fairway. However, he also forgets about rhythm and tempo, swings a little too hard trying to kill one and hits a weak, short fade that stops in the first cut of rough on the right.

"Everytime this week I've tried to hit it a little too hard, I hit that low heel cut, so that tells me that I need to use my normal pace swing and just swing, not try to hit it extra hard," he says.

He wanders over to Mark, hands him the driver, then goes to the cooler and luckily, there is an apple in there. He waits for Couples and Sieckmann to hit, then takes his first bite as he begins walking down the fairway.

Couples is eyeing his apple and although he doesn't say anything, Davis knows his fellow competitor would probably love a chunk. He tosses him the apple, Couples winks and after taking a couple of hearty bites, tosses it back. Davis then sees Lexie over by the ropes on the left and gives her a wave. He is relaxed and in control.

He is also well behind the drives of Couples and Sieckmann and with 280 yards to the front, has no chance of reaching the green in two, even though he has his 3-wood in his hands.

"I knew Freddie was going to knock it on or at least get it real close, so I had to keep mine in the fairway where I could set up a good wedge shot," Davis says.

Mark asks him what his target is and he says, "That big tree," and Mark says, "Yeah, that's a good target." Then Davis asks, "You think I can clear that hump?" Mark replies, "If you take it over the left side."

Davis takes one more look at the target tree, gets set up and does what he has to do. He hits a solid shot that comes up

226

forty-five safe yards short of the green. A fan in the gallery, impressed by the result, tells his companion, "See, the secret is to eat apples."

Like Davis predicted, Couples blasts a 3-wood onto the left side of the green, about forty feet below the hole. The crowd roars its approval and Davis knows that this could be the start of a surge by the man who is considered the best player in the world.

The beauty of Fred Couples's swing is its simplicity and the effortless manner in which he executes it. It doesn't seem possible that this man of average build (one inch shy of six feet, 185 pounds) can hit a golf ball so far. Rick Reilly of *Sports Illustrated* described his motion as "Vermont syrup—slow and sweet."

It is the swing that captivates you when you watch Couples play. He has been called laid-back, which he does not deny, and his swing is a mirror of his sleepy personality. He takes the club back slowly, sets it casually at the top, then thrusts it downward with a tempo that does not change from driver to sand wedge. Yet when club meets ball, ball flies. And flies. And flies.

Over the past nine months, not only has the ball been flying far, it has been flying straight. Starting with the U.S. Open at Hazeltine last June, Couples has played in 19 tournaments around the world. He won two PGA Tour events, the Federal Express St. Jude Classic in Memphis and the B.C. Open in Endicott, New York. He was *Golf World's* 1991 PGA Player of the Year, he won the Tour's Vardon Trophy (for best scoring average) and capped last season by winning the rich Johnnie Walker World Championship in Jamaica.

In addition, he finished in the top 6 in 10 of the other tournaments, including thirds at the U.S. Open and the British Open. And not to be forgotten was his brilliant play in the Ryder Cup matches as he led the United States to victory over the Europeans at Kiawah Island, South Carolina.

He has gone from being one of the great enigmas in the history of the Tour to the top of the professional golf summit. To many, the refrain is: "It's about time."

Couples was raised in Seattle, the youngest of three children.

His father, Tom, was an employee of the city's recreation department and for a time was a minor league baseball player so athletics were always big in the Couples household. As a youth, Couples played soccer and baseball as frequently as he played golf, but by the age of thirteen, he started enjoying the challenge golf presented and took an interest in practice as well as playing. He would go to Jefferson Park, a local muni in Seattle that had a driving range, where he would beat balls and play the short nine-hole course all day.

He attended an all-boys Catholic high school and played on the soccer and golf teams, but made his mark with his clubs, not his feet.

He chose to attend the University of Houston, made the golf team as a freshman and in 1978 and '79 was an NCAA All-American. Two of his Cougar teammates were current PGA pro Blaine McCallister and CBS sports announcer Jim Nantz. Nantz, who was a pretty good player, has been quoted as saying that when he saw the way Couples hit the ball, it made his decision to pursue a career in broadcasting a whole lot easier.

In August of '80, prior to his senior year, Couples went to Long Beach, California, to visit his girlfriend, Deborah, whom he had met the previous fall while attending a Houston football game at the Astrodome. While in Long Beach, he went to play golf, but when he arrived at the course, he found out that he couldn't play because a pro tournament, the Queen Mary Open, was being held. When told he had to be a pro to enter, Couples came back the next day, had a friend's father pay his $250 entry fee, and his days of playing for the Cougars were over. He tied for sixth, won $2,800, then decided to try PGA Qualifying School a couple of months later.

Armed with that silky, wonderfully tempoed swing, he survived Q-School and led all PGA rookies in earnings in '81. He then served notice that he was a player in '82 when he finished third in the PGA Championship at Southern Hills in Tulsa. He shot 66 on the final day, but just as impressive was his PGA Championship 9-hole scoring record of 29 during the first round.

He earned his first victory at the age of twenty-four in the 1983 Kemper Open on one of the finest courses in the world,

Congressional in Bethesda, Maryland, beating four players in a playoff, then surviving a wild victory hug from Deborah, who had become his wife. In '84, he gained a ten-year exemption by winning the Players Championship at Sawgrass. He tied the course-record of 8-under 64 in the second round, then held off a late charge by Lee Trevino to win by one.

It was then that greatness was expected of Couples. He was supposed to keep winning and winning and become the next great, dominant player that American golf fans had been pining for. But he did not win again until 1987 at the Byron Nelson Classic, and critics began wondering if he had the fortitude to win consistently on the Tour and take responsibility for his immeasurable talent.

He lost the Pheonix Open in '88 in a playoff to Sandy Lyle after blowing a chance to win on the 72nd hole. In '89, his loss to Christy O'Connor in his singles match on the final day of the Ryder Cup cost the U.S. the title. He won in Los Angeles in February of '90, but a propensity for missing short putts in the final round of the '90 PGA Championship at Shoal Creek cost him his first major title and again, the doubters clawed at him.

In March of '91, with Couples still spinning his wheels, Tom Weiskopf, in an interview with *Golf Digest*, said Couples had "great talent, but no goals in life. Not one. He's not as easygoing as he seems. You can see the pressure gets to him."

Couples brushed off the remark, but it did strike a nerve. He began re-evaluating his career and decided that working on the driving range and the putting green was a more productive way to spend time than sitting on the couch switching channels with the remote control.

He also sought advice from veteran Raymond Floyd, and he spent a week at Tom Watson's house in Kansas City just talking about golf. Floyd and Watson shared some of their knowledge with Couples and he was willing and eager to learn.

"I knew I was a pretty good player," he told the Associated Press. "I felt like I could go play this week, then go to the next week and not have to practice Monday, Tuesday or Wednesday and play again on Thursday and everything would be fine. There were weeks where I kind of threw away a good week because I didn't practice very hard.

"Six years ago, I tried just as hard. I just wasn't as good. People say they think I care more now. It's just that back then I wasn't as good as I am now. It's fairly simple."

Yes, golf has been simple for Couples lately.

"Fred has gotten so that he's separated himself from the other players," NBC commentator Johnny Miller told *Golf World*. "People said that would never happen again, but he's proven them wrong."

Couples told *Golf Digest* that his failure to win in the '89 Ryder Cup probably turned his career around.

"I'm not afraid to say I cried," Couples said. "Ray Floyd said, 'This will make you a better player. This is what the Ryder Cup is all about. It's about winning and losing. You didn't lose the Ryder Cup for us. We ended up tying as a team so we shouldn't feel too bad. This isn't the end of the world. You'll be back.'

"I decided that I really hated to lose. Now, when I'm in a golf tournament, when I've lost before or when I've done some things that caused me to lose, it now bothers me. Before, maybe I'd say I did my best and I'll get 'em next time. Now I look back at that Ryder Cup and think that maybe if I had just bore down and had that killer, killer instinct, maybe one shot would have been a major deal. After that, I felt like it was an experience that made me tougher in competition."

It was never more evident than in the '91 Ryder Cup when he posted a marvelous 3–1–1 record and was the largest reason why the U.S. regained the coveted prize from the Europeans. It was the stamp of approval he needed to legitimize his season. To that point, he had won in Memphis and Endicott to raise his pro victory count to six, but hanging over him were his lackluster performances in majors and in the '89 Ryder Cup.

"I proved that I didn't screw up a good year by not playing well in the Ryder Cup," he said. "The Ryder Cup was a blast."

"He hit it on so I'm thinking, 'You've got to hit your wedge in tight, you hit a good one on the hole before, do it again,'" Davis says of his third shot at the 11th hole.

He thinks he has hit a good L-wedge, but it hits just short of the hole, doesn't check up, skips by and winds up a disappointing twelve feet behind the cup. Couples then narrowly misses his eagle attempt and settles for a tap-in birdie to get to 14-under.

"Fred's made birdie so here's the time to make one," Davis says. Just as he is ready to putt, another fool in the gallery coughs in an obvious attempt to distract him. Unlike back at No. 6 when it bothered him, this time Davis is unaffected by the noise. As soon as he hits the putt, he says to himself, "Perfect, it's in." It is right on line, it breaks where he had read it to break, it has the right speed, all systems are go. Then one foot short of paydirt, a spike mark sends the ball off its path and the birdie is lost.

"I looked over at Freddie and he's rolling his eyes and saying, 'You got screwed there,'" Davis says. "Then Joe says to me, 'Man, you got screwed, that was a great putt.' That's what's so much fun about playing with Freddie, it's not like he's happy that I missed and he's on to his next thought, it's 'Too bad Davis missed that putt.' When I hit a good shot, he says, 'Good shot,' and vice versa. That makes it more fun.

"I won at Hilton Head last year playing with Ian Baker-Finch and we're good friends and we're going down the stretch and we'd hit and then we'd walk off the tee and talk and people are wondering, 'What are these guys doing, they're playing against each other and they're talking and being friendly.' There's no reason why we can't enjoy it. Sure, when I'm over my shot, I'm thinking about hitting a good shot and beating whoever I'm playing against, but after I do that, there's no reason why Ian and I or Jeff [Sluman] and I or Fred and I can't talk. I played against Mike Hulbert at Kapalua and we battled it out all day, went to a playoff, I lost and we went to dinner together that night. I'm not going to not talk to him for four hours because I'm trying to beat him. It's still you against the golf course."

One shot separates Davis from Couples, Mediate and Lyle. Yes, Lyle. The Scot has rebounded from a 2-over 37 on the front and up ahead at the 12th green has just made his third birdie in a row, a little 3-footer after a fine approach, to get back to 14-under.

Back at the tee, the art of positive thinking is being put to the test. Yesterday, it was here at the 12th hole that Davis met disaster in the form of a triple-bogey. He is back today, again atop the leaderboard, but not nearly as comfortably.

Couples is up first and he blasts a big, high cut into the middle of the fairway, a perfect shot. Now Davis has to fight the crashing inside his brain.

"I told myself to 'put it out of your mind.' Hit a good drive and this hole is easy," Davis says. "If I concentrate when I'm going through my routine, I'll do fine. If I concentrate on not hitting it to the right again like I did yesterday, I'll hit it right or left or somewhere, but it won't be straight. If all you're thinking about is going through your routine and hitting a good shot, it's easier to block those thoughts out of your head."

Davis' routine is flawless. His drive leaks a bit to the right, but not as bad as it did yesterday. The eucalyptus trees can't knock this one down and although it bounces into the first cut of rough, it is not a problem because he still has a clear shot to the green and the horrible memory of his tee shot here yesterday has been scuttled forever.

As he walks down the fairway, Couples asks him if his ball stayed in and Davis replies, 'No, it's in the right rough. I'm always in the right rough on this hole.' Then Couples sticks out his right hand, which is full of sunflower seeds courtesy of LaCava. Repayment for the apple back on 11. But Davis says, "No thanks," and they go their separate directions.

It's 138 yards downhill to the pin and Davis pulls out his pitching wedge. "Do you like wedge?" he asks Mark and Mark says, "You have to hit it pretty solid to get it there, but I like it because there's not much room behind the pin." Davis' shot checks up quickly and comes up 25 feet short of the hole. He grouses about not hitting it harder, but Mark says, "Hey, you hit a good straight shot, it checked up, you've got an easy putt up the hill, don't worry about it."

"Mark's been real good about not letting me complain about a pretty good shot and not letting me get negative about the way I'm hitting it," Davis says.

Couples has just 135, but he hits a terrible wedge that flies over the back of the green to the left. As soon as he follows through, he looks down at the ground, refusing to watch the flight of the ball. The whooping crowd is now quiet as the players make their way to the green because the favorite has put himself in a tricky predicament.

It grows even quieter when Couples doesn't get his chip all the way to the hole and leaves himself seven feet to save par.

Davis has a putt that he thinks is going to break about two inches to the left, but as he hits it, he realizes he has pushed it out about four inches to the right and as it gets closer to the hole, he knows it's not going to break back enough. "Dam," he mutters as it slides two feet by. He knocks that in for par, then watches passively as Couples reads his putt. It's straight, but it almost seems like Couples is trying to read some break into it. However he doesn't play any, rolls it right at the hole and it tumbles in to keep him at 14-under. The crowd lets out a roar and Couples tips his visor in appreciation.

Up ahead at 14, Jay Haas nearly makes a thirty-foot putt for birdie and his tap-in par leaves him at 13-under. From the fairway at 13, Lyle pushes his approach into the right fringe, pin-high, and Mediate follows with an excellent shot out of the left rough to within 10 feet. A birdie would tie him with Davis for the lead.

Back on the tee at the 422-yard 13th, Couples works his ball around the dogleg to the left with his 3-wood, but pulls it too much and he lands in the left rough. Davis sees how far down Couples has driven it and decides to also back off and use his 3-wood. Just before he hits, the crowd at the green groans as Mediate misses his birdie putt to the right and settles for par.

This is not the place to pull a drive, but Davis does. He had done it Thursday and Friday on No. 5 and it had cost him bogeys and he had also done it on Thursday at No. 2 and wound up with a bogey.

"I've had a few of those this week and that comes from trying to draw it around the corner rather than being happy at the corner," he says after watching his ball fly into a tree on the left side and drop straight down.

Luckily, he has a good lie, but he still has to play a low hook around the trees to get the ball to the green. Mark walks up to get a yardage from a sprinkler head, but Davis isn't quite sure it's correct so he checks it himself to be safe. He comes up with 204 to the front of the green, then 29 more back to the pin. Also, the hole is cut way left, just four yards from the edge.

Davis aims a 4-iron at the bunker on the right, hoping that it would move left toward the green. However, he catches it thin, the ball flies straight into the trap, bounces out and plops down into the deep rough on the far side of the bunker.

Davis starts walking toward the green, then pauses to watch Couples hit his 9-iron approach from 140 yards. He doesn't need the roar from the green to alert him that Couples has stuck a beauty in there about three feet below the hole. With Couples almost certainly about to make birdie, Davis knows he may go from one shot ahead to one shot behind unless he can get up and down.

Davis and Mark agree that it's ninety-four yards to the hole so Davis takes a half-swing with his wedge and slashes the ball out of the thick grass. The grass turns the club slightly, causing him to pull the shot left. The ball scoots past the hole and goes to the back of the green.

After checking the terrain, Davis decides to putt from the fringe. He has about two feet of fringe to get through, and that creates a problem.

"I was afraid that if I chipped it with the elevation change, it might not bounce straight, so I putted it," he explains. "And as always when you try to putt from the fringe, it took a little funny wiggle out to the right and got off line right away. You don't figure you're gonna make par from way back there, but it would have been nice to have a putt on the green."

Moments later, Couples rolls in his birdie and vaults into a one-stroke lead. Davis walks over to the new leader and says, "Nice putt," and Couples nods and says, "Thanks."

On the way to the 14th tee, Davis notices that Lyle and Mediate have both made bogeys at 14 and have dropped back to 13-under, so Davis is alone in second at 14-under, one behind

Couples. As Davis walks through the gallery, Robin and Lexie sidle up to him and Lexie shows off her Cracker Jack tattoos which she has affixed all over her arms. "Boy, you've got 'em all," Davis says to his daughter. "I don't want to take a bath," she says to her father, knowing that if she does, her tattoos will wash off. He laughs, gives her a kiss, then Robin says good luck and he steps through the ropes and onto the tee box.

Couples is speechless after launching a 6-iron over the green. With the wind blowing steadily from left to right, Couples aimed way left and tried to cut the ball into the pin, which is stationed 16 back and nine from the right edge. Actually, Couples should be feeling fortunate because if not for the gallery around the green, his ball would have gone down the hill.

Davis watches Sieckmann hit a 6-iron over the back edge and that is more than enough to convince him what club to hit.

"I'm like, 'What's going on?' After I saw it once I didn't need to see it again so I knew what I was hitting—it's 182 to the pin, the wind's left-to-right and it's helping—it's a smooth 7."

His swing is fluid, the wind leaves his ball alone and it lands softly, ten feet to the left of the pin.

Couples finds his ball in matted-down rough, pin high, but halfway down an embankment. With the hole cut just nine yards from the right edge, Couples will not have much green to work with. The first thing he has to do is move the gallery back on the right. Next, he asks a few photographers to re-position themselves and they comply. Then he begins checking the terrain from behind his ball, from midway between his ball and the flag, and then from behind the flag. Finally, he decides where he has to land the shot and in his mind, visualizes the ball arcing to that spot. When he is ready to play the stroke, his lips are pursed and his eyes are riveted on the patch of grass he hopes to hit the ball to. He then focuses on the back of the Maxfli, takes his sand wedge back just a few feet, moves it forward delicately yet purposefully and slides the clubface softly under the ball. It pops into the air and lands almost exactly where it was supposed to. It skips through the kikuyu rough, dribbles onto the putting surface and methodically makes its way to the hole, stopping two feet short and left of the flagstick. It is sheer brilliance and as he walks up the hill and onto the green, the crowd's loud cheering and clapping ringing in his ears, he looks at Davis and shakes his head, knowing that luck also had a role in the terrific result of that shot.

"He studied and studied on that one," Davis says. "He hit two pitch shots earlier that weren't that good, so he was giving that one a better look and he hit it just perfect. He came up and said, 'Damn, I can't believe that.'"

After Sieckmann's lag putt, Davis goes to work lining up his attempt to regain a share of the lead.

"It was uphill, just outside the left edge and I was real confident that I'd make that one," Davis says. "After I hit it, it was going and going and just before it got there, it looked like it wasn't going to break, but then it dove in at the last second."

Davis pumps his fist, retrieves his ball from the hole, then walks over to talk to Mark while Couples and Sieckmann clean up their pars.

"That thing tried to hang on and not turn," he says to his brother, and Mark says, "Yeah, I thought it did, too. You hit it so solid."

After hitting a truly terrible approach shot at the 15th, way right and over the green, Lyle hits a marvelous chip shot to within eight feet and eventually saves his par to remain at 13-under. Mediate's two-putt par also keeps him at 13-under, two strokes behind the co-leaders, Davis and Couples.

There are four holes to go, possibly more, and here is where the pressure starts to increase on the PGA Tour. Someone is going to win the tournament and everyone else is going to lose. There are no ties. Sure, win or lose, the first and second-place finishers will each bank six-figure checks, but winning is all that matters to these players. Careers too often are judged by how much money a player has won when in reality, victories are the only true barometer of a player's greatness. Jack Nicklaus is not the all-time career money leader, but is there any question who the greatest golfer of all time is?

Davis loves to make money because money allows him to lead the type of life-style that he prefers. But winning golf tournaments is what drives him to be the best player he can be. And as he walks to the 15th tee, victory is within sight. He feels mentally stable and is ready to meet Couples' challenge.

"Yesterday, the last seven holes, I was uncomfortable all the way in, but when I started today, I felt a lot better and then once I got going, I felt real good," he says. "You get nervous the last three or four holes when it's close, but most of the time that makes you concentrate better. You know you're nervous and shaky, but it makes you bear down and it's more fun than being behind and playing bad and having things go the wrong way. Actually, it's more excitement than nervousness. People might look at us and notice that we may be walking faster or something and they might think we're nervous, but it's not really nervousness, it's excitement because you're trying to win. You're enjoying yourself and you have all that adrenaline going."

Back on the fifth hole earlier in the day, Couples stood on the tee and although he seemed ready to hit his shot, he wasn't, so he called LaCava over to help him complete his preparation. All he wanted his caddie to do was reassure him that he had chosen the right club and he had picked the proper area to aim at in the fairway. On the tee at the 447-yard 15th, Davis needs the same type of help from Mark.

"I'm up, the wind is blowing strong up the hill, I teed it up and then I called Mark over," Davis explains. "I just wanted him to talk to me before I hit the shot so I'm thinking clear. The caddie's main job when you get going good is to keep you focused on what you're doing."

Davis hits a high fade down the left side of the fairway and is happy with the result. Couples then hits his tee ball down the middle, three yards past Davis.

In the fairway, Davis has to ask Couples who is away, he or Sieckmann, and Couples judges that Davis should hit first.

"I had 179 and it was way downhill because the pin is back right and that part of the green is lower than the front part," Davis says. "So I took 6-iron and I wanted to aim it into the swale, cut it into that hill and have it stay up on the right."

The pin is 28 back and five from the right edge on a green that is 37 deep. As Davis watches his ball fly toward the green, he says, "Get right, get down," but the ball is defiant. He had played it to the left of the flag and that's where it stays, hitting into the swale and rolling to the bottom, 45 feet away from the hole.

Couples decides to hit a 7-iron from 176 and he hits it just over the back edge into the fringe, 35 feet away, so neither player has a legitimate birdie opportunity.

On the way to the green, Davis asks LaCava if Couples hit 6-iron and learns that he had hit the 7. "Man, I can't believe he flew that over the green," Davis says.

Davis is facing an uphill putt through the swale and as he studies the shot, he remembers a similar putt that he had last year at this hole.

"I had one like this and I didn't get it over the hill and I left myself a tough putt," Davis says, "so I remembered it was slow."

Mark also emphasizes that it is uphill the first part and still uphill once it gets out of the swale, "So it's going to be slow and it's going to break."

Mark has taken the cue that Davis gave him back on the tee. He realizes his brother wants his opinion and wants conversation to keep his mind focused on the shot at hand. The rookie caddie is performing admirably.

Putter meets ball squarely and as the ball creeps toward the hole, Davis sees that it is right on line and five feet from the hole, he thinks he has made an improbable birdie. However, just as it gets to the hole and seems ready to curve in the side door, it stops.

"I can't believe I left it on that side of the hole," Davis says to Couples as he walks to the hole to tap in his par. "Usually they just dive into the cup." Couples replies, "Yeah, you'd think it would break down in there."

Davis repeats his lament to Mark as he watches Couples lag to two feet and tap in to stay even.

As Davis looks down at the green on the par-3 16th, a rush of confidence sweeps over him. He is thinking about winning the tournament right here and of winning a brand new Nissan sports car which goes to anyone who records a hole-in-one. He has a good feeling about this tee shot because the pin is cut just five yards from the left edge and thirteen back, perfect for a fade because if he happens to move it too far to the right, he has plenty of green to capture the ball. Yesterday, with the pin on the right, he overcut a 7-iron and wound up in the bunker on the right.

Mark tells him it's 167, but the downhill stature is neutralized by the fact that the wind is blowing in his face, so it's a solid 7-iron.

"I'm thinking, 'This sets up good for me, perfect 7-iron. Let's win the car.' That was my thought," Davis says. "Freddie almost won the car yesterday. So I'm trying to win the car and win the tournament."

Davis' practice swing is elegant and he recaptures that same motion when the ball is in the way. He hits it out over the left edge of the green and as if he was programming the ball's flight with a remote control device, it begins to fade right at the flag. It flies over the hole and stops eight feet behind. He may not be the fan favorite, but the gallery can't help but cheer the effort.

Mother Nature is calling and after he hands Mark the club, he ducks behind Couples on the tee, walks briskly outside the ropes to the left of the tee box and jogs down the hill to a Port-A-John. By the time he has finished, Couples and Sieckmann have hit their shots and as he makes his way back to the green, he looks and sees a ball back where his is, perhaps thirteen feet behind the cup.

The co-leaders and their caddies had been exchanging chit-chat throughout the day, but here at the 16th, it is quiet. Both players have makeable birdie putts and know that a deuce here could win the tournament.

Meanwhile, up at the 18th green, the huge gathering that has given the surrounding hill a stadium look is roaring as Jay Haas has rolled in a five-foot birdie putt to get to 14-under. Haas had hit a brilliant 5-iron cut shot from the right side of the fairway at the closing hole and his successful putt puts him alone at 14-under and the leader in the clubhouse. At 17, Mediate hits a pitching wedge approach that comes up a disappointing 25 feet short of the hole while Lyle hits a wedge out of the deep rough that stops about three inches from Mediate's ball. With the difficult 18th in front of them, each knows he has to make his birdie putt to get even with Haas, then hope Davis and Couples stumble coming in.

Back at 16, while Sieckmann is putting from thirty feet, Davis and Couples are eyeing their respective lines. After Sieckmann rolls his attempt two feet past, Couples really begins to go to school.

"I was watching Freddie and he took a long time to putt. You could tell he was bearing down on this one and I was thinking that he's liable to make one any minute, 'So if he makes his, don't worry about it, just putt your putt and try to make it,'" Davis says.

Couples strokes the ball and as soon as it starts to roll, the crowd begins rooting it on and just when they are about to explode into celebration, the ball slides underneath to the left and a huge groan fills the cooling air.

"By watching his I could tell that I'd have to hit it high up there to the right to let it curl back down," Davis says. "It was so soft, one of those ones where if you get it out there and get going to the hole, fine, but don't try to jam it in and get it five feet by."

With that in mind, Davis hits it too softly and the slower speed causes it to break more than he had planned and it slides underneath, just like Couples' did. The fans aren't nearly as distraught over this miss.

A look of disappointment creases his face as he walks up and taps in for par. He then walks over to Couples who says, "It's a bad place for the pin because it's sitting on the side of the hill and you don't have a chance to make it unless you're dead pin high to the right." Davis replies, "Yeah, you just have to lob those putts and hope they get in."

At the 17th green, Mediate and Lyle both miss their birdie putts and must birdie the brutal 18th to pull even with Haas.

Davis still has honors and he makes two practice swings as he waits for the crowd to settle down. Mark quickly comes over and says, "Keep your feet on the ground."

"He was reminding me to make a good swing and don't try to kill it," Davis says. "Those two practice swings I made, he noticed I was just up and down, getting a little carried away and out of my rhythm, so he was making sure that I stayed inside my swing. He was kind of laughing because they were loopy swings.

"That's the reason he's out here—to remind me of those things—and he's gonna do really well. Mark has done a really good job of helping me rather than just caddying. A good caddie will not get in your way, not do anything wrong or cost you any shots, but a great caddie will help you and make you play better. It's real hard to find a caddie who will help you."

Davis harnesses himself and plays a controlled fade into the right-center of the fairway. Couples follows with a bullet to the left-center of the fairway that bounds past Davis' ball.

The two walk together, their caddies out in front of them, and they discuss the unruly Los Angeles fans.

"You wish you could go tell every one of them what you thought, cuss 'em out," Davis says, and Couples replies, "Yeah, but you don't have enough time."

"The people are pulling for Freddie, but they bug him, too," Davis says. "People say, 'Way to go Freddie, you the man,' but that bothers him. He's learned to deal with it, but he'd rather not have to deal with it every time he plays. And it's only going to get worse if he keeps winning."

At 18, Kaneko makes a 15-foot birdie putt to wrap up an impressive 65 that gets him into a tie with Haas at 14-under.

Because Couples has outdriven him, Davis must set the course of action for the second shots. However, Davis really doesn't have a choice here. He has 280 to the front of the green and 310 to the hole and without a howling wind at his back, there's no way he can get home in two. The play has to be a layup. He chooses his 1-iron, aims it at the trap on the left and plays a fade that winds up in the first cut of rough on the right, 76 yards away from the hole.

Couples has 270 to the front and after seeing what Davis has done, he too asks for an iron and the crowd, which had been urging him to go for the green with a wood, reacts negatively. He takes a 3-iron, stands over the ball and surveys where he has to lay it up, then changes his mind, puts the 3-iron back and pulls out a 4-iron. The crowd got excited when he changed his mind, thinking he would opt for a wood, but again is disappointed when the 4-iron comes out. He plays a smooth shot into the middle of the fairway that finishes eighty-four yards from the hole with a better angle of approach than Davis will have.

"That's just a smart thing to do," Davis says. "The people were kind of booing him, they wanted him to go, but it's not smart. If he hits it 255, he's in the lip of the last trap. You want to get a putt at birdie, you don't want to be scrambling for a par. Especially after I laid up and he knows I'm gonna have a birdie putt."

There is no talk during this portion of the walk up 17. Each strolls with his caddie in silence, thinking about what type of shot will get his ball closest to the hole.

The tension has increased. Each player expects to get close to the pin on this next pair of shots and it will come down to putting. And a birdie here will likely lock up the title.

Couples plays first. His sand wedge hits below the pin and checks up quicker than he had hoped, twelve feet shy. The crowd loves it, but Couples doesn't and Davis knows Couples doesn't.

Davis is brimming with confidence. He has been hitting these little short wedge shots well all week and although the hole is cut tight to the right, just four yards from the edge and he has to carry a slight rise just in front of the right half of the green, he knows he can get this in close.

And he does. It takes one bounce ten feet short and right of the flag, then checks up for good just seven feet away. The crowd cheers, but not lustily, and Davis acknowledges them with a quick wave.

He knows Couples can make his putt, but he knows that no matter what Couples does, he's going to make his own birdie. He's so deep in thought that he momentarily forgets that Sieckmann is playing as well and Tom is away.

"Sorry, Tom, knock it in," Davis says in an apologetic voice to Sieckmann.

Sieckmann misses and taps in for par, leaving the stage to Davis and Couples. Couples again takes a long time getting ready to putt.

"Freddie's not a fast player and he's not slow, but he was a little slow on some putts today. He was working hard," Davis says.

Couples' putt looks perfect as it approaches the cup, but

breaks across the right edge at the last instant and stays out and the fans can't believe it. Actually, Davis is a little surprised, too.

"Great putt," he says to Couples, and Couples nods before tapping in for par.

Now Davis can take the tournament by the throat and start squeezing.

"I'm thinking, 'All right, this is your chance. You're due to make one,'" Davis says.

He and Mark study the crucial putt and talk about it as they read.

"I think it's most of the ball in the hole, but when it gets to the top, if it's going slow, it might break more," Mark says. "It depends on your speed. If it has a lot of speed it's not going to break very much. C'mon, knock it in."

Davis replies, "I will."

He looks calm and confident as he comforts himself over the ball. His routine is perfect, he strokes the ball solidly and it begins its roll to the hole. As it gets within three feet, Davis looks up and is practically ready to pump his fist in celebration because it is right on the line he had intended it to be on. Suddenly, it veers to the right and inexplicably misses the cup. There are not a lot of groans coming from the gallery. The majority of the fans are happy because now Couples is still tied for the lead. Davis stands still for a couple of seconds, staring at the ball, then the hole as he wonders how the ball stayed out.

"It's disappointing, but if you hit a good putt and you felt good about it, you can't get too upset," he says. "I would have been mad if I left it short and right of the hole, but I gave it a good roll."

Davis taps in his par and after putting the flagstick back in, Mark walks alongside him and says, "Hey, not a bad putt. Let's forget about it and go on to the next hole."

As he makes his way through the crowd to the 18th tee, Robin and Lexie join him for the walk and Robin asks him, "How did that not go in?" Davis just shrugs and says, "It got outside." Robin then says, "All right, get yourself a birdie here." Robin is starting to show signs of being nervous and Davis recognizes this and says, "Okay, I'll see you up by the green."

The fans around the 18th tee and a group of partyers, high above the tee enjoying the view from a deck off one of the magnificent houses on the hill, roar for Couples as he steps through the ropes. Davis and Sieckmann are barely noticed.

Davis is still up and as he looks out to the fairway, all he is thinking about is staying calm, picking out a target on the hill straight ahead, making a good swing and hitting a nice cut into the middle of the fairway, which he has done every day during the tournament.

He brings the driver around perfectly and launches his ball almost exactly where he aimed. It comes to rest in the left-center portion of the fairway.

"Great swing, that was perfect," Couples says to him. Less than a minute later, Couples has done the same thing, only his ball winds up in the right-center of the fairway. The fans on the deck whoop it up and Couples pumps his fist at them and that only riles them up more.

As Sieckmann is preparing to hit, Davis walks to the cooler to grab some bottled water for the walk up the hill.

"Going up the last hole, you like to have some water because you don't want to be standing in the fairway with a dry throat," he explains. "You need water so you can breathe. At the International last year in that altitude, I couldn't even breathe the last two holes, I couldn't even spit I was so dry. You get nervous, plus walking up that hill, you get out of breath."

Davis and Couples continue to remain composed. The scorekeeper asks jokingly if someone could "drag an old lady up the hill," and Davis says, "I need someone to drag *me* up the hill."

By the time they get to their balls, everyone knows what's going on. Haas and Kaneko are in at 14-under, Mediate has finished at 13-under an Lyle's bogey at 18 has dropped him to 12-under. Davis and Couples are either going to settle this thing in the next few minutes, or a playoff will be necessary.

Sieckmann hits first from 188 and he knocks his 6-iron over the back edge of the green. Not much of a reaction from the huge crowd. But as soon as Davis starts getting ready to hit his shot, excited murmurs fill the air.

244

Davis has 181 to the hole and he is thinking of only one thing: "I felt good, I felt like it would be great to birdie this hole to win it. I was hitting first so I can hit a good shot and put the pressure on him."

The shot plays uphill, but there is a fairly consistent breeze at his back. Last year at 18 on Sunday, Davis had a similar shot, hit a 6-iron and hit it over the green. He decides to use that knowledge and pulls his 7-iron out. The plan is to hit a high draw, aim it for the center of the green, but curve the shot to the left and have the ball release back to the hole, which is cut twenty-three back and five from the left on a green that is thirty-one deep.

Couples is doing stretching exercises over by his ball as he waits for Davis to swing. He stops when Davis is ready, then emotionlessly watches as Davis' ball shoots off the club and begins its climb toward the green. Davis has not pured it, the ball flies straight and never draws to the left. It hits in the middle of the green where he had aimed and stops thirty-five feet away from the hole. It is not the kind of putt anyone can expect to make, especially with a tournament championship on the line.

However, Davis says, "There's a lot of worse places it could be. It's not an impossible putt, I can still make it and win."

The crowd reaction is mixed. They almost begrudgingly cheer for his ability to hit the green under enormous pressure, but they are also happy that his birdie chance is slight and now Couples can stiff one and win.

Couples has 174 to the pin and his play is also with a 7-iron. He hits the shot crisply and as the ball soars through the air, the crowd becomes louder the closer it gets to the green. When it lands safely on the putting surface, they let out a huge roar. It sounds as if he has hit the shot to within two feet of the hole. Davis knows Couples will have at least twenty feet left for his birdie.

Couples waves to the cheering crowd, then looks into the CBS camera that is pointing at him and says to his wife back home in Florida, "Hey, Deborah, how are things at home?"

As the players stride to the green, the applause and cheering is even more boisterous than it has been all day. Davis and Couples have provided a stirring finish to the tournament and the fans are now heaping praise upon them, although the bulk of the cheering is for Couples.

Ever the class act, Couples invites Davis to walk with him onto the green to share in the adulation, but Davis realizes that the fans are rooting for Couples and he declines and lets his friend bask in the glory.

"Freddie said to me, 'C'mon, get on up here on the green,' and I just pushed him in the butt and said, 'Go on, this is for you,'" Davis says. "That was typical of the whole day. Freddie wanted me to walk up onto the green because he was kind of embarrassed about all that stuff."

After fixing their ball marks, Couples and Davis get together and Couples tells Davis to take his time and let the crowd get settled down and Davis agrees.

There is also the matter of Sieckmann, who is lost amidst all the hoopla. Sieckmann is just off the back edge in the gnarly kikuyu grass and is actually closer to the hole than Davis. Sieckmann can either play his shot onto the green, or because Davis is away, let Davis putt first.

"I told him to do whatever he wanted to do. I wanted him to call it," Davis says. "I think he just wanted to get out of the way so he decides to hit and then he hit a bad chip and I felt kind of bad for him. He's trying to make some money and he kind of got mixed up with all this stuff that was going on with me and Freddie and the crowd."

Sieckmann's first chip barely gets onto the green, so he decides to regroup and he marks his ball. Couples then begins cleaning up the area between his ball and the hole while Davis studies his putt from every angle.

"I was looking at that thing and I'm thinking, 'You deserve to make one, just make sure you get it up that hill.' It was really uphill and it was going to be slow. I thought it was breaking a little right and Mark said, "As hard as you have to hit it to get it up the hill, it's not gonna break that much."

When he is finally satisfied with the line and speed, he goes through his routine flawlessly, but does not hit a flawless putt.

"As soon as I looked up I said, 'Damn, it's gonna be short,'" he says. "That's the last thing you want to do. You don't want to blow it four or five feet by, but you want to at least give it a chance to get lucky and bounce in.

"Now I've got eighteen inches and Freddie looks at me like, 'What do you want to do?' And I know what he's thinking. If he makes his par, they're gonna go running to the 10th hole, screaming and moving. And if he holes his to win, mine doesn't make a bit of difference except money-wise. Again, he was being nice and saying if you want to finish, get it out of the way. It's a tap-in, but I'm nervous because you don't want to miss it and let Freddie be two-putting to win."

So Davis decides to take Couples's offer and finish the hole. However, after looking over the putt and getting over it, Davis backs away and goes back into his routine.

"I got up there and in my mind I'm thinking someone's gonna yell, 'Miss it,' while I'm putting this thing and that's all I could think about, so I stopped and backed away because that's no way to putt it. As soon as I back away, the whole crowd is like 'oooooh.' I was kind of laughing to myself because they don't understand, this is my way of making sure I make it rather than standing there and thinking goofy thoughts and missing it."

He returns to the putt and easily rolls it in. As Davis walks to the side of the green, Couples says, "Way to take your time," and then when Davis gets to where Mark is standing, he says to his brother, "I wasn't ready to putt."

"People thought that was embarrassing for me to have done that, but Bob Rotella always says if you're not ready, there's no reason to putt it, you might as well start over again. Even if you don't make it, don't miss it because you're not ready."

As Couples studies his putt, the crowd has stopped breathing. It doesn't seem possible that that many people can be so quiet. No one is coughing, sniffling, drinking a beer or shifting their weight. Total silence. Lexie is hugging Davis's leg and then he squats down like a baseball catcher to whisper to her.

"I'm thinking Freddie is going to make this, he's gonna pour it in there and it's going to be the storybook ending so I said, 'Lexie, when Freddie makes this putt, you go out there and give him a hug,' and she was like, 'I don't want to do it, there's too many people,' and I said, 'It's just like the hockey game last night.' But she wasn't gonna give him a hug."

There is no need to because Couples' putt drifts over the right edge by inches. The crowd lets out a huge groan of disappointment, but Davis' passive expression does not change. He feels as if Couples has given him another opportunity to win this tournament and now he is determined to take advantage.

"If he had made it, it's the same as if he makes one in the playoff to win," Davis says. "He still wins and I still lose and I'm happy for him and disappointed for me. But now I'm like, 'I've got another chance to win.'"

There is confusion and semi-bedlam around the green as the fans scramble away so they can get a spot somewhere on the 10th hole, the first of the playoff, to view the action. Others begin running down to the 14th, which would be the second hole if necessary.

In the scorer's tent, Davis and Couples take a little extra time to make sure their cards are correct. Tour official Mark Russell is on hand to make sure everything is right and when he sees that it is, he instructs the players to sign.

There is a sense of urgency all around because of television. Now that a playoff must be contested, TV may have to go past its allotted time slot, so the CBS producers are pushing the Tour officials to get the players over to the 10th tee and get this thing over with.

Couples is aware of this and asks Russell, "How long do we have, a half hour?" and Davis says, "We're gonna go get a sandwich, is that all right?" Russell chuckles and says, "That's fine, you guys tie, no playoff." This draws a laugh from both players and Davis says, "Well, I guess I can make it a little longer."

Extra marshals help to escort Davis and Couples to the tee. Now that there are just two players competing, Robin and Lexie will be allowed inside the ropes to watch and extra marshals are also needed to get them over there. Robin looks nervous and she says, "Davis has never won in a playoff. I hate these things." Lexie just looks confused as she sits nestled in her mother's arms, but she handles the excess of scattering people very well. The groups have to walk single file, right hands extended to the right shoulder of the person in front of them, to get through the mass.

Once they have made it safely inside and TV comes back from a commercial, two slips of paper are folded up and dropped into a hat. Davis reaches in, pulls out the slip with "2" written on it and says to Couples, "Well, that leaves one for you." Couples will have honors and Russell says, "Okay, Fred, play away." Davis and Couples wish each other luck with a smile and a handshake, then Davis walks to the right side of the tee box and stands next to Mark as Couples gets ready to hit his drive.

Couples does not wear a glove so after he takes a practice swing, he steps away and wipes the grip of his 3-iron. When he is satisfied with the feel, he steps back up, takes another practice swing, then coolly fades his drive into the left portion of the fairway and the crowd cheers approvingly.

Unlike earlier in the day, when Davis really didn't know what to hit because he hadn't laid up here, he knows exactly what to do. His routine is normal and he makes one of his best swings of the day, smoothing a 3-iron into the center, just two yards away from where his drive landed a couple of hours ago.

He is loose and relaxed as he walks to his ball, and Couples looks the same. They do not converse on the way down, each thinking about what he has to do. For Davis there is slight anxiety; he knows the playoff could come to a quick end because the 10th hole could present him or Couples a simple birdie opportunity.

"It's like it's more anxious than nervous," Davis says. "I'm thinking let's get a birdie because then it could be over and you get a result. And in a playoff, you know you have to make birdies to win, especially on this hole. I was excited to get out there and get going."

Couples hits first with a sand wedge from 112 yards and as his ball plops on the green and checks up as if he had yelled at it. The crowd screams with delight. Unlike on 17 and 18 when Davis knew that Couples' approaches weren't as close as the fans made them seem, he knows this one is in tight. In fact, it is five feet to the left of the cup and Davis knows that Couples is going to make birdie. Nothing is assured in golf, but Davis realizes that Couples is not going to waste this chance.

"When Freddie hit it in tight, I was thinking, 'All right, all you can do is hole it and win this thing right now,'" Davis says. "I've seen a lot of shots in the back corner get in close to the hole. I knew the yardage, I had just hit the shot here and made birdie a while ago, I knew that I could hole it."

His confidence pays off. He hits his sand wedge from eighty-six yards and the ball lands three feet to the right of the hole and spins back to within eighteen inches. It is a work of art and as he acknowledges the applause, he smiles shyly, yet proudly at Mark.

"When I hit it I was thinking, 'Oh man, this could go in, it's right at it.' It was exciting because I know that Fred is gonna make that putt ninety percent of the time. I knew I had to get in close, but the whole reason I hit it close was because all I was thinking about was holing it. I knew if I did, it was over. So that let me hit a good shot rather than thinking of just getting it on the green and having a putt at it. That was a good aggressive pitch shot, it wasn't one of those high lob shots. That shot, the wedge on 17, the one before on 10, those are the ones that make me happy."

As Couples looks over his putt, knowing that he has to make it to prolong the playoff, Davis muses with Mark and LaCava. He looks into the gallery and notices a woman on a man's shoulders with a cellular phone in her hand.

"Check this out," he says to the two caddies. "She's giving the play-by-play to somebody."

"Hey, this is LA, everyone in LA has cellular phones," Mark says.

After about a minute of reading the green, Couples steps up to his putt and is seconds away from pulling the putter back when a loud crash occurs over his left shoulder. He quickly backs away, then looks behind him to see what happened. A collapsible stool lived up to its name and collapsed, sending the man who was standing on it hurling to the ground.

"When that happened, I was thinking about what happened to Jeff Sluman at the TPC when the guy jumped in the lake," Davis says, referring to an incident in 1987. Sluman was standing over a six-foot putt on the second playoff hole at Sawgrass that, had he made it, would have defeated Sandy Lyle in the Players Championship. A college student, on a dare, dove into the lake surrounding the island 17th green and forced Sluman to back away from the putt. When he returned, he missed and eventually lost the tournament on the next hole.

"I was thinking now Fred's gonna miss it and that's gonna be a terrible ending. I'm thinking, 'Don't let this happen.'"

Couples is unfazed. He steps back up and calmly dunks the putt for birdie.

"Nice putt, given the circumstances," Davis says, and Couples replies, "Jeez, tell me."

Davis does not take his eighteen-inch tap-in for granted. He looks it over, sticks to his routine, then confidently strokes it into the middle of the hole to match Couples' birdie.

There is slight confusion as to where to go next, but Russell quickly points toward the 14th hole and the players and caddies begin walking briskly. The reason for the move from 10 to 14 is to accommodate TV. CBS has cameras ready and waiting at those holes so there is no transition needed. The walk is not a short one, though, and Davis jokingly asks Russell, "How did you guys pick these holes, you draw them out of a hat?" and Russell chuckles.

By the time Davis and Couples arrive at the tee, a huge crowd has already gathered and they have to be led through by marshals. As soon as Couples appears from outside the ropes, the fans whoop it up Arsenio Hall–style.

Davis is a little distracted by this because he pulls out his yardage book and starts figuring out what club to hit on the par-3 hole before realizing that he just played this hole, he knows it's 182 yards.

Couples had ripped a 6-iron over the green the first time around, but now, the wind has died down so Davis knows that his rival has the right club in his hands. He doesn't expect him to do anything other than hit this shot right at the hole. He is correct. The pin is sixteen back and nine from the right and Couples starts the ball in the middle of the green, then fades it into the pin. It lands softly and stops eight feet to the right of the flag and the fans begin sensing a victory for their hero.

"I watched him hit and it didn't look like he hit it very hard, so I figured I'd take a little bit off, go with the 7-iron and cut it in just like I did with the 7 the time before on this hole," Davis says.

As he takes his practice swing, he notices some fans moving behind the green and another group of fans yelling some sort of cheer, so he backs off and starts his routine over. Everything is repeated, the practice swing is fine, but when he goes after the ball, he swings too easy and his cut shot turns into a fade and it caroms off the right edge of the green and into the fringe up against the collar of the rough.

"My thought was 'Well, you kind of quit on it so you got what you deserved,'" Davis says.

It does not look good for Davis, but as he walks to the green, he tells Mark, "Ya know, it seems like a lot of playoffs are won on chip-ins."

It is positive thinking at its most positive. He figures that Couples is going to make his birdie. So in order to stay alive, he has to chip in. It is a thought that comes from supreme confidence in his abilities.

Davis has about forty feet to the hole, but he has to go up a little ridge, then about halfway to the hole, the green slopes downhill.

Couples asks him if his marker is in his line, and Davis says, "No, that's fine, I'm going up to the right of that."

Davis then asks Mark, "What do you think, should I chip it or putt it?"

"Well, it's up to you," Mark says, not really wanting to make the decision.

"Well, it's not lying real good, I think I'll just putt it, the fringe looks pretty good, doesn't it?"

"Yeah," Mark agrees. "It looks pretty smooth. You can make it that way."

The decision has been made and Davis takes out his putter. He picks out a spot about two feet above the hole to the right because the putt has plenty of break and the break is accentuated because of the downhill slope. It's one of those putts that if it is hit too hard, will steam past the hole. However, Davis also knows that he has to be bold and try to make it because if he doesn't, it won't

252

matter how far past it goes because Couples will probably make it inconsequential by making his birdie.

Davis strikes it solidly, but the ball gets off to a bad start because it scoots through the fringe, shoots hard off the lip and crests the hill with way too much speed. By the time it starts going downhill, Davis knows it's gone and he says, "Whoa, whoa, hold on."

It picks up speed every inch it moves, but then it starts to take the break and suddenly, it is motoring right at the hole. Now Davis is thinking he may get incredibly lucky and the putt might hit the back of the hole and drop in. Instead, it smashes into the right edge of the hole, is going too fast to fall in and it whips off the lip and slides eight feet past.

Now Couples has a decision to make. He can go ahead and try to pour his putt in, or play safe and not run the risk of blowing his by and then put the pressure on Davis to make his.

Davis tries to act like all is well so he fixes a ball mark in his line and reads his putt while Couples looks over his.

"I didn't want to stand there and watch and then all of a sudden have to go putt, I wanted to be prepared," Davis says. "I was making it like a regular round. I had it read and then was going to wait for him to putt."

But when Couples is ready to go and Davis gets out of his sight line, the feeling comes over him that he's not going to have to putt. He knows Couples is going to drain his eight-footer.

"You give a guy that many opportunities to win and he's gonna take it, especially Freddie," Davis says. "I gave him an opportunity to miss on the hole before and let me win and he didn't miss. I had a chance to win at 17 after he missed, and then I missed. He was off the hook too many times."

Couples' ball is halfway to the hole, rolling right on line, and he is already walking behind it, knowing that it is going into the heart of the cup. The crowd sees him moving and it starts howling. When the ball drops in, it is almost anticlimactic. Couples pumps his arm into the air, then raises both arms to the sky as the gallery cheers ecstatically.

"He poured that thing right in and my thought was 'At least he won it making birdie,' that was my first reaction," Davis says.

"At least he didn't miss it and then I go and miss mine. He made a good solid birdie and he deserved to win."

Davis walks up to Couples immediately and shakes his hand and pats him on the shoulder. Couples is then pulled away by CBS foot soldier Bobby Clampett, and he tells Clampett, "It's just one of my favorite courses and the people here really pull for me." Then he looks into the camera and says, "Hey, Deborah, whaddya think of that?"

Mark pats his brother on the back and says, "Great playing, too bad, but you played great."

Now, Davis has to get back to the press room where he will have to meet the media and explain how he lost, again, in a playoff. Counting his defeat at Kapalua, he is now 0-4 in PGA Tour playoffs.

"Now you've lost, you finished second and nobody wants to talk to you, TV's with Fred and then he's gonna get whisked off," Davis says. "And here we are again, I've lost another playoff and I'm getting sick of this lousy feeling. Looking back on the whole tournament, the way I played, I should have won by a lot. But if you narrow it down to today, given what happened today, Freddie should have won by a lot. He should have made birdie at one and been gone instead of double bogey. I didn't light it up, so he should have won."

Robin comes up to him with Lexie and they give him a hug and a kiss. There isn't much his wife can say to him, so she doesn't. Instead, she lets Lexie go to her father knowing that he will take care of her and it will get his mind off of what has just transpired.

The Loves climb into a minivan that has been driven onto the course for the sole purpose of transporting them back to the press room.

Once inside, Mark reiterates to Davis, "You played good, you didn't play great, but you're ready to go to Doral and the Players and play really well. You did a lot of good things."

Davis has to agree. He knows that this tournament was lost on Saturday when he had that bad stretch of seven holes starting with the triple bogey at No. 12. He hit the ball well, he finished the week with 24 birdies, and when you make that many birdies, you should win. This tells him that he didn't get much out of his game.

If he can just eliminate a few mistakes, he can blow a tournament wide open, and he can do it pretty soon.

"I'm disappointed, but I'm trying to see the good side of it," he says as he gives his pin sheet to Lexie so she can draw on it with her magic marker. "I didn't play as good as I can play and I still got beat by one of the best players in the world in a playoff. I don't even have to play perfect and I can beat everybody, that's the way I have to look at it. I can't say, 'Boy, I got bad breaks and the fans were against me.' I can't let my day end like that and feel sorry for myself.

"That's another thing Bob always says, 'Try to see the good things you did and try to build on them.' I made more birdies than anyone in the tournament and I made a bunch of mistakes, some bad swings, some bad decisions, misread some putts, and I still got beat in a playoff. It was a good week. If I had done ninety percent of the things right rather than 85 percent, I would have won going away. I shot under par every day and played pretty solid."

The van creeps along trying to avoid the masses who are heading back to the clubhouse and to the various parking lots. Robin sits in the backseat quietly, her arm around Lexie, who is seated between her and Davis. Davis watches his daughter draw on the pin sheet and a smile creases his face.

"Do you want to go to the Lakers game tonight?" he asks Robin. He has tickets for the family, and now that he isn't taking the red-eye tonight or taking care of the responsibilities that go with winning a tournament, going to the game is a viable option.

"We'll see. I'm not sure if I feel like it," Robin replies.

After about ten minutes, the van pulls up in front of the press tent and Davis gets out and takes Lexie with him. Robin and Mark are going to go to the hotel and pick up their bags from storage and load up the car, then come back for Davis.

In the press room, Lexie sits on the interview platform in front of Davis, doodling with her markers while her father answers the inquisitive media. The hot topic turns out to be the behavior of the fans.

"Freddie is a great friend of mine and I'm happy for him that people like him that much," Davis says at the same time Couples is sitting in the working area of the media tent making a phone call to Deborah. "He's super-popular and super-talented. But it's upsetting that people would come to a tournament to pull against me.

"When I'd miss a putt, it was like someone missing a putt against Nicklaus. They were happy for anything bad that happened to the other guys. I'm not mad about it, just disappointed."

Davis spends nearly a half-hour talking to the writers. By the time he is finished, Lexie has fallen asleep. He lifts her up and carries her out the door as Couples strides into the interview area.

Naturally, the first question posed to the champion regards the fans.

"I think the fans were more for me than anyone, but I didn't believe they were against him," Couples says. "I don't think the fans were discourteous, I just think they were having a good time."

Then, Couples is asked about his run-in with the fan on the way to the driving range.

"I didn't appreciate it," he says. "I have a smart mouth, too and I responded. It was stupid for him to say that and probably worse for me to respond."

Eventually, the conversation turns to golf and Couples explains how he was able to win his second Los Angeles Open in the last three years.

Davis is emptying his locker as Robin, Mark and Lexie walk into the barren room. The car is all packed and although Robin still isn't sure about the Lakers game, she is positive that she's extremely hungry. They talk about dinner plans, then file out into the chilly early evening Los Angeles air.

Another week on the PGA Tour has come to an end. The scoreboards are being taken down, the gallery ropes are being coiled, the grandstands are being dismantled. Tomorrow, Riviera will be returned to its members, and the professionals who held court for the past week will be flying or driving to Florida for the Doral Open in Miami.

"It's not as everyone perceives it," Davis says of life on the

Tour. "Freddie's not out drinking and partying and celebrating. He's taking the red-eye out tonight to Miami. Whether you win, lose, draw, whatever, when Sunday ends, you pack your bags, you go to transportation and turn your car in and ask for a ride to the airport or a hotel and you go on to the next tournament and try to do it again. It's a job. I didn't close the deal today, so now I have to go try and work on another deal."

Epilogue

The alarm is ringing in Davis's ear, signifying that it is 6 A.M. and time to get up and get over to Los Angeles International for the flight to Miami. He is tired and this early wake-up is a cruel reminder that he should have just come back to the hotel and gone to bed last night. Instead, he did go to the Lakers game and saw them lose to Houston, 105-97. Things just aren't the same anymore at the Forum now that Magic Johnson has retired.

As it turned out, things in Davis' life weren't the same anymore, either, thanks to what happened in the two months that followed his defeat in Los Angeles.

At Doral, he shot 71-68-68-67 – 274 and tied for fourth, three strokes behind ageless winner Raymond Floyd.

After skipping the Honda Classic in Fort Lauderdale, Davis tied for eighth in the Nestle Invitational at Arnold Palmer's Bay Hill Club with rounds of 74-70-67-71 for 282, far behind Couples, who stomped to a nine-stroke win.

Davis was on the verge of victory, his game never better, and he knew it. And then it all came together in a blizzard of great shotmaking.

After five top 10 finishes in his first eight starts of '92, Davis finally broke through and won the prestigious Players Championship with a splendid final round of 5-under 67 at the TPC at Sawgrass to beat Nick Faldo, Ian Baker-Finch, Phil Blackmar and Tom Watson by four shots.

It was a monumental victory. He won $324,000, but more importantly, earned a ten-year exemption on the PGA Tour, security that any player would kill for. It means he never has to worry about losing his playing privileges for the next decade.

"It's hard to think of everything this means," he told *Golf World*. "You don't realize what a ten-year exemption means until you have the chance to win one. This is the only thing I want to do for the next ten years."

It was his fourth career victory, more than any player on Tour under the age of thirty. And Couples, whose victory at Nestle and loss to Corey Pavin in a playoff at Honda vaulted him to the No. 1 ranking in the world, was moved to modestly say of Davis, "His game is probably ahead of mine. He hasn't won a major, but just because Mark Calcavecchia and Ian Baker-Finch have won majors, I don't think they're better than Davis. I like his game. He may not have won as much as he should have, but he's always there at the end. That's what I like."

Davis bypassed New Orleans to prepare for The Masters, but he couldn't get anything going at Augusta after shooting an opening 4-under 68. He closed with three straight 72s and tied for 25th, a distant nine shots behind the world's hottest player, Couples. Couples won for the third time in 1992 and also captured his first major title. And incredibly, on April 12, he passed the $1 million mark in earnings for the season.

Couples skipped the Heritage the following week and gave the stage back to Davis, as Davis won for the third time in his career and second year in a row at Harbour Town.

He took the lead with a 67 on Thursday and never trailed as he produced rounds of 67-67-68 to win by four over Chip Beck.

"It's a great feeling to win this three times, but to win twice in the same year . . ." Davis said. "I told my brother this was a great hurdle to get over, especially this early in the year. It's hard to believe I've won two tournaments and it's only April."

Mark O'Meara, who played with Davis on Sunday, said: "I admire him. The way he manages himself on the golf course is tremendous. He has the talent and potential to be one of the greatest players in the world. He's as good as Fred Couples. He's long off the tee, he hits great iron shots and he's got a great touch around the greens. If you've got those things, you're going to win golf tournaments."

Davis had them all, and then some, the following Sunday in Greensboro. He needed just 62 shots to complete the fourth round at Forest Oaks Country Club and he romped to a six-shot victory in the Greater Greensboro Open. It was the best round of his seven-year Tour career in addition to a course record.

He was within three shots of leader Rocco Mediate when play began, but when he birdied the first two holes, he jumped into the middle of the fray. He holed a 117-yard pitching wedge for eagle at No. 7, hit his tee shot on the 215-yard eighth to two feet and tapped in for birdie, made birdies at 11 and 12, holed out from a bunker on 15 for eagle and wrapped it up with a birdie at 16.

"I've had so many days where I finished and said, 'That could have been a 65,' or 'That could have been a 63,'" Davis said. "If, if, if. Today, there were hardly any ifs. This is almost the perfect round. Every time I looked up, the ball was going in the hole."

Tom Kite, who played with Davis and witnessed the majestic 62, summed it up this way: "Some people questioned his courage when he couldn't beat Couples in Los Angeles. But I think he's answered that question now. Fred's good, but Davis is not far behind, if he's behind at all."

Golf's newest rivalry was born. Couples vs. Love was being compared to the last great antagonists on Tour, Nicklaus vs. Watson in the early '80s.

In a nine-week period starting in Los Angeles, Couples and Davis each won three events and finished second once and became exclusive members of the $1-million-by-April-Club. By the end of the month, Couples was No. 1 in money (1,010,874) and scoring average (69.29) and Davis was No. 2 ($1,001,932 and 69.43); Couples was second in birdies (209), Davis was third (206); Couples was No. 6 in putting (1.733 putts per hole), Davis was seventh (1.736); and in the all-around stats, Couples was No. 1 and Davis No. 3.

They were being touted as the American players most likely to become grotesquely rich in the '90s. *Sports Illustrated* and *Golf World* did feature stories on the new dynamic duo. They were invited into press rooms before every tournament began, and because of their stellar play, often visited with the media the rest of the week. Crowds flocked to see them play and practice, and gawked at them wherever they went. They were asked to throw out first balls at a couple of major league baseball games. Suddenly, they became experts on any topic that was being discussed. The attention was incredible, their limbs were being pulled in every direction and neither felt comfortable with it.

"The rivalry was just a media thing," Davis said. "Fred and I share the same personality in that we want to win and if we don't, we don't care who beats us; we'll congratulate him and move on. The media was looking for something and that was fine.

"But it got into the summer and we hadn't won in a while, yet they still wanted to talk to us every week. We had a tough time dealing with that. They wanted us even if we shot 75. That was different. When we both started playing poorly, we tried to find time for ourselves and get back on our game, but it was hard. I had no concern about Fred or the money list, I just wanted to play well for myself.

"Hubert Green summed it up best. *Sports Illustrated* interviewed Fred and me and then they asked Hubert and he said that there were a whole lot of other guys who can play out here, too. He's right."

He was. Once April ended, Davis and Couples predictably cooled off. Couples idled himself for three weeks before the U.S. Open at Pebble Beach and while Davis played, enabling him to pass Couples and move into first on the money list, he didn't come close to winning. Neither threatened during the Open and some of the glare that had blinded them was shifted to Kite, who captured his first major title.

As the summer plodded along, Davis continued to struggle. At Muirfield for the British Open, Davis played wonderfully in practice and sincerely felt that he had a good chance to win his first major. After a first-round 73, he was nine behind co-leaders Steve Pate and Ray Floyd. Knowing he'd have to do something dramatic to get into contention, Davis played poorly on Friday, shot 77 and flew back to the U.S. having missed the cut by seven strokes.

"It was just one of those things where I was trying too hard to win rather than play my game," he said.

His final chance in the majors also brought disappointment as the thick, deep rough at Bellerive in St. Louis doomed him. He started miserably with a 6-over 77, brought it back with 71-70-72, but was never close to the top of the leaderboard. He finished 12 shots behind winner Nick Price.

"The golf course was set up so hard, if you didn't hit it perfect, you were dead," he said. "I hit a few bad drives every day and that's all it took. I thought the course was set up poorly and I got frustrated by that."

Not winning a major during a period when he was at the top of his game stung because he realizes that winning majors is the way the great players are gauged.

"I felt like I was going to do great in the majors," he said. "I went into all of them playing real well. I had good starts at The Masters and the U.S. Open and instead of just playing, I started playing to win."

With the majors out of the way, he set his sights on winning the money title. After the PGA, he trailed Couples by about $60,000. He never caught him.

He had planned for September to be his most inactive month, but he didn't intend to take the whole month off. He had to withdraw from the Canadian Open when his wrist began bothering him.

It wasn't until the Tour Championship was over and the money title had been decided—with Couples winning by $152,558—that Davis finally began to relax and get back to playing the way he had early in the season.

His timing—at least financially—couldn't have been better. there is no longer an off-season for professional golfers. The Tour Championship at the end of October concludes the official schedule, but until just before Christmas there is a big-money unsanctioned event to be played every week. This late fall period has been dubbed "Dash for the Cash" and Davis did plenty of dashing.

He teamed with Couples to win the World Cup team event in Madrid, Spain. The pair led throughout most of the four-day tournament, but blew their lead on the last day and had to rally dramatically to edge the Swedish tandem of Anders Forsbrand and Per-Ulrik Johannson. Davis birdied the 17th and he and Couples both birdied No. 18 to snatch the victory.

The following week, he won the Kapalua International in Hawaii. He had finished second two years in a row there, but he shot 65-71-72-67 and his 40-foot eagle putt on the 72nd hole beat his good friend Mike Hulbert by one shot. Hulbert had beaten Davis in a playoff at Kapalua in 1991.

Davis's roll continued the following week when he and Kite teamed up to win the Shark Shootout, Greg Norman's annual invitation-only party at Sherwood Country Club in Thousand Oaks, California.

In the JC Penney Classic, a team event that pairs a PGA player with a Ladies Professional Golf Association player, Davis and Beth Daniel finished second to Dan Forsman and Dottie Mochrie.

And capping off the post-season, Davis shot 72-75-70-66 to place third in the Johnnie Walker World Championship in Jamaica behind Nick Faldo and Norman.

In the six-week post-season period, he won approximately $645,000. Coupled with his $1,191,630 in official earnings, Davis had put together one of the most dominating seasons in PGA Tour history.

"I've been working on the same things for a few years," he said in reviewing his season. "I've stuck with them, haven't changed whether I'm playing good or bad. That has paid off. There were a lot of tournaments early in my career that I should have won that I threw away or blew and I think the more you persevere and the harder you work, luck is going to turn around your way.

"I holed out a lot of shots, holed a lot of putts this year. It all comes back to you. Early in my career I got some wins, but now I'm a better player when I'm in position to win. When I go back and look at what I accomplished, I accomplished a lot, but I see room for improvement."